D1275723

INTELLECTUAL
COMPROMISE
The Bottom Line

INTELLECTUAL COMPROMISE

The Bottom Line

Michael T. Ghiselin

PARAGON HOUSE
New York

First edition, 1989

Published in the United States by

Paragon House Publishers
90 Fifth Avenue
New York, NY 10011

Manufactured in the United States of America

Library of Congress Cataloging-in-Publication Data
Ghiselin, Michael T., 1939–
Intellectual compromise / by Michael Ghiselin.
p.   cm.
Bibliography: p.
Includes index.
ISBN 1–55778–065–X
1.   Science—Philosophy.   2.   Economics—Philosophy.
3.   Rationalism.   4.   Reason.   I.   Title.
Q175.G468   1989
501—dc19   88–22426
                                                                        CIP

To the memory of Jon Ghiselin
1935–1985

Contents

CONTENTS

Preface

An intellectual may be defined as somebody who rationalizes his prejudices. If such a pronouncement seems a bit cynical, consider what the word "cynic" originally meant. Contrary to what present usage might have us think, the school of Greek philosophers known as the Cynics, of whom Diogenes was the outstanding example, held as their fundamental doctrine that virtue is the highest good. So why did Diogenes carry a lamp about the streets of Athens, looking for an honest man? Surely not because he expected to find one. The story would have been ruined altogether, had he held the lamp up before a mirror.

Diogenes was telling people that pretension and hypocrisy stand in the way of good judgment, and therefore of genuine virtue. Those who equate virtue with an earnest belief in their own righteousness are not amused by such gestures. The hypocrite is most successful when sincere. So he wants to believe that the cynic's cynicism is like his own hypocrisy. And he would like us to believe that attributing base motives to behavior implies a belief that such motives are necessary or desirable.

Diogenes might just as well have been looking for a rational man

PREFACE

as for an honest one. In either case, however, it would be gross hyperbole to claim that nobody is ever honest, or that nobody is ever rational.
But one might insist upon stripping away at least some of the illusions
and hypocrisy that make it so difficult to be honest or rational. Or, for
that matter, virtuous.

This book is concerned with the rationality of science. It is also
concerned with rationality in general. Although it takes a rather cynical
view of how scientists conduct their affairs, it is basically a defense of
reason from its detractors. The kind of rational behavior that is here
attributed to good scientists is rational in a humbler, and less preten-
tious, sense than what we find in most discussions of rationalism and its
alternatives. It is the sort of "economic rationalism" that we find in the
conduct of our daily lives.

Therefore one might consider this a book on economics, and it is.
But it avoids the technicalities and the higher mathematics that fill the
learned journals of that discipline and sticks to the fundamental principles. The book might also be considered a work on sociology, for it
addresses many issues that interest sociologists. But it opposes much of
sociological theory. Or one might wish to read it as a work of natural
history—a zoologist's reflections on the laws of animal behavior as they
apply to his colleagues. There would be excellent reasons for catalogu-
ing it as philosophy, for it grapples with important questions of epistemology, metaphysics, and ethics. It also says a lot about psychology
and the history of science. Several minor branches of knowledge group
together into a non-discipline sometimes called "the science of science," but what is said here applies to the humanities as well. So
perhaps the best way to classify this book is to call it "criticism." It
certainly contains much social criticism, especially toward the end.
Criticism of academia by insiders like me has produced a vast literature, but I have made little use of it in the present effort. It owes more to
the inspiration of such predecessors as De Tocqueville, Taine, and
Veblen. A particularly knowledgeable reader may also note some parallels between this work and Machiavelli's *Il Principe* and Castiglione's *Il
Cortigiano*. These predecessors deserve high marks for their ability to
understand the behavior of those around them, but my intellectual
roots are really in zoology, not political science.

My own point of view is that of a professional evolutionary
biologist. I have also had the pleasure of studying the history of my

subject. As part of my effort to understand the evolution of reproduction and sex among plants and animals, I found that one can readily apply economic theory to explain all sorts of biological phenomena. The application of economic theory to human as well as animal behavior follows naturally, and investigative behavior follows in due course. So I am particularly pleased to acknowledge my debt to such predecessors as Adam Smith and Alfred Marshall.

I have profited from many years of firsthand experience in the laboratory and the classroom. As student, teacher, and researcher, in a diversity of institutions, I can discuss such matters as an insider. Thanks to the generosity of the Guggenheim and MacArthur foundations, I have been able to be a full-time scholar for some years, distancing myself from academia somewhat, and I hope adding to my objectivity.

I have presented a few lectures on the subject matter of this book to scholarly audiences. Although what I have said has seemed new to them, they generally agree with me, and without my having to back it up with statistics or other embellishments. Indeed, they only have to reflect upon their own experience to see that it all makes a great deal of sense, and they volunteer examples that tend to support my views. Furthermore, the authors of many works on metascientific matters often invoke explanations not unlike those suggested here. So I am pleased to acknowledge their contributions as having helped me to see the general pattern.

The manuscript has been read by several friends. They are by no means responsible for what I say, and are not to be thought of as having endorsed my views. Nonetheless I am grateful for their encouragement and assistance. Gordon Tullock, who is an economist and has written a book somewhat like this one, has helped me avoid blunders with respect to economics. David Hull, who is a philosopher of biology, and who is writing a book on the sociology of biologists, has gone through the manuscript with a somewhat different point of view. Elsewhere in this volume I acknowledge my many intellectual debts to Hull, who in some ways may be regarded as a collaborator even though we have never published anything together. Robert Root-Bernstein, who is writing a book on scientific creativity, has also given me the benefit of his erudition and good taste. William Bennetta has read the manuscript from the point of view of an intelligent reader much interested in the subject, and has provided me with excellent and detailed advice, saving the copy editor and me a great deal of work, and much improving the finished product. Seymour Kurtz provided good advice for the final revision.

While working on this book the following institutions have provided me with hospitality: Cambridge University, the University of Utah, the Istituto di Genetica Biochimica ed Evoluzionistica in Pavia, Italy, the Institute for Advanced Study in Berlin, and the California Academy of Sciences. The book was begun, and nearly completed, during the tenure of a MacArthur Prize Fellowship.

Chapter 1

INTRODUCTION

SCIENCE HAS BECOME THE ULTIMATE SYMBOL, AS WELL AS THE supreme example, of reason triumphant and of all that goes with it. Yet reason and its fruits are widely spurned. We live in an age when science, and even more so the technology that is so often confused with it, have many hostile critics, and not just those who long to return to the simple life of a preindustrial economy.

Some of the attacks upon science have been launched by those who feel threatened by its findings, and by the concomitant erosion of traditional values and accustomed authority. Or they look for some new alternative basis for conduct that seems incompatible with all or part of modern science. Others would have us abolish authority altogether—except perhaps for what might be called the authority of their own tastes and impulses. If there are no objective grounds for deciding what is true or false about nature, then *a fortiori* we can abolish standards in general.

The very rationality and objectivity of science have been called into question. Much of the criticism has come from those who have concerned themselves with the "sociology of knowledge," and from historians and philosophers who have fallen under its influence. There

1

is no consensus here, however. When philosophical criteria of rationality seem out of line with the data of history, there are various options. Such authors as Kuhn claim that science is irrational, and, going even further, Feyerabend claims that it should not be rational.[1] On the other hand, Lakatos and Laudan argue that science really is rational after all.[2] Some philosophers, such as Popper and his followers, have definite ideas about how scientists should reform their ways and become truly rational—according to their criteria of what rationality is supposed to be.[3]

This book reexamines the place of reason in science, and to some extent in human life in general. It seeks to solve the problem by replacing a philosophical conception of rationality with an economic one. Reasonableness replaces ratiocination. The result is a mixture of economics and the history and philosophy of science, with a substantial amount of psychology and social criticism added for good measure. Among other things, it is a contribution to the literature of institutional economics, and thus has some antecedents. It partakes of the tradition of Thorstein Veblen, whose *Theory of the Leisure Class* and *The Higher Learning in America* are in some ways ancestral.[4]

Both Veblen and I attempted syntheses of Darwin and Adam Smith. My book on *The Economy of Nature and the Evolution of Sex* has been looked upon as an early contribution to sociobiology.[5] However, it deemphasized genetics, and really was about what is coming to be called "bioeconomics." Among other things, it presented a long discussion on the principle of the division of labor. This attracted the attention of economists, because the topic had not advanced much since *The Wealth of Nations* appeared in 1776. In a paper entitled *The Economy of the Body,* delivered to the annual meeting of the American Economic Association in 1977, I showed how the division of labor can be applied to anatomy.[6] This was an easy task, for I am a comparative anatomist by doctorate, and for years had studied the division of labor in that context without realizing it. I suggested that economics and biology might be considered branches of a larger endeavor, "general economy." Later I defined "general economy" as "the study of how the availability and utilization of resources affect the organization and activities of organized beings."[7] There were precedents for this step. The connections are evident in the influence of Malthus on Darwin. And the greatest of nineteenth-century neoclassical economists, Alfred

Marshall, had said that economics is a branch of biology in a broad sense.[8] The connection becomes even closer when we realize that some historians of science have modeled their conceptions of scientific change upon the theory of natural selection.[9] Hence the present work extends a line of research that has attempted to explain history in the broadest sense in terms of economics in the broadest sense.

The extension of economic thought beyond the limits of pecuniary matters is a remarkable development in contemporary thought. Biologists now routinely employ economic metaphors, but they are only beginning to realize the extent to which economists already know about what they believe to be their original discoveries. The science of bioeconomics, analogous to biophysics and biochemistry, is still in its infancy. In psychology a substantial literature has developed on consumer choice, stimulating a considerable body of experimental work, even on the white rat.[10] In 1980 I attended a conference in Miami on evolutionary theory in economics and law, where, among other topics, we discussed attempts to apply evolutionary thinking to the common law.[11] The upshot is that law evolves not so much by rational decisions on the part of judges, but by a kind of trial and error analogous to natural selection. When people are dissatisfied with the law, they litigate. Judges vary the law fortuitously, as a sort of "mutation." People continue litigating until they are satisfied. Reason becomes far less obtrusive.

Biological thinking has similarly affected economics. In particular we have the work of Nelson and Winter, among others, on evolutionary economics.[12] The basic idea, which goes back to a seminal paper by Alchian, is that the more efficient firms outcompete the less efficient ones.[13] Similar ideas occur in the work of Boyd and Richerson on cultural evolution.[14] The cost of obtaining information can be very high, and one way of coping is to imitate persons of high status without really understanding the reasons for their success. Such evolutionary approaches are still in an early stage of development, and it is hard to say at present how far they will lead.

These days intellectuals are not expected to know anything about economics. Even those who do know something about it treat economics as if it were a social science and as if it were concerned with nothing but money. But its real subject matter is resources of every kind. Scarcity and competition affect all organisms everywhere, whether social or not, and they affect not just organisms, but machines as well. Neither do economic laws and principles apply only to the more mundane aspects of our existence. How much time we allocate to love or to art is just as much an economic problem as how much we allocate to work or to rest. We all strive for a good balance among our various needs. A scholar's life is no exception. So the economic aspect of science is not simply a matter of getting a grant renewed or keeping a job. The problem is all too often a matter of time. How much of it shall we devote to teaching, how much to the library, how much to the writing desk? No matter how hard we try, we can never work twenty-seven hours in a day.

Scientists, when talking about prospects for research, often use such expressions as "bull market" in molecular genetics. Such a metaphor is apt, and more than just a linguistic ornament, for it subsumes particulars under general laws of nature. If this is so, it is perfectly reasonable to take the next step, and turn such commonplaces into an area for serious research. There already exists a substantial literature on the pecuniary economics of research and education.[15] It covers such matters as the job supply and the effects of growing and shrinking budgets. But the nonpecuniary aspects have largely been ignored, with the important exception of a book by Tullock.[16] Furthermore, our baser motives have either been ignored or treated from a sensationalistic point of view in this literature. Although some people will discuss, in the context of moral discourse or political diatribe, the problem of sexual commerce in the academic groves, nobody seems to ask how many times one has to copulate with one's supervisor in order to be excused from a language requirement. Academic man is apt to get upset if such questions are asked. Perhaps he fears that his profession will be discredited. It may hurt him where it hurts most—in the pocketbook. Perhaps he fears that a lot of questions will be asked about himself, and fears the consequences. Or it may just mean a lot of work, with no return for his time and effort, responding to factors beyond his control and outside of his influence.

The extensive literature on science policy also has an economic aspect.[17] But although it often uses phrases such as a "free market in ideas," it is largely inspired by political science. Much of the science policy literature has been written by economists, but they have addressed the issues from the sort of managerial viewpoint that one

4

might expect from businessmen. We also have heard a great deal from bureaucrats, politicians, academic opportunists, and the administrators of large, mission-oriented applied science programs. Consequently the general public's philistine attitudes and habit of confusing science with technology are presupposed and reinforced.

When dealing with the intellectual economy we need to make a clear distinction between the academic and the scholarly worlds. By the scholarly world I mean the life of the intellect proper—the pursuit of knowledge, its preservation, and its transmission. By the academic world I mean the sort of infrastructure that, ideally at least, exists in order to support the scholarly world. Veblen made a similar comparison between industry and business. A lot of people make no such distinction, and that is part of the problem. The academic and scholarly worlds are presently so closely allied as to be hard to separate. This is especially true in Europe, where everybody takes it for granted that all eminent scientists are professors. These days there are very few "gentleman scholars" in the sense of those who live on private means alone. Even the scientists who work for public museums and other nonacademic research institutions often have faculty status at universities as well.

By no means let us treat academia as if it were another name for teaching. The communication of one's results is an integral and necessary feature of the scholarly life, and the printed word is but one vehicle for such communication. Lectures and discussions can be equally legitimate. However, we need to distinguish between teaching and certain other duties that may go along with it. Providing leadership and guidance for the young is an honorable and worthy way of making a living, and serving as baby-sitter or warden is at least socially useful. Administrative chores and faculty meetings may be tolerated as necessary evils. Many of the problems of the scholar arise from the difficulties of combining these various functions. The tendency for the values of the academic life to override those of the scholarly life is one reason why bad scholarship drives out good.

For the purposes of analysis the scholarly world will here be separated from the academic world as much as is feasible, by treating scholarship first and then seeing how academia enters in. A complete separation of the two, however, would tend to obscure the connections. We shall proceed through a series of topics, explaining why scientists, as such, behave as they do. The institutional complications are introduced gradually, with the amount of social criticism increasing proportionately.

Whatever the matters of social criticism and ethics that are considered here, the basic theme remains bioeconomics. This book attempts to integrate two major branches of knowledge. In so doing it aims at a more comprehensive synthesis, incorporating much sociology, intellectual history, psychology, and epistemology. Like every other biological process, thinking has an economic aspect.

This book also addresses some very fundamental metaphysical issues. The economic and biological perspective suggests a radically new way of envisioning ultimate reality—an opportunity for placing metaphysics itself upon a new foundation. To understand how any society works, we need a clear idea of what the fundamental units in that society are, and of how they work. Unfortunately "society," like "water," is a mass noun—i.e., no discrete units are implied by that term. So when we say that society disapproves of something, it is far from clear whether we speak of a social group itself, or of its component individuals. Such philosophical problems are by no means unique to the social sciences.

A new way of thinking about groups has resulted from an effort to solve one of the traditional problems in philosophical biology. This was the question of whether biological species are "real." The argument against their "reality" had been based upon a kind of nominalism, which is the notion that classes are mere abstractions and only individuals have real existence in nature. If species do not exist, except in the mind, their ability to evolve and to become extinct would seem downright contradictory. The usual solutions to this problem have been two. The first was to go along with nominalism, and agree that species are not real. Perhaps things other than species evolve. Perhaps evolution does not occur. The other solution was to reject nominalism, and affirm that classes, including species, are real. To this I have added a third: I deny the premise that species are classes.[18] I claim that species are individuals. Since nominalists and realists alike agree that individuals are real, the problem is solved. Indeed, others said the same sort of thing before I did, but nobody had paid much attention to what can be dismissed as nothing more than a metaphysical curiosity.

That species are individuals has been overlooked partly because the word "individual" has been used in two different senses. In biology, "individual" is usually synonymous with "organism." In logic and ontology, it means any particular, or single thing—whatever has to be designated by a proper name. It is contrasted with a class, or group of objects having certain traits in common, and designated by a class name. But individuals can be groups, most obviously where a group forms a unified whole. Good examples of such individuals are a club, a family, or the Milky Way. Maybe some individuals are absolutely simple, and contain no parts, but at least the familiar examples are wholes made up of parts. Each of us human beings consists of cells, and these in turn are composed of molecules. Molecules are made up of atoms, and we do not know how far this analysis may lead us. Just because there is space between the parts of a whole does not mean that it is not an individual: There is a lot of space between our component atoms.

The members of a class, such as the class of red books, do not share a whole–part relation. The only thing they share is the traits that cause them to fall within the class. In other words, they share only the defining properties, such as redness and bookness. Unlike classes, individuals have a particular position in time and space, and can change. A red book, being an individual, has to be one place or another, and can begin to exist or cease to exist. The class of red books is everywhere, and immutable, existing whether or not any red books exist.

Perhaps this will be more clear if we consider a person's relation to a class and to an individual of which he is a part. Let "John" be the name of a man. Like many other organisms, John belongs to the class of males. It makes sense to say "John is a male." John might also belong to, in the sense of being a part of, an individual called the United States Army. But it would be nonsense to say "John is a United States Army."

One reason why the individuality of biological species is not obvious is the fact that the component organisms in a species do not always exist in direct physical contact. Sex, however, does the trick. Biological species form reproductive communities, or families of the most extended sort. The thesis that species are individuals was largely ignored, or even dismissed as preposterous, for several years. For some purposes one could get along conceiving of species as if they were, in fact, classes. For historical reasons that we need not go into here, modern philosophy has tried to interpret every object in the universe as if it were a class—even an organism! But problems arise when we attempt to fit evolution into the philosophy of science in general and that of biology in particular. Species do evolve.

There are no laws about particular objects (individuals). Rather, all the laws of nature, without exception, refer only to classes of objects, and are true irrespective of space and time. It was this point that caused the philosopher David Hull to accept the thesis that species are individuals, even after having rejected it for several years.[19] Hull changed his mind upon reading a book in which J. J. C. Smart asserted that biology is not a science. Sciences, Smart maintained, are supposed to have laws, and there are no laws about *Homo sapiens*. Hull realized that no biologist had ever made such a claim. But neither had any physicist claimed that there are laws about Saturn. The laws of biology are laws about classes of species—inbred species *versus* outbred species for example—not about any one species in particular. This insight has been the basis for Hull's research program ever since.

There has been a great deal of resistance to the thesis that species are individuals. But it continues to gain adherents, partly because evolutionists have long treated the individuality of species as a tacit assumption. Another reason is that it helps to solve a wide variety of problems. One is tempted to ask what else besides a species might be an individual, and hence be able to change indefinitely while nonetheless remaining the same thing. Hull has addressed the problems of intellectual evolution by treating such entities as individual research traditions, individual ideas, and individual theories from this point of view.[20] In paleobiology various authors, especially Eldredge and his collaborators, have been led to ask about the ontological status of different kinds of groups.[21] Above the level of the species, genera and higher units may qualify as individuals, but these are just lineages that share a common historical origin and nothing more. As such they cannot "do anything" for the simple reason that they are not integrated into functioning wholes. Organisms copulate, species speciate, but genera do not generate. One result of such insights has been a fresh, if rather controversial, look at macroevolutionary mechanisms. Among my own contributions has been an effort to extend the scope of investigation to cognitive psychology, epistemology, and related areas.[22] It would be rash to prophesy how far such investigations will lead.

INTRODUCTION

The individuality of species bears directly upon bioeconomics, because the fundamental units or individuals in biology are economic ones, and so too are the laws of nature. The properties of the living world are the consequence of economic processes, both past and present. That world has been, and it continues to be, structured by the availability and utilization of resources. I once suggested that species are to biological theory as firms are to economic theory. The point was that different kinds of competition occur within and between economic units. This analogy has its limitations, however. Species are not productive units, and it might be better to compare them to a sort of market in which genes are exchanged. Nonetheless, the forces that hold species together are economic forces, and by shifting to an economic perspective, a host of problems, philosophical as well as biological, can be solved.

The economy of the intellect differs in detail, but not in principle, from the economy of nature, of which, indeed, it is an integral part. Data are resources. Theories are capital goods. Scientists and schools form competitive and cooperative units. Understand general economy, and you have the key that will unlock some of the deepest mysteries that surround our existence. For us, as organisms, ultimate reality is economic reality.

Chapter 2

SOCIOLOGY OF KNOWLEDGE VERSUS ECONOMY OF RESEARCH

IN THIS CHAPTER I EXAMINE TWO CURRENT APPROACHES TO THE explication of science, namely the logical and the sociological, and propose an alternative, the economic.

The logical approach has developed out of traditional philosophy, especially from what has rather misleadingly been called the "philosophy of science." At least tacitly it invokes the Greek ideal of the philosopher, dispassionately examining premises and seeing what conclusions follow from them. Its model for knowledge is mathematics, especially geometry, in which the Truth is known by demonstration, and hence with apodictic certitude. A deduction from true premises cannot possibly be false. The geometrical model has always enjoyed immense repute, especially where the validity of premises seems not to be at issue. The "quest for certainty," as John Dewey put it, has been a virtual obsession among philosophers.[23]

An inductive ideal has long coexisted with the deductive one. Pure mathematics enjoys its certitude only because it is a formal discipline. It is not "about" anything in particular. Science, on the other hand, asserts something about the material universe. We must ever face up to the incertitudes and imperfections of our premises.

11

"Inductivists" have tried to maximize certitude by reasoning from premises that, to them, seemed beyond question. Their goal was to raise an intellectual edifice upon an unshakable foundation of hard fact. Alas, the premises have repeatedly collapsed under the weight of further investigation. Inductivism of this sort was very popular in the nineteenth century. It became particularly difficult to defend when the physics of Newton was replaced by that of Einstein. It is still sometimes invoked in the context of scientific discourse, because not all scientists have taken the trouble to reflect upon such matters. Popular writers and scientists playing to the galleries are especially apt to presuppose it.

The hypothetico-deductive model of scientific reasoning provides a more realistic explication of how scientists can and do proceed. It treats the premises not as certain, but merely as conjectures, or hypotheses, to be tested in the light of new investigations. Hypotheses are provisional, and must ever remain so. They can never be "proven," in the sense that a theorem can be proven by a mathematician. But at least in some sense it is possible to refute them. If our premises imply what we can show to be false, it follows logically that something is wrong with those premises. If atoms are indivisible, then they cannot be split. Split one, and we know that atoms are not indivisible. Therefore scientists ought to proceed by trying to refute hypotheses. The resulting position, which is often called "refutationalism," tends to treat the search for truth as mainly an effort to get rid of error. It does not account for where hypotheses come from in the first place, and its advocates generally do not claim that it does. Discovery and verification are thought to be two quite different things.

This "H–D model" has been the basis for much discussion of how scientists do their research, and of how they ought to do their research. According to Popper, one of its leading champions, scientists ought to bend over backward to refute hypotheses.[24] They also should prefer those hypotheses that are most readily amenable to refutation. They should not embrace untested hypotheses. And those hypotheses that cannot be tested have no legitimate place in science.

Much research on the history of science, my own included, shows quite convincingly that refutation is one of the basic operations in scientific research as it is actually conducted.[25] Scientists do in fact strive to refute hypotheses, and such refutations have led to major advances. Nonetheless, the inadequacy of simplistic refutationalism

12

has long been evident. Often scientists refuse to reject an hypothesis when the data contradict it. Even the best scientists occasionally salvage their theories with so-called "*ad hoc* hypotheses" that explain away the difficulties and immunize their work from criticism. Likewise, scientists often embrace hypotheses long before a serious effort has been made to test them. An opponent of refutationalism might use such facts to refute refutationalism itself. But an advocate of refutationalism might just as well say that scientists ought to clean up their acts. So we ought to ask whether the goal is to describe science or to reform it. It does not seem reasonable for philosophers to dictate rules to scientists when they cannot agree among themselves upon how to evaluate the rules. Popper embarrassed himself by telling evolutionary biologists how to do their work, claiming that something was wrong with the theory of natural selection, but ultimately he admitted his error.[26]

Be this as it may, it is both philosophically legitimate and descriptively accurate to maintain that scientists can refute, do refute, and should refute hypotheses, provided that such refutation is not the sole criterion by which the truth is established. We need not embrace as an ideal the refutationalist notions that scientists *always do* maximize certitude, or *always should* maximize certitude. Nonetheless, for many just such an ideal has become the main, and perhaps only, criterion of the rational.

An alternative to the foregoing rationalist views holds that science either is not, or should not be, rational. This thesis is advocated by many who study what is called the "sociology of knowledge." This movement has been strongly influenced by Marxist thought, though not all of its supporters are Marxists. The dialectic approach, whether Hegelian or not, tends to conflate social interaction with logical inference. And sociologists would not be sociologists if they did not believe that society is important.

The sociology of knowledge strives to explain science in terms of what societies do, rather than in terms of what the organisms that make up those societies do. In dealing with science, this means that there is a kind of social unit, perhaps called "science," which really explains things, and individual scientists do not matter. It would be silly to contest the obvious facts that scientists do not work in absolute isolation from one another and that they are affected by social influences.

Nobody who is reasonably well informed about the history of evolutionary biology, for example, will deny that religious and political sentiments have profoundly affected the subject. We need only reflect upon the Huxley–Wilberforce debate and the effects of Lysenkoism on biology in the U.S.S.R. Surely, if we want a complete "science of science," we need to understand such matters.

There is a real threat to scientific freedom here, because the sociology of science can market itself as a managerial tool. If decisions about science have to be made upon the basis of extra-scientific considerations, and if sociologists are the experts, they stand to gain a great deal.

The value of legitimate work on the societal complexities of research can hardly be contested.[27] But it does not tell us the whole story of how scientists in fact conduct their research, and it tells us still less about how they should conduct their research. Sociologizing historians of science have invented a mythical pair of factions called "internalist" and "externalist" historians. Internalists are supposed to deal with intellectual history pure and simple, whereas externalists restrict themselves to the social influences. I have myself been berated for doing internalist history. As a professional comparative anatomist I was most puzzled by this charge. We biologists do not accuse our colleagues of doing "internalist anatomy," or "externalist ecology." We study the organs, the environment, or both, depending upon the kind of problem under investigation. When we engage in academic mudslinging we use a different assemblage of epithets.

Sociologists often claim that the group, rather than its components, must be treated as the "unit of analysis." Their arguments rest upon metaphysical premises that might as well be laid to rest here and now. They tell us that individuals are capricious, and that a scientific treatment of any subject has to deal with classes. The trouble here is that groups of scholars, such as The American Association for the Advancement of Science, are no more classes than the fellows themselves are classes of cells. Like biological species, social units are *individuals* in the ontological sense of wholes consisting of parts.[28] They are analogous to the Milky Way, not to the class of galaxies. To be sure, there are no laws about individuals, but individual societies are no exception.

In sociology, the legitimate laws would have to be laws about

14

classes of scientists, classes of scientific organizations, or something like that. And if individual scientists are capricious, so too are individual scientific organizations, schools, peer groups or whatever else you may choose to name. Furthermore, only individuals can do anything whatsoever, and the things that wholes and their component parts do may be quite different. Organisms, but not species, reproduce. Species, but not organisms, evolve. Organisms think. Societies do not. We must have very good reasons for treating science as if it were the product of committees, even if there is a certain amount of truth to that thesis.

Central to much irrationalist sociology is a tendency to deny the reality of truth itself. We meet with a kind of pyrrhonism or epistemological nihilism: "It's all subjective, so I'm right." We are told that truth is "relative," not "absolute," whatever that is supposed to mean. Such opinions are very popular among those who, for whatever reasons, resent modern civilization in general and science in particular. If nothing else, the success and prosperity of science makes its academic neighbors a bit jealous. In the context of a discussion on the nature of science such an attitude foredooms the discussion itself to failure. Without some conception of the truth as more than opinion vulgarized we have no basis for the objective evaluation of anything. Granted, our knowledge of the truth can never be perfect, and granted too, that certitude is a matter of degree, we have been presented with a mere attitude, not an argument for abolishing the distinction between true and false.

Feyerabend, who once was my colleague at Berkeley, tells us that in science "anything goes." This was just the sort of attitude that was popular with the Telegraph Avenue drug culture of accursed memory. Of course Feyerabend is so given to hyperbole and persiflage that it is sometimes hard to fathom his real sentiments. If all he means is that we scientists ought to make our own rules, and not take philosophers too seriously, all well and good. But not just anything goes.

Irrationalists have been particularly assiduous in their efforts to discredit the notion of scientific progress. They claim that the growth of scientific knowledge is not "cumulative." Instead of error giving way to truth, one error is replaced by another, and what is accepted at any given moment is attributed to the condition of society. In other words, the legitimacy of a theory is like the acceptability of some fashion in clothing.

15

These arguments are partly descended from an erroneous conception of progress, inherited from nineteenth-century social science, which has served as a straw man. In the metaphysics of Adam Smith, Herbert Spencer, and many others, progress was treated as providential, perhaps necessitated by the natural order. God had ordained that things would change for the better, at least for the most part and in the long run. Progress was built into the "social organism" as the adult organism is preordained in the fertilized egg. Social Darwinists, Marxists, and many others have embraced such historicism. Hence it is understandable that the idea of progress has been labelled an "ideology." But it does not follow that progress should be spurned as a fact.

Such arguments as are provided against the reality of progress may have a certain plausibility. Who would deny that a reduction in infant mortality tends to be offset by a higher death rate from the infirmities of old age? It is very hard to deny progress in some of the applied sciences. Progress in the struggle against smallpox has in fact been crowned with success, insofar as that disease has been wiped off the face of the earth. What about the pure sciences? In taxonomy we find our catalog of animals, plants, and microorganisms vastly expanded over the last two centuries. Turning to nature itself, the standard example is the eye of the archaic cephalopod *Nautilus*, which is like a camera without a lens and is a crude device beside the lensatic eye of a squid or an octopus. In biology, evolutionary progress is an aspect of objective reality to be studied. To pretend that it has never taken place would mean never getting credit for discovering its laws and causes, and for documenting its history.

Among the most influential thinkers in the irrationalist camp has been Thomas Kuhn, whose book *The Structure of Scientific Revolutions* has been the center of much discussion about scientific change in general.[29] Kuhn attempted to develop a model for scientific change based upon a unit more comprehensive than the idea, the experiment, or the theory. He called this unit the "paradigm." Originally a paradigm was an "exemplar"—an accomplishment such as Newtonian physics. The term also meant a group of assumptions, procedures, beliefs, methodologies, and the like, shared by a community of scientists. Kuhn also distinguished between two kinds of science. In "revolutionary science" a new paradigm is introduced, often replacing an older one. In "normal science," the paradigm remains unaltered, and research consists of "puzzle-solving." When the paradigm ceases to provide solutions to puzzles, it is said to break down, and a new paradigm may be devised to replace it.

A host of commentators have discussed both the strengths and the weaknesses of Kuhn's approach. In my own work on Darwin I came to appreciate some of the inadequacies and suggested some modifications.[30] For one thing, Kuhn's approach was non-evolutionary. He was after all a physicist, not a biologist, by training. I have suggested that paradigms evolve. Or, as I. Bernard Cohen puts it, scientific ideas are "transformed."[31] They also have to come from somewhere, and an important source is from interdisciplinary transfer. I have also suggested some stages in their evolution, to be discussed later on. Kuhn's model of the history of science looks rather like Baron Cuvier's pre-Darwinian theory of successive special creations. At best it can be said to invoke a kind of saltation. Evolutionary biologists for good reasons prefer change by steps, not leaps—though running very fast at times is perfectly acceptable. But my most important point is the suggestion that paradigms are the property, not (as Kuhn maintains) of scholarly communities, but of individual scientists. Kuhn wrote me a letter saying that he considered a personal paradigm analogous to a "private language." I am still not quite sure what this allusion to Wittgenstein was supposed to mean. However, Peter Munz, who studied under both Popper and Wittgenstein, has discussed the latter's influence on Kuhn at some length.[32] According to Munz, Wittgenstein early on attempted to erect a philosophy of science based upon atomic facts or truths established by observation. That effort fell to pieces, and Wittgenstein was then driven to claim that intellectual discourse is nothing more than a language game played by a group of people who accept a set of conventions. A paradigm shift is thus little more than a change in the rules. If one accepts the Popperian view, Munz says, one is not led into this sort of nihilism, because scientists are criticizing hypotheses, not working from one established truth to another. It is a kind of intellectual natural selection.

In the same spirit, Stephen Toulmin argued that a community of scholars ought to be viewed as a diverse population, not as a homogeneous unit consisting of like-minded persons.[33] Likewise, Hull has argued that Darwinism is an "historical entity"—an individual, and an evolving unit that changes through time, much as a biological species does.[34] Darwinism is a lineage, not a mere succession of objects.

Efforts to transform paradigm theory are not to be confused with efforts to replace it with something totally unrelated. Kuhn makes the good point that Lakatos's "research programs" and his own "paradigms" are variations on a theme.[35] This in spite of the fact that Lakatos, originally a mathematician, was definitely a rationalist. Furthermore, when we view scholarship as a matter of evolving historical entities, novelty becomes more readily intelligible. To say that Lakatos and I have merely extended and applied what Kuhn did would obscure what really happened. From the point of view of evolutionary taxonomy a human being is a modified fish, and even a modified protozoan, but some important changes have occurred in the last billion years. Indeed, Kuhn's views in the two editions of *The Structure of Scientific Revolutions* differ in many respects, and they continue to evolve.

Whatever the merits of his versions of paradigm theory, Kuhn did raise some issues that deserve particular attention in the present study. For one thing, he pointed out that revolutions and their effects may be long delayed. The anomalies and inadequacies of an accepted paradigm may become downright scandalous before a new one is evoked. Furthermore, once a new paradigm has become available, not everybody embraces it, even when it is obviously superior. (Often, it has been claimed, a school persists until its members retire or die of old age.) However, examples of the opposite pattern are known, with paradigms sometimes arising before the old one reaches a state of crisis. The Darwinian revolution is a good example. Darwin had developed an articulate paradigm by the early 1840s, but did not publish his work until 1859.

The fact that Darwin's views came largely from outside of biology proper—from geology *via* biogeography with a crucial addendum of economics—makes one wonder whether the failure in puzzle-solving is really crucial. Among the most controversial aspects of Kuhn's views is that paradigms render theories incommensurable. Given different points of view, one cannot choose between alternatives. If one cannot decide upon a rational basis, irrationalism would seem to follow by exclusion.

The notion that science evolves through efforts to solve problems was central to the pragmatism of John Dewey. His was the first important effort to base a philosophy of science on Darwin's accomplishment, and Dewey should be considered the founder of the evolutionary approach.[36] Unfortunately his effort was not particularly successful.

18

He was too much of a relativist, perhaps because he could not shake off the Hegelianism of his youth. Be this as it may, if scientists do anything, they at least try to solve problems. They also invent problems. One problem leads to another. Hence a scientist has to be judged as one whose task is to devise and solve problems. Of course that is not all they do, and they are not the only people who do it. We could equally well judge artists and statesmen on the same basis.

The fundamental thesis to be developed here is that scientists are explorers, not prophets. Their enterprise is rewarded not by certitude, but by discovery. Theirs is an economic, not a philosophical, rationalism, impelled by a desire to obtain the greatest amount of credit for producing the greatest contributions to knowledge. Calling a scientist an explorer implies that science is a risk-taking enterprise in the face of uncertainty. The outcome of investigation need not be foreseen from the beginning, and the goals may change as opportunities appear. A prospector who sets out to find gold is not a failure if he finds diamonds instead.

There are distinct economic tradeoffs between certitude and discovery. It is reasonable to seek what one wants in the most promising places, especially where we now have the least knowledge, for it is there that we are most apt to find the greatest reward. For this reason it would be folly to behave like a caricature of a Popperian, and devote years of labor to making sure that one's hypothesis was rigorously tested before doing anything else. One might lose one's priority, and furthermore someone else would get credit for taking the next step. Therefore it makes perfectly good sense for a scientist to be concerned with certitude, but only in order to guide the investigation along the more promising channels, avoiding gross mistakes if possible, but nonetheless forging boldly ahead.

There is nothing reprehensible about a scientist making mistakes. Error is part of the overhead of doing research. It can be reduced, but never eliminated. The best scientists can even be expected to make more mistakes than do the mediocre ones, for the best scientists do the most research. It is they who will work on the most difficult problems, and venture into the areas of greatest risk. Of course they will not be profligate of their capital, and they will cut their losses when that is called for. But an obsession with avoiding error either wastes time through attention to trivial details, or dictates investment in safe, low-yield enterprises. Hence the best scientists are bold but not rash, cautious but not timid.

A refusal to falsify an hypothesis, even in the face of anomalies, also makes good economic sense. A theory is not just a product. It is a resource, and a most valuable one. Inventing a good hypothesis is not easy, in spite of what those who have never done so may claim. The time spent attempting to invent hypotheses may be wasted, especially if an available one is acceptable. Furthermore, the inventor of an hypothesis possesses something of a monopoly on it, at least for a while. He is the one who will get credit should it turn out to be true, and often he is in the best position to develop it. Giving up such a valuable resource before its potential has been explored would be folly.

It should make equally good economic sense that scientists will differ among themselves with respect to how much evidence is required before they accept or reject an hypothesis. They differ with respect to how much they stand to lose or gain. For obvious reasons, he who invents a paradigm stands to lose or gain a great deal.

Another consideration is the cost of retooling. A scientist may not have the time, or feel it worth the effort, to learn a whole new body of data, theory, and methodology. In the face of uncertainty it might be reasonable to keep the old mill running until one is fully convinced that the investment in a new one will yield sufficient return. Perhaps it would be better to view the matter as remodeling the old mill, in which case there are certain obvious constraints. It might be wise to liquidate, perhaps changing fields, going into administration, or taking early retirement. For someone with idle capital, perhaps an older scientist who has run out of problems, or a younger one looking for a promising future, the inducement to embrace a new paradigm might be particularly attractive.

Probably such economic considerations underlie much of the apparent conservatism that is said to exist among scientists. At least this seems an attractive alternative to societal influences, personality structure, or senescence. The available empirical evidence tends to discredit the notion that scientists become less inclined to switch paradigms as they get older. [37] Indeed, we should expect those who either never really made it, and those who still have something important to contribute, to be particularly attracted by new opportunities.

A good example of a scientist who changed paradigms at a fairly advanced age is Charles Lyell (1797–1875), the father of modern uniformitarian geology.[38] Lyell opposed evolution in his early writings, but the views he presented in them were seminal to the contribution of Darwin. Even when *The Origin of Species* appeared, Lyell hesitated, then championed evolution in his book *The Antiquity of Man*. His action has been treated as an edifying instance of scholarly discipline, and of course it was. But we should not overlook how sensible it was in terms of what Lyell gained. His earlier contributions stood largely intact. He had an opportunity to make yet another. Why should he have wasted the last years of a magnificent career by engaging in rear-guard actions in defense of error?

Economics suggests that we might view the behavior of scientists as they get older in a somewhat different light.[39] Scientists experience diminishing returns upon their publications. All else being equal, each publication yields less than the previous one in terms of prestige, income, academic advancement, and other rewards. The precise reasons for this are inadequately understood, but it is not difficult to see what goes on. The first paper to be published should bring the greatest benefit, if for no other reason than because it makes a world of difference whether one has published at all. Additions to the stock of papers do less and less, however, to increase the relative size of one's contribution. Thus, the second paper doubles the contribution, the third increases it by one third, and by the time one gets to paper 101, the increment is only 1%. Somebody with 100 papers would probably not be considered 100 times as famous as somebody with only one paper, but even if he were the diminishing returns still apply.

The *caeteris paribus* assumption here is of course somewhat unrealistic. As scientists gain experience the quality of their publications should increase, to some extent offsetting any depreciation of the scientist through obsolescence or deterioration. Furthermore the stock of papers tends to depreciate. A certain level of output is needed to maintain a position as a productive scholar and to enjoy the benefits of that position. Nonetheless scientists are apt to have less of an incentive to maintain a high level of productivity as they get older, and this may militate against changing paradigms.

We also need to consider the effects of academia. Publications, recent or otherwise, are of greatest value to an academic when seeking employment, especially when seeking to move to a better job or when threatening to do so in order to be promoted. To the extent that older academics have less mobility, that should tend to reduce their productivity. Because untenured faculty have less job security, they should maximize publication, but for advancement within an institution only a certain level of publication is required, and resources might better be allocated to faculty politics and perhaps even teaching.

As scholars and academics get older, furthermore, they get more and more opportunities for advancing themselves by doing things other than research. Given a certain minimal scholarly reputation, there are plenty of opportunities to run things, both scholarly and academic. Looking at it from the opposite point of view, an academic scientist who gets back into the laboratory upon reaching retirement age probably has motives other than just crass expediency.

Economic thinking also suggests a better theory of paradigm replacement and development. We might consider something analogous to what Rostow calls "the stages of economic growth."[40] In my earlier discussions on paradigm theory, I proposed a terminology for such stages, but at the time economic considerations were rudimentary at most. As a model we might consider what happened in the mining business in the nineteenth-century American West. Initially there was a stage in which prospectors sought for ore. They were soon followed by claim-jumpers and miners, and later still by heavily capitalized and technically skilled industrialists who worked the more difficult bodies of ore, and even reworked the tailings. So too in science we have creative thinkers, plagiarists and opportunists, and those with big grants and command of the latest technology. Of course the same person can often play more than one role. There are many, however, who make it a business of "skimming the cream" off an area, then getting out. Others become experts in applying some technique or apparatus to areas opened up by others.

The earliest stage in the economic history of a paradigm would obviously involve its invention. It would be a supremely creative period, in which a theory took shape, perhaps as an alternative to some older one. Close upon it would follow an illustrative stage, in which the potentialities of the paradigm are worked out. Here the basic consideration would not be so much whether some hypothesis were true, but whether the new paradigm would solve old problems and generate new ones. It might very well involve the development of new methodologies, new instruments, and data of an unfamiliar kind. The practitioners might have to learn a quite different way of thinking, and perhaps unlearn old ones.

Just getting accustomed to novelty would require a considerable amount of time and effort. There would then come a period of verification, in which hypotheses were tested within the context of the paradigm itself. A subsequent period of exploration would involve the extension of the paradigm to larger contexts, including even different branches of knowledge.

These stages of invention, illustration, verification, and exploration are of course not kept perfectly distinct in practice. Some testing of hypotheses is always going on as a matter of routine. Nonetheless one might expect that different kinds of economic activity will be emphasized as time passes.

When a new hypothesis becomes available it is apt to be greeted with more enthusiasm and less criticism than a refutationalist philosophy might deem reasonable. The hypothesis is loosely connected to all sorts of problem situations, but the fit of the hypothesis to data can be very loose. At this stage the optimal stratagem is to get one's name associated with as many problems and tentative solutions as possible. The fun begins as the competition heats up, the opportunities narrow, and the rewards go to those who manage to eliminate some of the competing hypotheses. Testing becomes more stringent, methodology more cumbersome, and the data more abundant and sophisticated. Perhaps the main problems are solved. The choice is to look for new ones or work on the residual ones with less prospect for return. A paradigm shift can always start the whole process over again.

The history of evolutionary biology is as good a source as any for examples, and the "modern synthesis" that led to the so-called synthetic theory in the middle of this century is particularly instructive.[41] The creative breakthrough occurred in the 1920s, when it was realized that genetics does not create the difficulties for evolutionary biology it originally appeared to. The document most often cited as crucial is R. A. Fisher's book *The Genetical Theory of Natural Selection*, published in 1930, though as good scientists and good historians we must give much of the credit to Chetverikov, Haldane, Wright, and a few others.[42] Fisher's book helped make a great deal clear to the scientific community, and it may well be taken as the beginning of the illustra-

23

tive phase, which extended through the 1930s and 1940s, leading to the emergence of the synthetic theory, which was perhaps less of a synthesis than a mixture. It is rightly called synthetic, however, insofar as there were contributions from workers in various fields. There was Dobzhansky's work on the genetics of natural populations among animals, and that of Darlington and later Stebbins on plants. There was the work of Rensch and that of Huxley on the structure and growth of animals. Simpson was the leading figure in the study of fossil mammals, and Mayr clarified our understanding of speciation and geographical variation.

Of course a great deal of inventive and verificational work went on during the illustrative period, and there is no obvious point at which it gave rise to the verificational one. It might be sensible to regard the period after the Second World War as transitional, and date the beginnings of the stage of verification from around the time of the centenary of the publication of *The Origin of Species*, when a lot of basic assumptions began to be reexamined. The architects and the hod carriers alike built up a rather shaky edifice. It has stood up remarkably well, but only thanks to some extensive reconstruction. Much was published with but minimal justification on the basis of data.

The synthetic theorists largely took it for granted that natural selection could evolve features that exist "for the good of the species." Darwin had realized that this was not possible, but only in the mid-1960s did we begin to appreciate how seriously this mistake had affected the synthetic theory. A more critical attitude with respect to such matters has strengthened the theory and given another generation of researchers a new area of rich opportunity. A host of entrepreneurs, including myself, have cleaned up by going through the literature and showing how what was claimed to benefit a species actually benefited individual organisms or individual families. Such a pattern is precisely what one might expect. One generation covered a vast amount of area with scant resources. A later generation supplied its deficiencies.

The great irony here is that we keep finding how much better a job Darwin did than the rest of us. One might even say that our position is more Darwinian than neo-Darwinian and that the synthetic theory was abandoned, not just corrected. But this, too, is intelligible in economic terms. To invent a whole new conception of the universe, let alone an hypothesis or a paradigm, requires both considerable talent and a great

24

deal of work. Few have been willing or able to devote the amount of time and effort to coming to grips with the fundamentals that Darwin did.

It seems to me that we are now in the midst of an exploratory stage in evolutionary biology. That, at least, is one way to look upon efforts to synthesize biology and other branches of knowledge. This is the rationale that underlies evolutionary approaches to the evolution of culture, including that of science, which seem at the moment at least to be flourishing. But once again we need to bear in mind that the various stages overlap, that they are matters of emphasis, and that they occur together. Probably a better application of a stage theory will have to take a more detailed view, focusing upon separate areas of investigation, and not taking so sweeping a conception of things.

These days a fair number of biologists are telling the world that a new revolution is at hand, and that the synthetic theory is dead, soon to be overthrown by a "new evolutionary paradigm."[43] Perhaps there will be such a revolution, but the particular persons who are making such claims are not those who are apt to bring about the change in question. They try to sell us a new product without providing evidence that they can deliver something better. Their so-called "crisis of Darwinism" is a media event. What they have proclaimed as alternatives to the existing theory turn out to be minor improvements at best, or perhaps rediscoveries of truths and errors alike that are old hat to anybody who has mastered the literature. Their attacks on the synthetic theory turn out to be directed at textbook travesties, and not at the body of knowledge available to the scholarly community. If major improvements are to be made, they will be made by those who have in fact understood the present paradigm, who really know what its strengths and its weaknesses are, and who exercise some real creativity. At least this will be so if the examples of Copernicus, Newton, and Einstein mean anything; and those of Vesalius, Harvey, and Darwin.

It would be folly to prophesy what is going to happen to evolutionary theory, beyond the obvious point that it is going to continue flourishing. In the summer of 1966 an acquaintance remarked to me that a lot of people were getting out of molecular biology, and going into neurobiology, because molecular biology had "solved all its problems." When I was a graduate student at Stanford, Professor Ehrlich said to me "Go into phylogeny and you will starve." These days molecular biology is flourishing as never before, and my second grant to apply it to the phylogeny of animals has been funded. The people who get the credit are those who do the work, not those who tell the world that it cannot be done.

This is a good point at which to discuss the problems that beset anybody who attempts to elaborate a theory of how anything "develops" or "evolves"—words which are used interchangeably in French, but fortunately not in English. Theories of change are often modeled upon an implicit or an explicit analogy, such as the development of an embryo or the evolution of a species. Freud's theory of oral, anal, and genital periods was based upon a fanciful comparison of early stages in the formation of the embryo, which (at least when he received his education) were thought to be paralleled by very early stages in the history of multicellular animals.[44] Likewise, theories of cultural evolution have been strongly affected by the notion of orthogenesis, which means that lineages are programmed to evolve in a certain way, much as embryos are.

If we are to avoid the pitfalls of analogical reasoning, we need to be aware of the limitations of analogy in general and of the ones we use in particular. In applying economic principles to investigative behavior, however, we are not making fanciful and superficial comparisons. Rather we are subsuming particular cases under more general laws of nature. Even if we want to call that analogizing, the theses here developed are scientific hypotheses, and the only legitimate grounds for believing them to be true is the empirical predictions that they generate. Skill in the use of analogy is no different from skill in applying any other among the various factors of production.

Scientists are not just explorers; they are enterprising ones, always looking for opportunities to exploit their talents and other resources. Hence they have strong incentives to abandon old paradigms and embrace new ones depending upon where the opportunities seem to lie. Therefore scientific behavior is not to be explained merely in terms of going along with the crowd. We deal with a diversity of entrepreneurs, competing among themselves, and varying in their talents, their opportunities, and their inclinations. Novelty is a major inducement to change, for it holds out the prospect for opening up new territory to be explored.

In our correspondence, Kuhn took strong exception to my suggestion that one reason for abandoning a paradigm is boredom. But I daresay that such motives explain a great deal. We are disinclined to do the same kind of job over and over again, even when this renders some valuable service. The very desire for novelty attracts the best minds to the most challenging tasks. This emphasis upon novelty is not without its diseconomies, as we see when fields get left untilled soon after being opened up to cultivation. But this is perhaps the crucial consideration. In the traditions of Kuhn and Popper, what is often called "demand-side economics" seems to be a tacit assumption. Because scientists are enterprising, and seek "business opportunities," they think for themselves. For the very same reason, their search for truth involves far more than just casting out error. It involves the exercise of the creative imagination, the active search for new opportunities, and the attainment of fame and glory as a reward. A comparable misconception occurs in theoretical biology, among those who see competition as a purely negative force, and also in the philosophy of biology, among those who view natural selection as if it were nothing more than culling out the unfit. The future belongs to those who take advantage of their opportunities.

That scientists maximize the quantity and quality of discovery is not to deny that they do anything else. They are not given credit for discoveries until they have made these available to other scientists, who in turn use them as resources for making further discoveries. Thus scientists are both producers and consumers of capital goods. They also market and distribute the goods that they produce, and shop for those they use. The result is a very complicated economy, but one that can be explained in terms of a relatively small number of basic principles, as we shall see in chapters to follow.

Chapter 3

ECONOMIES OF THINKING

LET US NOW EXAMINE, IN GREATER DETAIL, THE CONTRAST BETWEEN rationalism in a philosophical sense and rationalism in an economic sense. Many words have more than one "opposite." "Normal," for example, has a *contradictory:* "non-normal." It also has various *contraries:* "abnormal," "subnormal," and "supernormal." "Abnormal" and "subnormal" are considered undesirable, "supernormal" has favorable connotations, and "non-normal" tends to be neutral. So too with "rational." We have its contradictory: "non-rational," and also "irrational," as well as various other contraries. "Irrational," like "abnormal," is a pejorative term. It means acting contrary to the dictates of reason. "Unreasonable" is a fair synonym. But "rational" suggests not just reasonable, or acting in accordance with the dictates of reason, but actually reflective, intelligent, even downright intellectual.

A child getting a good night's sleep is not exercising the higher intellectual faculties, but neither is he behaving irrationally. Rather he is doing what everybody would consider perfectly reasonable under most circumstances. If his mother were a scientist, it would be equally reasonable for her to leave a great deal of her daily routine, both on and off the job, to habit, and not constantly reflect upon every little detail of existence. Her intellect is a valuable resource, one that ought to be focused upon the really important problems. She should be devising and executing experiments, theorizing, reading the professional journals, and revising her manuscripts—not finding the best way to drink a cup of coffee.

If we intellectualized everything we would have no time left for what really matters. So we put our brains to work where we hope they will do the most good. This is not to say that the average citizen has given much thought to matters of economic policy in daily life. We learn our routine partly by a sort of trial and error, partly by imitation and conformity, partly by the advice of others. Even the way in which scientists do their research is largely the result of accepting, without much reflection, the common procedure among their colleagues. They were shown how to do research by their teachers, and unless somebody complains they are not apt to give it much thought. After all, if what everybody does seems to work perfectly well, why bother to reflect about it? One answer is that under certain circumstances the usual procedure gives the wrong answer. Knowing the rationale for at least some of one's actions separates the scientist from the technician—and education from mere training.

Economists have a long and venerable tradition of viewing human life as if everything were optimal, and as if all were the product of intelligence and planning. Adam Smith, in *The Wealth of Nations*, referred to an "invisible hand," which was supposed to keep the economy working at its best so long as man did not interfere. Somehow the universe had been organized so as to insure that private interests would automatically lead to the public good. Smith was a deist. As such, he believed that God takes no active role in worldly affairs; instead He has ordained laws of nature to provide for our needs. Such a concept of mechanical Providence justified a laissez-faire policy. One might compare it to the notion of *vis medicatrix naturae,* or the healing power of nature, which turns out to be a not unreasonable basis for medical practice. There is a good reason to think that natural selection has optimized the parts of the body for the well-being of the whole. But then again, the organism's ability to heal itself has its limitations.

In economics it is indeed legitimate to invoke optimizing forces provided that these have real existence. Likewise, positing an optimal state makes it easier to solve certain kinds of problems. Taking it for

30

granted that the economy has the same sort of structure God would have given it, in the exercise of His omnipotent power and unlimited beneficence, is going too far.

Nonetheless, individual producers and consumers do make reasonable decisions about their economic activities, and the result tends to be a more efficient and productive economy. Our efforts to get the most for our money bring down the cost of goods. All this can be granted without having to make each and every customer a perfect judge of what is the best buy. The limits of economic rationalism are intelligible in terms of evolutionary biology. Economies and ecosystems will be optimized only to the extent that deoptimizing forces, including ones rooted in self-interest, do not counteract the optimizing ones.

Whether a truly optimal state does exist in any particular case has to be investigated by competent economists and ecologists. Such a decision is not a matter of philosophy or theory, but empirical fact. Deciding what our economic goals ought to be is of course another matter. Economics does not tell us whether we should spend money on luxuries or give it to charity, but only how to get the most for our money. So too the advantages, in the struggle for existence, of being able to make rational judgments are sufficiently obvious. But precisely because we are not the product of some intelligent and foresightful creative act, but rather the consequence of mindless trial and error, we should not expect perfection in our rational faculties either. Nature may appear to be a perfect artisan, but actually she produces cheap consumer goods *en masse*. Heedless of the consequences, she produces whatever the market will bear.

Given an evolutionary perspective, the inadequacies of our intellects are readily intelligible. Our faculties did not evolve in order to solve abstruse metaphysical puzzles, but as a consequence of their usefulness in solving the problems that arose in our ancestors' daily lives. That the intellect has evolved such capabilities as it does possess shows how useful it can be in dealing with the practicalities of survival and reproduction. We are able to know the truth because such knowledge is useful. However, we should not expect our nervous systems to be set up so as to maximize the apprehension of truth. Discovering the truth can be expensive, and what really counts is attaining effective results. Hence the brain might well be expected to engage in certain

31

shortcuts, giving cheap and easy solutions that do the job well enough. We should not expect the mind to contain perfect representations of ultimate reality or of things in themselves—even if that were physiologically possible.

Evolutionary speculation in economics has suggested that decision making is not so much a matter of "optimizing" as it is of "satisficing."[45] By this it is meant that we do not consider all of the possibilities open to us and choose the best, but select one that seems acceptable under the circumstances. We might shop for an automobile, not by visiting every dealer in town, but rather by allowing ourselves to be satisfied with the fact that the second dealer offered a better price than the first. Critics of satisficing theory have pointed out that from a certain point of view satisficing is also optimizing. Shopping consumes a lot of time and effort. As one goes from one merchant to another, the probability of finding a better buy decreases, and therefore the return on shopping time goes down. In other words, effort devoted to shopping gives us diminishing returns. Ideally, a balance ought to be struck between the value of time and the economic gain realized through lower prices and more desirable goods. Practically, one uses rules of thumb in efforts to approximate that ideal.

A scholar engaged in searching the literature might very well satisfice instead of optimize. One is supposed to read the literature that bears upon one's research to find out (among other things) if one's views are original and give credit to one's predecessors. Ideally one ought to look everywhere, and in some cases that has been accomplished. However it may not be feasible to cover the literature perfectly, and it is not necessarily worth the effort. In many cases one does not know where all the relevant materials have been published, and in others it is hard to decide what is in fact relevant. I suspect that the common practice is to keep looking up references until one experiences diminishing returns. A balance will be struck between the amount of effort further search would involve and the estimated probability of missing something important. But such "optimal foraging" will only be optimal in a very crude sense.

So too with efforts to test hypotheses. A scientist is supposed to do some experiments and otherwise gather evidence before publishing, perhaps by ruling out some alternative hypothesis. There are also standard precautions to be taken in making sure that the study is valid.

This at least has the effect of reducing the volume of literature. But one can never be sure that one has ruled out enough possibilities or taken enough precautions. So rather than collect more and more evidence, it makes sense to check out the most obvious possibilities, publish, and hope for the best. A naive Popperian is apt to lose his priority.

Satisficing can lead to serious difficulties. To accept a solution is one thing, to get stuck with it is another. Ideally every hypothesis should always retain its provisional character and be subject to replacement by some alternative. Often this happens when new evidence becomes available. However, an hypothesis may become a "fact" or a tradition, so that it is presupposed in later work. New results may then be interpreted so as to render them consistent with the hypothesis, either by discarding them or by explaining them away. Apparent lack of contradictory evidence then becomes the basis for an argument in favor of the hypothesis. The theory can be supported by arguments that beg a question that ought to be at issue or even by arguments that are downright circular. Early in the nineteenth century the marine biologist Edward Forbes found that as he dredged the sea bottom at ever greater depths, the number of animals decreased. Extrapolating from his data, he hypothesized an "abiotic zone," below which life did not exist. The "fact" of an abiotic zone militated against the study of deep-sea animals. Relevant data were thrown overboard both literally and figuratively! It was only when extensive sampling by the *Challenger* Expedition in the 1870s turned up an overwhelming body of data that the notion of an abiotic zone was finally abandoned altogether.

Another example of an assumption becoming a fact is evident in the history of biogeography and continental drift.[46] For perfectly good reasons nineteenth-century biogeographers were skeptical about a possible southern connection between the animals and plants of different continents, even though some of the data were highly suggestive that one had existed in the remote past. Hypotheses about sunken continents and land bridges were shown to be unnecessary, though the possibility of a very old connection was not ruled out. Later it was suggested that the continents had moved. This was resisted partly because of biogeographical arguments that presupposed the permanence of continents. The epistemological circle here was broken when independent evidence from geophysics made continental drift a compelling hypothesis.

Such incidents are common, but not inevitable. A competent scientist who knows what the premises are and who can cope with the reasoning process should come to the right conclusions, even without having to draw upon evidence from outside the system. But there is no particular reason why a scientist should be expected to know what premises underlie his research. To find out what these are takes a great deal of effort. Not everybody feels inclined to read hundreds of books and journal articles, especially if they are written in several different languages. Few scientists are taught to inquire into the validity of their most fundamental premises. They are taught to be critical, but only at a relatively superficial level. To spend much time on such matters would be pedagogically inefficient. It would create a need for additional space in scholarly journals. It would keep people out of the laboratory. When basic premises are reexamined, it is usually because some exceptional person recognizes an opportunity to do the job better. A few people enjoy that kind of work. Sometimes a point is reached at which it obviously has to be done.

The psychological literature provides some grounds for thinking that refutationalism is not part of our ordinary daily routine. Wason presented his subjects with a series of numbers generated according to a rule, and had them try to guess what the rule was.[47] Then he asked them to test the hypothesized rule by guessing what should be the next number in the series. The best strategy here would be to propose a number that would refute the rule. Thus, if the hypothesis was that the series progressed by increments of two and if the next number predicted by that hypothesis was six, the most efficient way to get the answer would be to ask if five were correct.

Wason's study, and others like it, show that subjects try to confirm, not disconfirm, their hypotheses. Evidently such procedures work out fairly well in ordinary day-to-day life. Usually we are not trying to test hypotheses, but to find the ones that work. This suggests that natural selection has programmed us to engage in induction, even though there is no logical justification for it, and even though it is not always the most effectual procedure.

Natural selection itself is an inductive process, not a hypothetico-deductive one. There is no effort upon the part of natural populations to be critical, and test the efficacy of their adaptations. In a world in which they did, we would find deer experimenting with their ability to escape from mountain lions. Species themselves cannot engage in critical thinking, or plan for the future, so a certain amount of maladaptation is inevitable. The imperfection of adaptation that results because natural selection is inductive provides the kind of critical test for the theory's validity that unsophisticated persons have failed to appreciate.

Another explanation for our tendency to want to confirm hypotheses may be that we find it difficult to think up disconfirming instances, and therefore we try the confirmation strategy first. Helsabeck found that it is very difficult to think up counterexamples.[48] Probably the process involves a lot of work and a good imagination. A good practical logician is adept at counterexamples precisely because others are apt to miss them.

It would seem that people in general are born optimists. Considering how dreadful life sometimes gets, this may have considerable survival value. Many a struggle is won on the basis of sheer persistence. If hope often fails it sometimes pulls us through when the odds are against us. Our attitude toward chance is a case in point, especially as manifested in gambling. The casino plays by the odds, thereby exploiting "human nature." Most people will commit what is called the "gambler's fallacy"—assuming that, even with a fair coin, a run of heads increases the likelihood that the next toss will be tails. A number of psychological studies show that man is not a very good intuitive statistician.[49] We tend to use crude approximations and rules of thumb. Even to professionals, the principles of statistics and probability theory are not all intuitively obvious. Furthermore their application may involve a great deal of work, and becoming adept at this is not easy. In other words, the cost of problem-solving may become prohibitive, and it makes sense to use imperfect tools.

Yet in spite of the imperfections of the common intellect, we are fully capable of becoming good statisticians, good logicians, and effective refuters of hypotheses. When we do understand the principles, we apply them where they are apt to do the most good. We focus upon important problems, especially those related to survival and making a living. He who runs a casino will calculate the odds or else go out of business, but the incentives are different for the customer whose sole motive is to have a little fun. In science there is no question that mistakes occur in the manner of reasoning; but scientists learn to avoid them. We now possess improved instruments and better methodology because these are valuable resources in the conduct of research, not because of considerations about "right thinking" in the abstract.

The notion that science is common sense writ large has been seriously downgraded in recent years. One reason is that some of the truths of science are counterintuitive. Perhaps judgment here is biased by the desire of academic specialists to make "the scientific method" a monopoly of some elite. Be this as it may, there would seem to be some truth in the "common sense" theory of the scientific method. Our conception of the reasoning of primitive man has been prejudiced by excessive attention to the nonrational sectors of his intellectual economy—to magic, religion, art, and political affairs. But in fact the economic life of primitive man reveals an immense amount of skill, particularly on the part of hunter-gatherers. This skill results from intellectual sophistication as well as from richness of experience. Several recent anthropological studies emphasize this point. For example, the ichthyologist Johannes studied the fisheries of Palau. [50] He was profoundly impressed, not only by the erudition of the fishermen, but by their ability to devise and test hypotheses. This makes a great deal of sense. If one wants to study adaptation, the place to study it is in the sort of context in which it evolved.

If this is so, then why do we find all this putatively nonrational behavior in primitive and civilized man alike? Why all the magic, the superstitions, the ideology, the successes of demagogues? Exactly the same answer applies, and an economic basis is equally evident, only here we deal with another sector of the economy. Man is a social animal, and does not live by bread alone. What really counts is getting into the gene pool. Beliefs and thought processes are used to control the behavior of others so as to achieve, in general and for the most part, maximal reproductive success. Here truth is often irrelevant. It might be downright suicidal to believe what is felt to be detrimental to one's neighbor's interests. Man is born wise, but society makes a fool of him.

Another sort of mental economizing is apparent in our habit of oversimplifying. Simplicity in our thinking may have certain advantages, insofar as it may lead us to generalize and attend to what is most important. But we may screen out what seems to be noise at the risk of missing a signal. In biology a good example is "typological" thinking—conceiving of groups or even of single objects in terms of idealized models or stereotypes. (Such stereotypes are often equated with Platonic Ideas or essences, so what philosophers call "essentialism" is an approximate synonym for what biologists usually call "typology.") It is easier to think about an exemplar of a group than about each of its members individually. For purposes of calculation, an idealized example having no corresponding object in the real world may be the best way to conceive of the group. In doing so, however, we tend to screen out the diversity that characterizes the actual objects. "The Human Being" becomes a white, adult male, but she could equally well be an Asian infant. Hence one root of racism, ageism, and sexism. We accept a social stereotype, and only revise it under pressure. Or, in dealing with individual people, we may rely too much on first impressions. Whatever the adverse social, political, and economic consequences, it saves a lot of work if we ignore human diversity.

In systematic biology the effects of typological thinking are notorious. The enormous variability within species was grossly underestimated, and the same is true with respect to the diversity of life at higher levels in the taxonomic hierarchy. Treating one kind of animal or plant, or even a fair sample, as if it were representative of all organisms has led to crude overgeneralizations time and again. Some of the blame for typological thinking must be ascribed to the pedagogical economy. It simply is not feasible to present students with anything remotely approaching a fair sample of organic diversity. Biology is taught largely by reference to "types"—Man and the Frog perhaps. In the behavioral sciences we are apt to be saddled with the White Rat, the Monkey, and the College Sophomore. That such typology really poses difficulties is clear from the amount of effort scientists have devoted to correcting the resulting distortions.

We take all sorts of analogous shortcuts in everyday life, frequently using rules of thumb where calculation might give a far better result.[51] Many people will go to more effort to save 10 percent on a tendollar purchase than they will to save 1 percent on a one hundreddollar purchase, even though the amount saved is exactly the same. Evidently we find it easier to compare the proportions than the absolute quantities. This suggests some intriguing possibilities. Consider a familiar optical illusion:

The upper horizontal line looks longer than the lower one. Some people, especially with practice, can compensate, ignoring the lines on the ends and perceiving the horizontal lines as equal in length. However this takes considerable effort. Such illusions are not much of a problem in everyday life. Under ordinary conditions attending to the length of the entire figure should be the reasonable way to judge the length of the part.

An even more striking psychological phenomenon occurs in what are called "ambiguous figures." A "duck-rabbit" can be seen as either one kind of animal or the other. Most of us, at least, cannot see both at once. Rather we experience "Gestalt switches," and shift back and forth from one to the other. Such figures have been invoked as analogous to incommensurable paradigms. [52] Just as we cannot perceive the duck and the rabbit simultaneously, it is claimed that we cannot regard a theory from two different perspectives at the same time. But do ambiguous figures really bear upon this issue? We can put a pair of identical figures side by side, or just look at one figure in different ways at different times. These psychological limitations merely reflect the way in which our visual equipment happens to be organized. Perhaps it would be too costly to be able to see a duck and a rabbit at the same time. In the natural environment in which our nervous systems evolved, an organism is either a duck or a rabbit.

Of course those who have speculated about paradigm incommensurability have other reasons for believing in it. Among these reasons we have the implications of the fact that paradigms and theories are unique and diverse individuals—a fact readily overlooked. Obviously no two individual objects can be meaningfully compared in everything whatsoever. Biologists have this kind of problem all the time. Consider, again, a duck and a rabbit. A duck has a gizzard, a rabbit has teeth. Both care for the young, but are we to compare the size of the rabbit's litter with the number of eggs the duck lays, or the number hatched? Such incommensurability does not inevitably prevent biologists from coming up with useful generalizations. The feathers of ducks and the fur of rabbits are not commensurable in every respect, but both do serve as insulation in warm-blooded animals, and their efficiency as insulation can indeed be compared in a meaningful way.

Perhaps the incommensurability thesis would not be taken so

seriously were it argued on the basis of concrete instances. In my experience most of the difficulties scientists have with respect to comparing one another's views result from a lack of mutual understanding. Consider two scientists, whom we shall call John and Mary. It may be that John understands Mary's paradigm, and Mary understands John's. Perhaps neither can understand the other's paradigm. On the other hand the relationship might be asymmetrical, with John understanding Mary's paradigm, but Mary not understanding John's—or Mary understanding John's paradigm, but John not understanding Mary's. In this case, the scientist who understands both paradigms will be able to decide what sort of evidence would allow a choice between the two, but will not be able to convince the other.

Any number of influences may militate against consensus among scientists having different approaches, backgrounds, and techniques. Perhaps understanding a competing paradigm requires esoteric knowledge, or a special background. Theoreticians and experimentalists, botanists and zoologists, physiologists and ecologists, are all apt to think about the same problem in different ways. In Chapter 1 I discussed the history of my views on the individuality of species. I had a very hard time persuading David Hull, a philosopher who had been applying the techniques of modern analytical philosophy to taxonomy, that species are not classes but individuals. Indeed it was several years before he came to the same conclusion on quite different grounds from my own. The problem here was not so much a matter of incommensurability, as of a different way of solving problems, and the need to ask some very penetrating questions about fundamental premises. Philosophers of biology and philosophical biologists are apt to ask very different questions. Once Hull realized what was going on, he was very effectual at persuading philosophers. He could speak their language and appeal to the kind of evidence they would accept. To put this in economic terms, we must not presuppose what are called "perfect markets" in the economy of the intellect. We do not all possess complete information about costs, opportunities, and the availability of resources.

The very data of perception do not present themselves as a random survey of the material universe. The brain selects and enhances its raw materials, correcting truth and error alike. Psychology is profligate of instances. The "blind spot" on the human retina results from an imperfection in the "design" of the eye—perhaps the consequence of

39

fortuitous events that occurred well over half a billion years ago. There are no photoreceptors where the optic nerve enters the retina. But only when we use a special apparatus is it obvious that the brain fills in the missing parts of our visual field. That the brain should do so makes good economic sense; we would waste resources if distracted.

But such "computer enhancement," or whatever we may wish to call it, may have its price. In reading we screen out minor discrepancies such as transposed letters. Both written and spoken language possess a certain amount of redundancy that facilitates communication. Non-redundant language is parsimonious of words, but costly to interpret without error, so an economic balance is struck between redundancy and brevity (Zipf's Law). [53] If our main task is to understand a written paragraph, it makes sense to ignore the blemishes in typesetting. But any such habit militates against our success in reading proof. I remember once typing a manuscript, and detecting an error only because the lines in the original and in the copy were of different lengths. I read the two lines several times, but could see nothing; only when I took the two sheets of paper, put one on top of the other, and then held them up to a light did the error stand forth! Reading for content and reading for accuracy are two different activities; trying to do both at the same time is inefficient because neither is done as well as it might be. In a later chapter we shall examine the economic principles of combination and division of labor which explain such matters.

We might expect scholars to impose both fortunate and unfortunate emendations on the text. Old manuscripts, particularly ones in dead languages, have to be reconstructed, not just scanned. This requires much time, effort, and skill. A good historian of science knows the books that an older audience was familiar with, and also the objects written about, such as animals and plants.

One experiences the same kind of challenge in trying to read the literature in a field other than one's own. It helps to do some background reading and look up technical terms. This, however, requires time and effort, and we are apt to take shortcuts. When biologists write about philosophy they have difficulties with such terms as "deduction," "value judgment," "objective," and of course "individual." Yet there is nothing unusual here. The French *demander* is not to be translated by the English "demand," the German *Gift* by the English "gift," or the British *corn* by the American "corn." Learning a language is costly, and even the best translations are imperfect. But contrary to what has

40

occasionally been suggested, such constraints upon our ability to communicate do not justify notions of incommensurability. They only tell us that a lot of work may be necessary before the message gets across.

Traditional philosophy has overemphasized language to the detriment of content. Words, after all, are cheaper to talk about than the underlying propositions and thoughts. It seems excessive to claim that language structures our perceptions, and extreme versions of this notion are not taken very seriously these days. Nonetheless we do have some evidence for interactions between our words, our thoughts, and our perceptions. Some data are available with respect to connections among psychology, anatomy, and art. The three are not unrelated, for artists have long been interested in visual perception and in the structure of the body, the better to achieve their effects. The research tradition of Leonardo da Vinci and Albrecht Dürer is continued by such moderns as Gombrich. Historians and philosophers of science have attended to such phenomena, and have tried to relate them to paradigm theory. Anatomical drawings are anything but photographs accurately depicting the *Ding an sich*. Rather they mirror the views of the anatomist, including the theoretical presuppositions of the time. But the same is true of sculptures and paintings. Chinese artists and English artists draw the same scene very differently. This happens not so much because they live in different perceptual worlds as because they have been taught to draw in different ways. Artists learn a series of rules for producing work, and do not depart from these any more than they have to—just as scientists generally refrain from doing radically different experiments or writing papers widely diverging from the traditional format. He who breaks with tradition and nonetheless gets pleasing results is naturally esteemed a genius.

Oscar Wilde, reversing the old saying that art imitates nature, suggested that nature sometimes imitates art. It seems to me that what art really imitates is imitation. So does science. Practitioners of every craft follow certain rules to get a particular kind of product. Doing otherwise might deprive us of our livelihoods. One produces a series of paintings, or short stories, or experiments, perhaps with a certain amount of diversity, hoping that each will be followed by something which, if not better, will at least fetch an acceptable price in the marketplace.

The anatomical documents thus far examined by historians have to do with certain theoretical traditions. In Galenic physiology, the heart was thought to have pores between the ventricles. Leonardo da Vinci and Vesalius searched for these in vain, but drew them anyway. It remained for Harvey to deny their existence, not so much because he did not find them, as because his theory implied that they did not exist. Now, what profound epistemological conclusions are we to derive from these happenings? As a professional comparative anatomist I am rather disinclined to indulge in ethereal speculations here. The explanation is simple, mundane, commonplace, and economic. Anatomists do not have the time, opportunity, or inclination to check every last detail of accepted fact against the testimony of the scalpel. Rather, they ask questions that are apt to give important new results. Unless they have some compelling reason for departing from tradition, they will not do so. In Harvey's case the compelling reason was a theory predicting a host of novel implications, and the nonexistence of the pores was but one of them. The notion that anatomy is a "descriptive" science, like the notion that economics is not a mathematical one, is a superstition popular only with those who know nothing about it.

In teaching anatomy we of course want at least a good sample of the accepted facts to be checked through reference to specimens, rather than merely embraced on the basis of authority. Many significant discoveries have in fact resulted from chance observations in the pedagogical laboratory. One of my advanced undergraduates turned up a hyaline rod (called a crystalline style) in the stomach of a gastropod. I knew that it was not supposed to be there, and we published a paper together.[54] But she was taking a course in which original research was expected. The ordinary student in a conventional course will probably not be motivated to focus upon even a glaring anomaly. Furthermore, the mind needs to be prepared for such anomalies, for otherwise it will not recognize them as such.

The great invertebrate zoologist Libbie Hyman once pointed out that students will not see objects unless they are told to look for them. In my experience they will see them even if they are not there. After all, students are rewarded for doing as they are instructed. Students are required to make drawings because this forces them to attend to the specimens. Their drawings tend to look more like the illustrations in their textbooks than the specimens they use. The same applies to their professional elders. In reviewing manuscripts of biology textbooks for

42

publishers I have noted a great deal of derivative illustration. Pictures are copied out of other textbooks, and many generations may have to be traced if one wants to find the original. At each stage the figures are "improved upon" one way or another, sometimes with odd results. Even so, mistakes are readily overlooked. One may have to know a little physiology to appreciate the fact that the esophagus should lead to the stomach, not to the bladder. This situation is more than just remotely analogous to what went on in the history of medieval herbals, whose illustrations, copied out of other herbals, became rather surrealistic.

In all such cases we see economic forces at work. It is easier to copy drawings than to draw from nature, or from the understanding of nature. I should add that this phenomenon of imperfect copying is not in the least restricted to science. Art historians and anthropologists have studied the evolution of designs and artifacts from this point of view.[55] And there is a substantial psychological literature based on having people tell stories, then repeat them to another person. The analogy with mutation and natural selection (or artificial selection) is all too obvious.

Among my early discoveries was an organ, which my predecessors had overlooked, in the reproductive systems of certain gastropod mollusks.[56] The nidamental glands, which form the coverings around the eggs, were supposed to consist of two parts, the albumen gland and the mucous gland. A close look at the egg masses themselves revealed not two layers, but three: the albumen was separated by a thin layer from the mucous. By such maneuvers as dissecting a slug killed in the act of laying eggs I found out which tissues secrete which product. It turned out that although there were only two names, there were three organs, one of which, the albumen gland, is often missing. The third organ had been observed and called a "winding gland" by a nineteenth-century anatomist. This name suggests that it is a long tube of small diameter. Actually it is a folded structure. However, it was drawn exactly as the name implies—as if it could be unraveled like a long hose.

Here again, there is no reason to invoke metaphysical obscurities, when a little straightforward economics and psychology will do. My predecessors were morphologists, not functional anatomists. They were interested only in the arrangement of parts, and not in how the system worked; but this was crucial to my research on why the animals had

43

evolved the way they did. We definitely were operating under different paradigms, and these determined what we would look for, but they did not determine what we saw when we took the trouble to look. It only happens that morphologists are not interested in function and do not invest time and other resources in studying it. Of course we can enumerate any number of instances of commensurability between paradigms, and never rule out the universal particular of at least one incommensurability effect. But for the same reason biologists have difficulty ruling out the possibility of spontaneous generation, the inheritance of acquired characteristics, and sea monsters.

There is nothing unusual about the eye playing tricks on us, although the more spectacular instances do not occur every day. Once I was reading a passage on Chinese art in a book by Gombrich.[57] With my peripheral vision I saw an illustration, and below it a series of Chinese characters. I looked again, and found a series of English letters. But the characters had indeed been visualized, and interpreted as realistic Chinese characters, if perhaps the sort one might envision in a dream. This can be interpreted as an extreme case of "visual set," with the brain enhancing the image in the wrong way. It is like a hunter actually "seeing" a deer which turns out to be a man. Ask somebody the following question: "If the word 'joke' is spelled 'j-o-k-e,' how does one spell the white part of an egg?" You will probably be told how to spell "yolk," not "albumen."

In our daily lives we occasionally misidentify a person or other object at a distance, or under other conditions where visual cues are scant. Minute anatomists have the same kind of problem when they push their optics to the limits of resolution. They try to see everything they possibly can, and often see things that are not there. The classic example is Hartsoeker's figure of the human spermatozoon, with its tiny homunculus, or preformed embryo, in its head. Perhaps the most conspicuous feature of early development in many animals is the cells that make up the embryo: but these are rarely evident in the drawings that predate the cell theory (1838). Even Darwin, whose work on the minute anatomy of barnacles was exceedingly meticulous, thought he saw antennae in the developing embryos in a place where we now know they do not occur. Under such circumstances we might well ask whether it is the brain or the instrument that causes the problem. A good answer would be that the brain *is* an instrument.

44

ECONOMIES OF THINKING

One reason for believing in scientific progress is that better microscopes, better theories, and better brains do correct our erroneous impressions. When we get an improved microscope, with higher resolving power, the incertitude vanishes, much as the light of the sun drives away the phantasms of the night. By the same token it is not a bad thing, but only a mixed blessing, that the brain enhances its perceptions at the risk of error. An occasional mistake is the price we pay for an ability to make do with data of marginal quality that nonetheless may be very useful in the conduct of our daily lives. A good scientist pushes his instruments to the limits of their capacity, for it is there that he is most apt to find the treasure he seeks. He labors in darkness and makes the best of the least flicker of light that might illuminate the path toward truth. Experience teaches that the best light comes from within—it is the light of reason.

Chapter 4

AGAINST AUTHORITY

SCIENTISTS HAVE A PECULIAR ATTITUDE TOWARD AUTHORITY, AND one that does not seem altogether consistent. On the one hand they profoundly resent its influence, and will tell you that in science the only real authorities are facts. On the other hand, they gladly invoke whatever authorities might be useful in furthering the acceptance of their work. In the present chapter we shall examine the reasons for such apparent inconsistency, and consider the role that authority actually does play in the economy of the intellect. In a few words, authority turns out to be a cheap substitute for the genuine article.

The issue of authority in science is complicated by the fact that so many contemporary philosophers attempt to make the truth a matter of social consensus. Even Popper, a strong supporter of democratic values, attributed the objectivity of science to its social character.[58] This gets everything backward. If you were on an island all by yourself and wanted to know whether a certain fruit was poisonous, you could easily design and execute a scientific experiment to find out. You could perhaps try eating a very small amount and see if it made you sick. After all, nobody in his right mind wants to die. It is in the context of society, not apart from it, that we lose control of our objectivity. When somebody is hired to show that a food or drug is or is not harmful, the outcome is very likely to be affected by who pays the bill and who might be sued for damages. Such agent–principal conflicts are notorious.

Likewise a graduate student can be in real trouble when the experiments do not turn out the way his major professor hoped they would. (A good example of this is provided by Provine.[59]) Scholarly discipline is corrupted by the desire for eminence, money, and all sorts of other amenities. Such corruption occurs as a result of social pressures, and pressures to the contrary would not be needed if these did not exist. But the notion that society is the hero here is a myth that finds a ready market. The friends of society would dearly love to stand in a position of authority, and to have us believe that authority itself is a good thing.

We are told that scientific knowledge is a "public affair," therefore not a matter of private judgment. This is supposed to imply that the scientific community, not individual scientists, should decide what is true. This thesis perverts the whole spirit underlying the perfectly legitimate principle that science ought to be "public" in a quite different sense. It was supposed to mean that the criteria of judgment ought to be equally accessible to each and every one of us—individually. Anybody ought to be able to carry out the requisite observations and experiments and judge for himself. Mystical insight has to be ruled out, because there is no way of evaluating it intersubjectively. When one authority tells us one thing, another authority something else, all we can do is conclude that one or the other is wrong, and perhaps both are. Pyrrhonists and skeptics are inclined to argue that because the experts disagree upon a given matter there is no basis for forming a sound judgment. Of course the authorities disagree. One way to become an authority is to make oneself disagreeable. But this says nothing about the legitimate canons of evidence and the merits of the dispute.

A most flagrant abuse of analogical reasoning is seen in efforts to compare a scientist to a litigant in a court of law. Consider what sort of tribunal this is supposed to be. Of what transgression does anybody stand accused? And what does the jury conclude? One juror says "I was bored stiff, and went to sleep." Another says "I couldn't understand a word," and a third remarks "I'll run a few experiments and let you know." The so-called jury is anything but disinterested, for it is they,

48

not just the litigant, who will suffer if they err. They will have to decide for themselves, individually, how to conduct their future research. And they will have to answer to a "higher court," which will reward or punish them in the light of evidence yet to be gathered. Supposedly scientists are being judged by their peers, or equals. But how should we decide who is equal to whom? The better the scientist, the fewer peers he has, and the very best, by definition, is unequalled. It is presumptuous to pass judgment on one's betters, and degrading to acknowledge them. Why should anybody want to be judged by anything so fallible as a human being anyway? Let future experience determine the issue.

Scientists are occasionally asked to testify in court. They frequently express resentment about the way in which they are treated and do not think very highly of the legal profession. This is because the rules of discourse in a court of law are very different from those in science. The sort of adversarial proceedings that go on routinely in courts of law are considered bad manners among scientists. And scientists giving testimony are expected to express the sort of certitude that would discredit them in the eyes of their colleagues. The situation is unfortunate, and I am not sure what should be done about it, but at least it helps to underscore the difference between a scientific community and a law court.

Among scientists there exists nothing analogous to a contract binding them to accept the judgment of others as to the merits of their work, or stipulating that the scientific community will decide what is right. If others disagree, it may be reasonable to accept their opinions, but a more appropriate action may be to gather more evidence. So far as science goes, the adverse judgment of the scholarly community may only mean that recognition may have to be deferred. If so, it will be all the more handsomely rewarded. When a new theory comes into the world it has to be advocated by a minority. Furthermore it would be irresponsible for a scholar to accept the judgment of the community if that community is wrong, for all would suffer in the long run. Individuals have the responsibility of judging for themselves, as best they can, irrespective of communal opinion. A scientist who fails to tell the truth as he sees it is a coward at best and a traitor at worst.

On the contrary then, any contract that exists among scientists must stipulate that authority will be ruled out altogether. This constitutes at once the loftiest ideal and fundamental cultural significance of science itself. Because the truth is exalted above everything else, science becomes a living symbol of justice and of the rights of each and every citizen of the world.

One might contend that a certain kind of authority plays a legitimate role in science, in spite of its limitations. After all, money would still be useful even if it really were the root of all evil. We need to be careful here, however, because what looks like authority might be something else. One might argue that a community of scholars possesses a greater store of skills and expertise than any one of them does. True, but we must not treat this as grounds for collective judgment. A scientist asks some colleagues for opinions about a new hypothesis. He need not be asking for opinions as such, but rather for facts and arguments, the better to judge for himself. He himself still bears full responsibility for making the decision. Nor would it be wise for him to rely upon colleagues when deciding what is true. A disciplined scholar is not supposed to trust his own opinions, so why should he trust anybody else's opinions?

It is true that our ability to check up on everything we read or hear is limited. But we make some effort along those lines. In principle there is nothing to prevent our having firsthand knowledge based upon observation and experiment. If we doubt anything in a book on zoology, we can examine a specimen, and quite often we do.

Thus we find an economic constraint here. Another's eyes and brains substitute for our own because, if nothing else, life is short and time has to be allocated efficiently. If all scientists decided to cease exercising their higher intellectual faculties, and relied on the judgment of authorities, nobody would really judge anything and research would come to an end. Furthermore, one always has the problem of deciding which authorities to consult, and that too would have to be determined on the basis of authority. Should we perhaps seek a consensus among them, or ask them to vote, when they disagree?

In the popular press we are always reading that "most scientists believe" such and such. Who cares what most scientists believe? We want to know what the *best* ones believe, especially those in the best position to evaluate the topic at issue. Even better, we would like to have them explain the issues clearly, and in such a manner that any intelligent person can judge for himself. There are ways of checking the credentials of a putative authority. As a biologist who has taught premedical students, I know enough to detect gross incompetence on the part of a physician. The average citizen finds it more difficult however, and has to rely upon professional reputation. He can indeed go from one doctor to another, and see if he feels better, but that is the crude sort of empirical research that only serves to make the same basic point.

Authority, then, is a cheap substitute for the real thing. We pass the buck to the experts instead of doing the job ourselves. But we are suspicious of authority, and for good reasons. The authorities will not necessarily act in our interest, especially if they lack incentives for doing so. Quality is always expensive and one would expect charlatans to flourish where the quality of their work cannot readily be evaluated by consumers. One can hire an expert to evaluate an expert, or decide that it is cheaper or more effective to do the work oneself. But ultimately one has to make the decision and bear the consequences.

Some theories are easier to evaluate than others, and to that degree they are accepted upon the basis of intrinsic merit. William Harvey's book *De Motu Cordis et Sanguinis in Animalibus* established beyond reasonable doubt that the blood circulates.[60] The book is praised for many virtues, among which was its overthrowing of the physiology of Galen, whose authority in anatomy had already been weakened by Vesalius. Nobody has to rely upon authority to decide whether or not the blood circulates. Just roll up your sleeve and press on a vein. The vein will swell on the side away from the heart. Such "ocular demonstrations," as Harvey called them, are simple in more than one sense. The reasoning is straightforward and the results are compelling. Note that this particular experiment does not require expensive apparatus, esoteric background information, or long chains of arguments to make the point. We are not always so fortunate, however. I have actually seen blood flowing through the capillaries in the web between a frog's toes, observing a connection that clinched the matter. But obtaining the animal and setting up a microscope is a little more trouble than just rolling up one's sleeve.

Good science aims at a cheaply produced and readily evaluated product. Bad science, especially bogus science, wants the cost of evaluation to be downright prohibitive. In place of simple experiments we have cumbersome apparatus, monopolized by its proprietors. Instead of plain English, we have an esoteric jargon. Rather than clear and decisive results, we find a massive accumulation of data that bear little if any relation to the issues. Everything is made to look difficult, not easy, hiding the shoddiness of the product from its consumers.

Scientists can only pass judgment on the basis of whatever resources happen to be available to them. Were this point better understood, the results of various studies on the behavior of scientists would no longer seem anomalous. For example, certain shifts in opinion within the scientific community occurred without those who changed their minds having read what may be called the "seminal" papers, in which the crucial evidence was presented. A good example from geology is the acceptance of continental drift. The notion that the continents move around a lot was accepted after a long delay, on the basis of some compelling new evidence, but without everybody reading the papers in which it was presented. We may detect a tacit assumption in the reasoning here. It is presupposed that scientists ought to have read the documents in question. What a preposterous notion! The scientific literature is enormous, and although the better scientists do read a great deal, they are exceedingly selective. The overwhelming majority of scientific publications are read, if they are read at all, only by a tiny minority of specialists. They are not even written to be read, but to be cited, and, so to speak, "for the record." That they are supposed to be readable does not imply that they are read, any more than the fact that every experiment is supposed to be repeatable implies that somebody will repeat it.

The publication in which a theory is first presented is rarely the best place to go for information about it. This is partly because the first publication may be designed for little more than establishing priority. The theory of evolution by natural selection was first presented to the scientific community by Darwin and Wallace in a brief, joint publication in the *Journal of the Proceedings of the Linnaean Society* for 1858. The compelling evidence appeared in *The Origin of Species*, which was published on November 29, 1859. Although this book was, and still is, well worth reading, like many others it became outdated in some respects, and went through six editions in Darwin's lifetime.

Scientists are inclined to read the latest editions of the latest works, a step not always optimal, but hardly unreasonable. Much of their reading is in the secondary literature, especially review articles or summaries of recent developments, which are usually intended for a somewhat broader audience than is the primary literature made up of research reports. It takes a considerable amount of time for a paper to affect the secondary literature, and to pass from author to author. As the process of citation and re-citation goes on, much is lost and distorted. Therefore there are some obvious benefits to consulting primary sources, but scientists are very selective about that kind of reading, and only a few do much of it, at least outside of a very narrow area.

Scientists by no means treat the literature as their only source of information. They attend meetings, go to lectures, converse with one another, and utilize the grapevine. Science is not strictly a literary culture, and this creates difficulties for those who would try to understand it by studying the literature alone. It would be foolish for a scientist to accept or reject an hypothesis simply on the basis of what he has read. He ought to bring every resource at his command to bear upon the matter. The goal, after all, is not to evaluate the literature, but to discover what is true.

A good scientist will surely possess a certain amount of privileged information and be particularly adept at using his personal expertise. We can only expect that the author of a paper will present one kind of evidence, whereas the reader will use another. The reader will rely heavily upon his own data, which he trusts and understands, and the use of additional evidence will make the judgment more secure. If the evidence is of a different character, it may be strongly confirmatory. Furthermore, we need not look for the "confirmation" of a theory in the traditional sense of a logically compelling argument. It suffices that the innovation looks like a promising lead. One reason why *The Origin of Species* appealed to paleontologists was that it transformed the fossil record into a rich source of novel and important problems. In 1859 the data of geology were not inconsistent with evolution, but neither did they appear to support it. Darwin argued that the fossil record was incomplete, and paleontologists got to work. Their results were most spectacular, and they won fame and glory as a reward for their enterprise.

There is no necessary connection between the arguments that a scientist presents in favor of his views on the one hand, and those that lead him to embrace them on the other. Remember that valid inference in science is a matter of private judgment, not public pleading. A good scientist will accept the theory that is true, and not the one that will merely impress his colleagues, granting agencies, or common fools.

After all, ultimate success depends upon being right. Short-term success is of course a different matter and the conflict a source of major difficulties.

Each scientist, being a unique individual, possesses a peculiar assemblage of resources, endowing him with a partial monopoly. This means imperfect competition, segmented markets, and diversity of product. It is anything but inevitable that two scientists will possess the same resources for evaluating a theory, experiment, or other commodity. Indeed, there is every reason for them to have very different resources. In my own research I can test various theories, thanks to the fact that I know a lot about animals. This, among other things, is one result of having taught invertebrate zoology for many years. I can hardly take it for granted that a botanist and I will share more than a small common fund of knowledge about the details of organic diversity. But even zoologists often find it hard to follow a long discussion about chaetognaths, myzostomids, acochlidiaceans, and echiuroids. These animals are marine, and not common at most places on the seashore. Most of the marine biologists who do know about them are not particularly interested in many of the theories upon which the data might be brought to bear. Hence theory in biology tends to neglect them, cutting itself off from a wide range of relevant experience. Zoology is not quite as biased in favor of the Bird as psychology is biased in favor of the White Rat, but there are some parallels. Knowledge allows one to test theories, but ignorance prevents the fact of their having been tested from becoming generally known.

Thus scientists often find it difficult to communicate, especially on a short-term basis, and this creates all sorts of constraints and bottlenecks in the flow of knowledge through the intellectual economy. For the long-term prosperity of science as a whole, as well as of its practitioners and other beneficiaries, discoveries should be made available with efficiency and with dispatch. Therefore a scientist who makes a discovery ought to disseminate it in the best possible way, and, as a reward and as an incentive, to receive credit for doing so. It also makes good economic sense that he should do at least some of the work of communication himself, because as discoverer he is apt to have a better understanding than others do, much as a firm that produces a machine should reasonably be expected to have some conception of what might be done with it.

Sometimes, however, the consumers of theories and other scientific goods are in a better position to find applications than are the producers. When scanning electron microscopes became available their applications were largely realized by users who had peculiar needs. Producers of instruments often market them and service them themselves, in order to be able to find out how well their product performs and what their customers' needs might be. Efforts to establish such "linkage" are less conspicuous among producers of raw materials.

Nonetheless it behooves the consumer to seek out resources. Drug companies provide physicians with information about their products, but it would be foolish for a physician to rely upon that source alone. Likewise a good scholar takes some initiative, and actively seeks for facts and theories he can use.

Remember that a scientist is both a user and a producer of capital goods. The use of various factors of production means that there are economic tradeoffs and diminishing returns. If a scientist devotes time to marketing, that time must be subtracted from somewhere, perhaps from more creative work. If he is particularly talented at research, the scientific community as a whole will suffer in proportion as he diverts resources from production to marketing beyond a certain point. So the better his research the less he ought be held responsible for communicating it, though of course nobody should let communication take care of itself. The consumer also has a limited number of hours to devote to surveying the literature and listening to lectures, and this time too has to come from somewhere. Naturally scientists will appreciate good efforts at communication, and will reward those who do the job well.

Such considerations help us to understand why priority of publication is so important, and why being "right" in the long run is so strongly emphasized. A delay in communication will decrease the rate of assimilation of a discovery. Priority based upon publication, or at least some acceptable public means of disclosure, provides an incentive for getting discoveries onto the market where they can be used. It also provides an incentive for scholars to find out what others have done. We get credit for giving credit to our predecessors.

Good scholars are very sensitive about priority, especially their own. Robert Merton has shown that when scientists claim not to be interested in matters of priority, they generally do so in the context of a dispute about their own priority.[61] Their diffidence does not, it seems

55

to me, reflect dishonesty. Rather, it is the usual hypocrisy everybody exercises under circumstances that call for being a good sport. Merton suggests that the scientist's concern for priority is the result of the fact that priority is basic to the reward system. This obviously explains a great deal. If it were just a matter of immediate self-interest, however, we would not experience a sense of indignation when someone attempts to receive credit for another's contribution. It is a breach of decorum when one gives the wrong person credit or fails to give credit at all. Were credit not given where credit is due, science as an institution could hardly exist.

It makes a certain amount of sense that credit should be given more for discovery than for communication. Striking a proper balance between the two may be difficult. When a message fails to get across it may be far from obvious whose fault it is. If I see a crime being committed and inform the authorities, but the authorities fail to act, I have done my duty as a citizen and am not responsible if the crime goes unpunished. But there are limitations to this principle. I have not done my duty if I inform the authorities in Greek verse. In science, the most effective communication is through what are called the "best" journals—those that are most widely cited, most widely circulated, and perhaps even most widely read. There is a serious question here of what are the minimal requirements for achieving priority. If it simply becomes a matter of competing effectively for exposure in these journals, then obviously the whole system is corrupted. Every time one wants an excuse for doing sloppy scholarship, or for denying a competitor his priority, one can say that the paper one failed to read or cite did not appear in the right place. The maneuver becomes particularly insidious when the members of certain cliques, national subcultures, and linguistic communities read each other out of the scientific community as a whole.

It makes bad economic sense for credit to be given only for what appear to be the right views at a given moment. Hence the criterion must be being right in the long, rather than the short, term. One can, of course, be fairly flexible about what is meant by "right," and make one criterion be opening up a fruitful line of investigation. But certainly "right" does not, and should not, mean pleasing to the authorities of the day. Again, standing up to the authorities is esteemed an act of the utmost scientific virtue, which explains the high esteem in which certain scientists of the past are held. They become semilegendary culture heroes, for good reasons.

We have to give the discoverer a vested interest in his discovery, for the same reason that we give patents to inventors. This is the efficient way to ensure that the intellectual economy will flourish. The alternative to patents is "trade secrets." These do exist in science, but it can hardly be desirable that resources so useful as facts and theories should be held off the market while their discoverers exploit them at leisure. So if somebody keeps a discovery secret he receives just retribution when somebody else publishes first—provided of course that the real issue is not something else, such as premature publication.

Remember, however, that in giving credit to scientists we judge them as explorers, not prophets. More is involved than just finding out who published what first. Scientists are rewarded for following up fruitful leads and developing areas of research. Consider the analogy of someone who invents a better mousetrap. He persuades others that it is a good product and sells stock in a company that produces it. He and his stockholders become rich. But what about those who failed to invest in the stock? Have they anybody to blame but themselves? Would it be better to appoint a committee of experts to determine which products should be manufactured? Why not let the committee tell the consumers what kind of mousetraps to buy? There are certain advantages to freedom of choice and to individual responsibility in the intellectual marketplace.

Government depends heavily upon the authority of scientists for advice about, and justification for, its activities. Such topics overlap somewhat with what is discussed in chapter 5, where I treat the economics of evaluation in detail. Here I only want to suggest a few problems created by the use of experts in deciding how research funds should be allocated.

The federal government of the United States invests heavily in research. Some of this research is performed in government laboratories by its own employees. This arrangement has certain advantages. For one thing it keeps the government more closely in touch with what goes on in the laboratory. But because it puts science under close bureaucratic control, it encourages the sort of research that bureaucrats readily justify to politicians. This helps to explain the low quality of research carried out by the Department of Agriculture.

The quality of research done through contracts and grants naturally depends upon the ulterior motivation for its being done. In these terms, the lowest level of research is performed merely to demonstrate that a particular policy is desirable. Having outsiders do the work gives the factitious appearance of scientific legitimacy, at least so long as it is not evident how the outsiders are manipulated so as to obtain the desired results. As a professional marine biologist, I have seen a lot of transparently cosmetic environmental research. For example, there are countless studies showing that marine life survives perfectly well at certain temperatures, but which fail to point out that its reproduction is adversely affected. The popular way of deciding whether a pollutant is harmful is the "L.D. 50," which tells one the concentration that kills half of the animals exposed to it. Just imagine what would happen if effects on human beings were judged that way.

Ulterior motives are not necessarily bad. The United States Navy used to provide a considerable amount of support for pure science, partly because oceanography turned out to have all sorts of unexpected applications during World War II, and partly in order to maintain good working relationships with scientists whom it could ask for advice and assistance in time of need. A lot of excellent marine biological research has been carried out in Antarctica, in order to provide the United States and other nations with reasons for being there. It is sometimes hard to draw the line between research, reconnaissance, and outright espionage. The point is suggested by a remark once made to me by a graduate student at Scripps Institution of Oceanography: "We all work for the CIA." Be this as it may, such ulterior motives may lead to good science. It is hard enough as it is to get scientists to go to Antarctica, and one inducement is letting them work on whatever interests them.

The National Science Foundation is supposed to support basic research, and it has considerable motivation for doing that job well, and for appearing to do so. One mechanism whereby that is accomplished is the participation of scientists in peer review. When a scientist (or group of scientists) submits a grant proposal to the NSF, copies of the proposal are sent to several reviewers (called a board). These reviewers are asked to evaluate the proposal, give a brief report, and rate it in comparison to other proposals. The reviews, together with the proposals themselves, are evaluated by a panel of scientists who deal with all the proposals in a given area. Although the NSF staff has some authority to override the recommendations, they are definitely constrained by them. There is a general tendency to play it safe, which makes it difficult to support a controversial proposal.

My own experience as a reviewer led me to suspect that there are serious problems with respect to reviewing. In order not to rely upon mere impressions I interviewed seven tenured biologists from four universities. The sample size is obviously too small for statistical treatment, but the responses to my questions about how they react to proposals sent for review confirmed my suspicions. For one thing, the choice of reviewers was sometimes quite poor. They are often sent proposals in areas where they have little if any expertise.

One encouraging sign, perhaps, was that the reviewers did not follow all the guidelines for evaluating the proposals. They tended to deemphasize social benefits, and to evaluate the proposals in terms of what they felt would be good for pure science. Less encouraging was the fact that they used very different criteria for ranking the proposals. In part this resulted from having no information about other proposals. The four reviewers who had served on panels told me that they had a fair idea as to whether a proposal they got in the mail ranked near the top, the middle, or the bottom of proposals in general. Otherwise, they simply had to guess. However, they did not take the rating scale at face value. Among other things, they knew that only a small percentage of the proposals would be funded. For some this evidently meant dividing the proposals into two categories, the top 10 percent and the bottom 10 percent. One informant told me that he rated two-thirds of the proposals in the top third.

Analogous problems occur with letters of recommendation, such as those that are part of applications to graduate school and medical school. The authors of such documents are often asked to rank students numerically, but know full well that any ranking below the top 10 percent will ruin the applicant's chances. I suppose one could justify ranking everybody in the top 10 percent by saying that one writes letters only for the very best. The content of the letter can give more useful information. For instance, when recommending a student on the basis of performance in my invertebrate zoology course, I was able not only to rank the student, but to tell how tough the competition was. A great deal of professorial time gets expended on letters of recommendation. This is partly because the professor himself has to bear the expense of producing such documents. Few students realize that they would get better results if they applied selectively, and learned how to say "please" and "thank you." In the case of job applications, where scores or even hundreds of candidates may be available, it would make sense if letters were requested only after a preliminary screening. But nobody spends a dollar to save somebody else ten.

Chapter 5

EVALUATION AND ITS INCENTIVES

IDEALLY, AT LEAST, SCIENCE IS BOTH FREE AND ENTERPRISING. THE ideal is not realized, however, when science is corrupted by society—by government, academia, and other extraneous influences. Here short-term interests lead to all the diseconomies to which cooperative and competitive systems alike fall prey. The scholarly life degenerates into a vast system of institutionalized buck-passing, and authority becomes a shoddy good that drives sound judgment out of the market. Group decision-making replaces the initiative of the individual, both as producer and as consumer of knowledge. There is no dearth of excuses for what goes on. Among the worst of these excuses is "quality control."

The evaluation of manuscripts for scholarly journals illustrates how the system is supposed to work and what all too often goes wrong with it. When a manuscript is submitted for publication, it is supposed to be reviewed. That is to say, the editor sends it to a group of putative experts in the field, who are asked to express opinions as to whether it is appropriate for publication. Responsibility for deciding what gets published rests with the editor, but he is supposed to take the advice of the reviewers seriously. The editor has an incentive for making a proper decision because he is accountable for the prosperity of the journal.

Those who read the journal and perhaps subscribe to it might withdraw their support if dissatisfied with the editor's decisions.

Sometimes journals are supported by professional societies, sometimes they are run as business ventures. They may derive income from government, from academic institutions, from philanthropy, or from "page charges" borne by the author and perhaps subsidized by grants. Journal editorships usually are unpaid, though there are many exceptions. Even so it must be remembered that we are not here dealing with a strictly pecuniary economy. The editor gets lots of emoluments, including the sort of power that he can use in subtle and perhaps mischievous ways. Doing a good job as editor can be intrinsically satisfying. Authors and readers alike are sincerely grateful for a good performance, and are apt to reciprocate. At Berkeley when I was there, editors got time off from teaching, and perhaps were spared less rewarding chores.

The editor's disincentives to good performance are clear enough. Editing a journal consumes much time. Therefore an editor is apt to cut a few corners. One way to do this is by superficial judgment, perhaps by excluding manuscripts that are highly original or otherwise peculiar. Another is to pass the buck to the reviewers. Let them make the decision, and perhaps even take some of the blame for what happens. It may, however, be difficult to evaluate the opinion expressed by a reviewer, or even to find someone qualified to judge. Self-interest on the part of the editor can complicate matters. If the editor wants a paper to be published, he sends it to one group of reviewers. If he wants it to be rejected, he sends it to another group of reviewers. This procedure is not unlike what governmental agencies do when contracting for bogus research. They send out requests for proposals, then fund the one most likely to give the desired results. If the desired results are not forthcoming, the report is filed away and not made available to the public.

The reviewers' incentives and disincentives are a bit less obvious. Rarely are the incentives pecuniary, but doing the job well builds up a considerable fund of goodwill, which might be reciprocated, say, by finding it easier to get one's own manuscripts accepted. But doing a very good job will perhaps lead to spending all of one's time reviewing manuscripts instead of doing research. When reading a paper in manuscript means getting early access to it the incentive can be very strong, provided of course that the reviewer is interested in the content of the paper. The motive for such interest might be mere curiosity. More likely is the possibility that the paper will be relevant to the reviewer's research. The reviewer may wish to help the author to improve the paper, and may even be motivated by a desire to benefit science.

The reviewer also has an opportunity to sabotage a rival's research. Blocking publication means that the author has to submit the article to another journal, perhaps a less prestigious one, at the cost of considerable effort and delay, perhaps with loss of priority. This maneuver can be coupled with plagiarism, the opportunity for which provides another major incentive to reviewers. (Sabotage and plagiarism are treated more fully in a later section of this book.)

The reviewer submits a written commentary, not inappropriately called a "review," to the editor. These reviews are often anonymous, and for most journals this is the standard policy. But sometimes they are signed, especially at the reviewer's request. An author is apt to take a signed review more seriously than an anonymous one, and may be grateful for the help even if the review was somewhat negative. Nothing really prevents a reviewer from communicating directly with the author, and this sometimes can lead to interesting discussions. David Hull signed his review of the paper in which I first suggested that species are individuals rather than classes. The long series of letters that ensued left us disagreeing, but only temporarily. George Williams signed his review of my paper on hermaphroditism, and we initiated a correspondence about the adaptive significance of sex; later both of us published theories about sex which are still being debated.

There are several reasons why reviews are generally anonymous. Should the author feel abused, as often happens, he may try to get even. If the editor is stacking the deck against the author by selecting hostile reviewers, the author may not like it. Or the editor may wish to conceal his poor choice of reviewers. The reviewers themselves are likewise constrained. It is not in their best interest to have an incompetent performance generally known.

Anonymity makes it easier to indulge in plagiarism and sabotage. Also anonymity is supposed to foster candor. In a signed review one is apt not to give the real reasons for disapproving of a manuscript. Telling somebody he is stupid and incompetent is not apt to make friends, especially when the charge is well founded. However, the author has no way of assessing the quality of an anonymous review apart from the review itself. If he knows who the reviewers are, he can better decide whether to take their advice and accept their judgment. We should observe that there are ways of finding out the identity of reviewers. The result is a lot of speculation, guessing, reading between the lines, and even espionage. A professor at the University of California at San Diego learned to recognize the typewriter of a professor at Berkeley, and she had the good sense not to let him find that out.

Sometimes the manuscripts themselves can be submitted anonymously, with no indication of the author's name. The occasional proponents of such "blind reviewing" are not the sort of people who publish much, and it is obvious why. A scientific paper does not exist in a little world all its own. It forms part of a series or corpus of works, and cannot be evaluated in isolation. A scientist routinely must refer to, and discuss, his earlier publications. Furthermore, his colleagues will recognize his work, at least if it has the sort of individuality that characterizes most good research. Only a few scientists are in a position to do a given piece of research. Each will probably apply a slightly different approach, perhaps using different materials. Writing styles differ. On top of all that, everybody in a given area has some idea of what the others in that area are doing. Results are communicated informally or at scientific meetings, alluded to in earlier publications, and otherwise publicized. Blind reviewing would add too many complexities to an already Byzantine procedure. The costs would be altogether prohibitive.

Ideally there should be one, and only one, reason for a paper not being published. This is that the reviewers' comments persuade the author himself that publication is not desirable. Here the author, as an autonomous individual, is deciding what is appropriate. For obvious reasons, such a utopian ideal would never work in practice. A good scientist, or even a mediocre one, never publishes a bad paper if he can help it. But a good academic does, and this is the root of the evil. A great deal of effort would be saved were more emphasis placed on quality control where it does the most good: in the early stages of production. The reviewing ought to be done before the paper has even been submitted for publication, and in fact much of it is. One asks colleagues for their opinions, and expresses one's gratitude in various ways.

In my experience there are two kinds of "helpful" reviews. One is by a reviewer who wants the manuscript to be published, and makes every effort to provide useful advice that might improve it. The other is by an adversary or rival who attacks it at every vulnerable point. Even if the adverse criticisms are entirely destructive, one at least knows what to expect after the paper has been published, and can perhaps answer objections in advance. Mere effusive praise is of little use, though it may encourage the author and help get the work into print. The worst reviews are addressed only to the editor, give no assistance to the author in improving the manuscript, and consist of excuses, character-assassination, and lies. They are always anonymous.

Reviewing has been studied experimentally. Peters and Cecci took twelve published articles from twelve American psychology journals, made some minor changes, then resubmitted each to the same journal in which it had been published. The main difference was that the addresses of the purported authors were no longer those of major institutions, but of imaginary places such as the "Tri-Valley Center for Human Potential." The results of Peters and Cecci's study were published, together with commentary from a substantial number of scientists, especially editors and former editors, in the journal *The Behavioral and Brain Sciences*.[62] The rate of detection of this fraud by editors and reviewers alike was only 8 percent. For those papers in which fraud was not detected, sixteen of the eighteen reviewers recommended against publication, and the articles were rejected.

This study evoked considerable dismay upon the part of some commentators, and not only because it raised some ethical questions about experimenting on human beings. The reactions show some definite patterns. In the first place, not everyone seemed to realize how little the scientific literature is in fact read. This by itself goes a long way toward explaining the low rate of detection. One might argue that the reviewers were not appropriate, perhaps because they mainly read other journals. If so this would tend to indicate that the editors made a poor choice.

Many commentators were dismayed by objective evidence that institutional labels correlated with the ease of acceptance. Such phenomena, however, are common knowledge, and have an obvious economic rationale: brand-name recognition. Everybody from textbook publishers to people applying for grants is more or less aware of it.

65

Scientists want jobs at big-name schools because this implies a valuable endorsement, and not just because these schools have other good resources. Everybody knows that papers from such institutions are apt to be read more widely than those from ones of lesser standing. It is much easier to rely upon such cues than to decide for ourselves what to read.

An unknown commodity has to possess some peculiar features if it is to penetrate the market. One reason why postdoctoral fellowships exist is that a young scholar can become affiliated with a recognized institution, perhaps have his name appear as a coauthor with some luminary in his field, and thus advertise himself before entering the job market. Harvard University has long exploited this situation by hiring young scholars to do the pedagogical drudgery at low pay and without any hope of permanent employment. In recent years lesser institutions have gone even further, providing teaching jobs with no opportunity to do research, so that the career, as well as the job, is soon terminated. Such cost-cutting measures have obvious economic advantages, and the institutions themselves do not have to bear the costs of liquidation.

Among the more striking results of Peters and Cecci's study was the frequency with which manuscripts were turned down on the grounds of "serious methodological flaws." The perceptive onlooker will easily see that this should be labeled not a reason, but an excuse. Science deals with uncertainties; and, its methods being fallible, any piece of research might be improved through better techniques. Since everybody thinks he knows a lot about methodology, methodology provides a cheap and easy source of justifications for saying "no." To evaluate a work on its own merit requires much effort and at least some competence. Some of the commentators noted that the rejection rate in psychological journals (about 80 percent) is different from that in other fields. This aspect of the problem has been studied extensively, and it turns out that the probability of acceptance is directly proportional to the ease of evaluation. In some fields (especially the humanities) the rejection rate is very high; in others (especially the physical sciences) it is considerably lower. A common explanation has been that this difference has to do with the "rigor" of the field, or with "hard science" *versus* "soft science," whatever that is supposed to mean. There may be some truth to this interpretation. However, there are several other reasons why a contribution might be difficult to evaluate. If a problem is easily solved by straightforward techniques there should be little difficulty determining whether the results are sound. Often, however, the most interesting problems are also the most challenging and difficult ones. Their solution often requires new and untried techniques. In many fields, the material which is most easily published is least often read and (for most of us) least worth reading, particularly works of purely descriptive hod carrying. The system militates against creativity, initiative, and even candor. Authors learn that they may be penalized for saying anything that might irk some reviewer. They are induced to shun controversy, to toady up to those in charge of running the discipline, to stick to the facts, and to do "safe" work.

Peters and Cecci made it obvious that the reviewers were not always doing their job well. Perhaps this happened because of laziness, but this is merely a label. Economics as usual provides the answer. Scientists, like everybody else, have a limited amount of time. To review a manuscript properly might require a full day's work, or even more. That time has to be subtracted from somewhere—perhaps the laboratory, perhaps the classroom. There are many good reasons for not wanting to allocate much time to a review. One may not be interested in the manuscript; one may suspect that the editor has already made up his mind not to publish the paper.

Good reviews are indeed written, but this happens when, by chance or by design, the manuscript falls into the hands of somebody with a genuine incentive—not duty, but self-interest. This usually means a scholar actively engaged in research that somehow relates to the subject matter of the manuscript. It could mean an older scholar with considerable experience, though younger ones often do a very good job too. This is not, however, because of youthful idealism. Young scientists have pretty much the same desire to advance themselves professionally that older ones do. A young scholar will not be asked to review a manuscript unless he is known by the editor to be particularly well qualified. The task of reviewing being novel and interesting, the young reviewer has an additional reason to work long and hard at it. Add to this the desire to please, and perhaps a less busy schedule, and it all makes perfectly good economic sense. Thus the problem of having good judgment brought to bear upon the decision as to what gets published turns out to be largely a matter of choosing someone who is properly motivated. Making that decision requires skill and effort, and these again are in short supply.

The economist David Laband used empirical data to find out

whether there was any relationship between the quality of a paper, as assessed by how frequently it got cited, and the length of time it took for the paper to be reviewed.[63] His data showed no such relationship, although he did find that papers got through faster if an author was from Harvard, and slower if an author was female or if the paper was long or empirical. If reviewing does improve papers it is because the authors, rightly or wrongly, believe that a better paper will be more readily accepted for publication.

When I was a young Research Fellow in Malacology at Harvard's Museum of Comparative Zoology, one of the folk heroes there was an entomologist named Forbes. I don't know how old he was, but his pure white beard reached almost to his waist. Early in his career he submitted a monograph on butterflies to a journal, but the editor turned it down. His response was neither to revise and resubmit, nor to send it to another journal. Instead he laid the manuscript aside and waited thirty years until the editor died. He then submitted it unchanged, and the new editor accepted it.

To explain why the evaluation of grant proposals can be even worse than the evaluation of manuscripts would be depressing, and not altogether necessary, for the same basic principles apply. So too with fellowships, scholarships, academic positions, and prizes. Such matters will be treated in passing as this discussion unfolds. For the moment let us be content to point out that when a scholar and teacher finds himself turned into a professor the results can be rather demoralizing. One prepares for a career in the library, the laboratory, and the classroom. Reality soon catches up. One sits at a desk, contemplating a stack of manuscripts for review, grant proposals to be written or evaluated, letters of recommendation for undeserving students who won't be accepted anyway, tenure reports, questionnaires. . . . It is not research that keeps teachers out of the classroom; it is paperwork.

Such academic circumstances go a long way toward helping us to understand why authority pervades the intellectual world to such an extent. Academia has usurped the function of exercising the judgments appropriate to scholarship, and not just within the learned community. Authority is what the public demands, authority is what academia supplies—if for no other reason than because shoddy goods drive out the competition. Producers and consumers alike may be unhappy about this state of affairs, but they go along with it. Our whole educational apparatus is geared up to present a public image of the scientist as prophet. The emphasis is placed upon the answers, even though it may be dimly recognized that the questions are what really matter.

Consider a standard laboratory exercise in an undergraduate chemistry course. The student is told to carry out a series of tests that will identify a certain substance in a bottle. By a very simple screening procedure, the student is able to eliminate a series of possibilities, and rightly conclude, say, that the unknown substance is potassium bromide. Although such an exercise has its place, it differs from everything but the most routine drudgery in a real laboratory. The student's problem here has already been formulated, whereas in real science much of the challenge is to invent the problem itself. The pedagogical problem is soluble because the teacher has set things up so that it will be soluble. Unlike a real scientist, the student is not expected to invent the technique for solving the problem. There is but one legitimate solution, and this too has been determined from the outset. And so on.

Except for the most fortunate, students do not experience, or even witness, real science until they get into graduate school. The fortunate ones are those who take part in research as undergraduates. It is well established, but not so well appreciated, that precisely such experience has been a major factor in causing scientists to opt for their vocations. The cost of involving undergraduates in research is prohibitive, because so much individual attention is necessary. Proponents of the lecture system might reply that the students learn the answers just as well without individual attention. But that is precisely the issue. How well do they learn to ask questions? Those who are interested in improving the teaching of science might well ask how much science is being taught at all.

The economics of pedagogy explain a great deal. In theory, education is supposed to develop the talents of the citizen. However, those who teach are also expected to function as baby-sitters and wardens. Education comes to be identified with keeping the rising generation out of circulation and otherwise controlling its behavior. All this must be accomplished at minimal cost, and authority is cheap. It is much easier to tell somebody the answer than to teach him how to find it for himself. In daily life answers are not necessarily given in order to supply information anyway. Often the main function of the answers is just to shut people up. And in dealing with the young, failing to tell the truth is not even considered reprehensible.

Naive persons are especially likely to lose confidence in an expert who does not know all the answers. People fear that if authority in one area of our lives is eroded, the effects will spread. Inevitably one would have to teach the young how to tell the difference between good authority and bad authority. Not only would that threaten the established order, it would necessitate a great deal of work.

Of course good teachers, like good parents, will strive to do the best job they can. There is no reason why they should not sincerely desire to benefit the young, whether from benevolence, duty, pride of workmanship, the sense of earning an honest living, or whatever other reason. But this does not diminish the countervailing economic pressures. Answers are much easier to evaluate than questions, particularly when the questions themselves are hard to devise. Hence students will tend to be evaluated in terms of a fixed array of "right" answers to questions presented rather than evoked. Although some creativity and personal initiative is cultivated in spite of the disincentives, it is sobering to realize how little such benefit accrues to the average citizen. Even those manifestly destined to become scientists are required to swim against the current all the way to retirement.

Neither students or teachers are rewarded for being candid about what they do and do not know. For many the rude awakening does not occur until the doctoral orals. Everywhere one is rewarded for making a good impression, even when certain eccentricities are indulged. In theory, getting and keeping a job at a university depends upon the quality of one's work, but there are prominent disincentives to evaluating performance on the basis of real merit. There is no cheap and easy way to tell a good teaching performance from a mediocre one. In some universities students are given questionnaires. These are often scored "objectively"—i.e., by counting responses of a given kind. This necessitates that the questions will bias the outcome one way or another. At Berkeley one of the questions asked of my students was "Is he a master of his field?" The next question definitely was not "Just what is his field, anyway?" Furthermore, the average students have just as much say in these matters as the very best, and this is not an unmixed blessing. The proper time to evaluate a teacher is after a lapse of some years, when the long-term effects can be more readily appreciated.

But let us not pretend that asking the students to fill out such questionnaires is more than a charade. The real reason for them is to give the appearance that the students are having a say in who gets advanced in rank. If one really wants to find out who the good teachers are, one simply gets to know a few students and waits until they volunteer the information. Those in charge want somebody to teach the courses nobody else will, and otherwise to get the chores done. Yes, of course good teaching ought to be rewarded, but in academia its official recognition is little more than a public-relations gesture. If you want to know what society really awards its truly outstanding teachers, the answer is found in history: a cup of hemlock or a crown of thorns.

Academic judgment of research is apt to be reasonably searching and conscientious, but only to the degree that scholars have a vested interest in the performance of their colleagues. Not only do they benefit from the good reputation of their institutions, but having someone competent around for advice and collaboration can be very useful.

It is better not to carry competence too far, however. A competent person may be asked to take on too many responsibilities. At Berkeley my colleague Daniel Mazia joked that one should "develop a reputation for lovable incompetence." Competence also makes one's colleagues look bad by comparison. One reason why it is so hard to upgrade a mediocre institution by bringing in good people is that it may displease the existing staff.

Even with good intentions, academics can cut a few corners and not do the job of evaluation as well as they might. Superficial criteria are all too readily applied. One is always tempted to count the number of publications—anything but read them. Another stratagem is to pass the buck, either to a committee or to some outside authority. In the former case there is at least the incentive that the members of a committee do not want to be stuck with an inferior colleague. An outsider might have the advantage of not being involved in local politics, but then again he might be somebody's professional rival. The department will probably make up its own mind anyway, and will solicit the kind of advice it wants in order to legitimize its actions.

A number of forces promote high-grade mediocrity. If somebody's work is unusual, it will be hard to evaluate by any standard. If it is controversial, there will never be a consensus and one will have to do a lot of work finding out just why it is controversial. What academia really wants is a product that sells and gets no complaints from the customers. Instead of real creativity it is apt to promote mere "trendiness." Some academics thrive on controversy, but for many it is just a

71

marketing technique. In some quarters controversiality becomes contentiousness, an effort to gain publicity by contesting every point.

The authoritarian image of science is projected to the general public. Simply telling people the answer is far cheaper than explaining the issues in terms that a layman can understand. The answer will be the most simplistic one that the expert can get away with. Only when the layman feels unhappy with the answer he is given will he exercise anything like the critical faculties. The problem is exacerbated by institutionalized buck-passing. Because academics can sell their services as experts, they have a vested interest in the authoritarian conception of science. Bureaucrats are always appealing to experts to justify their decisions. Industry does likewise. So does everybody.

Thus the truth becomes monopolized by a guild run by and for the experts. The layman is not privy to the decision-making process, or even allowed to know how the decisions are made. He has to take the experts' word for it. But then suppose the experts disagree. At worst, the whole system breaks down and loses credibility. Anything goes, as Feyerabend puts it, and pseudoscience takes over. The general public can't distinguish astronomy from astrology, and they let their gurus tell them what foods to eat. One system of authority replaces another, and with it goes the authority people ought to respect: the authority of reason, fact, and solid accomplishment.

Some years ago a petition was circulated among the biology departments in California universities and colleges. It asserted that special creation is not a scientific hypothesis, because there is no way in which it could be refuted by experiment or observation. This was intended as an argument for not teaching special creation in the public schools, as some were advocating at the time. In a faculty meeting I pointed out that, on the contrary, special creation is a perfectly good scientific hypothesis, as could be seen from the fact that Darwin had refuted it in 1859. The logic here was a bit compelling, and nobody could come up with a rational objection. After all, biologists are every bit as justified in rejecting special creation as astronomers are in eliminating the hypothesis that the earth is flat. Some of my colleagues argued, nonetheless, that endorsing the petition would be the expedient way to handle the problem. In other words, we were being asked to behave like politicians, not honest scholars. The department never responded. Good scientists do not lie.

Creationists, to be sure, are not constrained by scholarly principles. This is clear from their practice of reiterating arguments that have long since been refuted. A professional scientist who did this would lose credibility. The creationists however are presenting misinformation to naive persons for the first and perhaps the last time in their lives. In higher education the scholarly community exercises some responsibility both individually and collectively for the content of books and courses. At lower levels education is controlled by government and manipulated by business. Biology textbooks intended for the use of secondary school students are deliberately written and edited so as to mislead the readers. In modern college-level texts the material on evolution of course comes first, the better to show how much about life is otherwise unintelligible. When I took biology in high school the information on evolution was in the back of the book, and we never got that far. The current practice is basically the same: do not tell the students how evolution is used to explain the living world.

Take something as simple—and as basic—as classification. In modern biology the various groups of animals and plants are historical units—branches of a genealogical tree. Such genealogical classification occurs in a variety of other historical sciences, as in the language families of historical linguistics. If one wants to deceive high school students, one does not tell them about common ancestry. Rather one tells them that classifications put similar things together, and does not tell them why. It would be a most curious phenomenon were the existence of Latin concealed from students of Spanish and French. When discussing what purports to be the evidence for evolution, the most compelling evidence, which is biogeography, is simply ignored, and the difficulty of interpreting fossils is treated as if it somehow casts doubt upon the rest of biology. Somehow, the consensus of scholarly opinion for over a century becomes what "some life scientists believe."

One might argue that not telling the truth about science is somehow different from lying about it. Perhaps not calling the fire department is not quite the same thing as arson, and deliberately leaving poisons where children are apt to eat them is not quite the same thing as murder.

Lying to schoolchildren is big business. So is lying to their elders. Indeed those very elders pay handsomely to have their children taught, by precept and example, to become liars themselves. And their neighbors' children too. The morality of lying to children is one issue. The legality of doing so in order to circumvent the Constitution is another. Whether such practices corrupt our entire society is something else again. But if there is any realm of human experience in which the advantage to telling the truth is manifest, that is science. Good scientists do not lie.

Of course scientists do lie all the time, but not when they are being good scientists. As academics, scientists are paid to lie. They lie to the general public, they lie to their students, they lie to their colleagues, and they lie to themselves. A lie is often the cheapest way to control the behavior of those around one. In dealing with the young, lies are not only socially acceptable, they are often rendered obligatory by legislation. If the skillful liar has to be careful to avoid getting caught, this is just one of many social skills that academic man is supposed to master. What really prevents scientists, as scientists, from lying is another matter. It will be discussed in a later chapter.

The public tends to confuse science with technology. Again this is symptomatic of treating scientists as prophets rather than explorers. But what of the disease itself? That this confusion between science and technology is indeed a disease is manifest from the recurrent complaints of pure scientists at misunderstanding and lack of support. It is also apparent from the anger and resentment they feel at the actions of politicians, who slop the trough with money for scientifically worthless but politically attractive "research." It would be easy to blame the politicians, and perhaps curse the general public, for such goings-on. But consider the economics of pedagogy and child-rearing. If you want to get a child to swallow some medicine, the easiest way may be to put it in a glass of soda-pop.

Because it is an easy sell, one is always tempted to market science as if it were technology. Convincing someone that he ought to spend money to cure heart disease, cancer, and stroke is far easier than explaining to him why he should invest in discovering general truths about the living world. Everywhere the citizen is bombarded with appeals to the utility of science, but it is always utility of the crassest and most immediate sort. Scientists are happy to have themselves portrayed as if they were motivated by a desire to serve materialistic interests. Of course, it brings in the money, or so they think at least. Small wonder that the public receives the impression that the way to solve problems is to throw money at them.

Science tries to optimize discovery. It invests resources where they are apt to give a high return. It does not invest resources simply because it would be nice to know how to pull certain stunts. To do so would divert resources away from the problems that are soluble, and in science happiness can be defined as soluble problems. At any given moment some kinds of problems will be easier to solve than others. If a certain disease happens to be curable, then somebody is very likely to take advantage of the opportunity and devise a cure. Otherwise the best policy is to do something else and bide one's time. A development in some other area, perhaps an unanticipated one, frequently changes the whole picture as to what problems can be solved.

There is nothing peculiar or mysterious about a scientist working on the more soluble problems. A good farmer plants the crop that will yield the highest return, given the state of the market, the soil, the climate, the cost of seed, and other factors. He does not attempt to plant tomatoes in the fall simply because people would enjoy eating them in the winter. Likewise a good general attacks where the enemy is weakest, and does not squander his troops in attacks on impregnable fortresses. To be sure, if some fool will pay a farmer to plant tomatoes in the fall, the farmer might be happy to go along with the arrangement. And if politicians order a charge of the Light Brigade, we can only expect to pay the price in carnage. It all boils down to a matter of incentives and responsibility. The principle of self-interest will work, but not if institutions fail to take advantage of it.

Chapter 6

THE MODULES
OF THE MIND

SEE ONE AMERICAN UNIVERSITY AND YOU HAVE SEEN THEM ALL. Everywhere one finds departments, committees, presidents, deans, full professors, associate professors, assistant professors, graduate students, seniors, juniors, sophomores, freshmen, the library, the gymnasium—you name it. So too with the classrooms and the classes. All are much alike in many respects: homogeneous and modular. So many units for a major, a little more for honors. There are very good reasons for this. A whole functions better when the parts are uniform and mutually compatible. Economists have traditionally invoked a "principle of interchangeable parts."

In explaining such matters it helps to begin with concrete and familiar examples. Therefore let us consider the physical plant before the intellectual one. And let us begin with a portion of the physical plant so ubiquitous that anybody can provide copious examples from memory: what is somewhat euphemistically called a "lavatory." Most people haven't given it much thought, but whenever one goes into such an installation one finds striking evidence of homogeneity among the appliances. In any lavatory the sinks, soap-dispensers, and such are apt to be identical. The advantages to this modular homogeneity are

77

economic. They largely have to do with the costs of construction, maintenance, and use.

An architect designing a building saves a lot of time if each installation is basically a variant upon a common theme. When one equips a lavatory with ten identical toilets, one can send in just one order to a single firm for the lot of them, probably getting a quantity discount. The plumber who installs them will perhaps have to think a bit and even read some instructions while working on the first one, but will soon get the hang of it and install the rest much faster. Likewise, using the same kind of pipe and identical connectors throughout will make it easier to put the entire system together. Once everything is working the installation will be easy to service and clean. One set of spare parts may suffice for occasional repairs. Whoever cleans the facility will not have to reflect much about the features peculiar to each toilet, for the simple reason that there aren't any. And the habitual users will save time if they know precisely where everything is and how it functions.

Modularity relates to what are called economies and dis-economies of scale. One saves by purchasing larger quantities of toilet paper, but the savings are less if one has to buy more than one kind of it, even from a single supplier. Likewise a homogeneous lavatory needs fewer connecting pipes, and the janitor wastes less time in going from john to john. The bigger the lavatory, therefore, the lower the costs. However, the cost of carriage creates problems here. Central rather than dispersed facilities means that the users must spend more time getting to them. This situation gives rise to a complex pattern of diminishing returns, with a tradeoff between savings at the lavatory and the costs of getting to it.

If savings in janitorial wages are preferred to savings in user time and effort, we get one outcome. We get quite another if the user's time is relatively expensive—expensive, that is, to the person in whose interest the facility is built and operated. In a profit-making corporation, we would expect those who are paid the most to be placed in close proximity to a lavatory, those who are paid least to be situated less conveniently—and perhaps everybody admonished to retain wastes as long as possible. In academia, the convenience of administrators, professors, and students is given the obvious ranking in priority.

There is a minimal size for a lavatory. Say, one toilet and one washbowl. But a larger installation can have a different ratio—say one washbowl to two toilets—thereby eliminating bottlenecks and downtime. Furthermore, a small lavatory cannot enjoy certain divisions of labor, such as into toilet and urinal. Hence size furthers heterogeneity, rather along the lines that Adam Smith had in mind when he remarked that "the division of labor is limited by the extent of the market." In having a dual function for a particular apparatus one saves both in cost of capital expenditure and space occupied; but one loses such advantages as having different amounts of water used in disposing of different materials.

Heterogeneity of fixtures allows one to accommodate heterogeneity among users. It makes it easier to provide optimal services for people of different sizes, ages, sexes, and physiological conditions. Doing so can still be costly, as in providing special facilities for the handicapped. In general we try to design a fixture to meet the needs of the average user—perhaps a hermaphrodite who is five feet tall. It is not so much social discrimination as economics that causes problems here.

Not every feature in a lavatory has to do with straightforward optimality theory. A lot has to be explained in terms of history. English toilets differ from American ones because they were developed separately, as were electrical systems and much else. Economics has to be treated as an evolutionary science, in which laws of nature and statements about individuals both play important roles.

Given such theoretical principles and laws of nature as obviously apply here, we should expect to find modular professors flushing modular toilets, teaching modular courses to modular students, writing modular books about modular topics, and in short living thoroughly modular lives. Of course with something so mundane as the lower physiological functions it hardly matters. But let us turn to the higher intellectual functions, and to their products.

We may begin with books, considering them first from a structural point of view. Most of the books we encounter are organized in the same basic way, and this has definite advantages. In general we can take it for granted that the title will be in front, followed by a table of contents, then the subject matter, and the bibliography and index at the rear. We know where to look for such features. It would be inconvenient if some books began at what for us is the last page. Books in Chinese and Hebrew have such an arrangement, but this is just a convention—like driving on the left side of the road in Britain and Japan. The advantage derives not from any particular pattern, but from homogeneity as such. In some ways it would be a good thing if all books were the same size. A lot of shelf space would be saved. Also it would tend to reduce the cost of production, hence the price. The trouble is that books are adapted to different functions. An atlas ought to be large, a traveler's phrase book small. There are some less obvious considerations. A set of books ought to be nearly identical in appearance, for that makes it easier to keep the volumes together. When books are of different sizes and colors, however, it is much easier to find and recognize a given volume.

Diversity in the content of books has definite advantages. Begin with the limiting case: identity. A publisher may of course reasonably run off 100,000 identical copies for the benefit of an equal number of purchasers. I might even buy two identical copies of the same dictionary for my personal use, if I needed one for the office and another for my library at home. A large academic library will often keep several copies of a single work that is much in demand. Nonetheless the forces working toward heterogeneity are evident whenever we consider the needs of individual consumers. The works of a given novelist may be similar in many ways. Having enjoyed one of them, we are apt to read several. We may reread some of our favorites. But it would be most eccentric to own one hundred copies of a single novel, and to read one copy after another. We crave a certain amount of diversity in our reading.

The scholarly literature is a somewhat different matter. The producers and consumers alike have motives of their own, motives of which not everybody is fully aware. In this discussion let us focus upon what will be called "the scientific paper." This is considered the primary medium of what purports to be communication among scientists. (There are entities that do not fully fit the narrow definition of a "paper," such as books, monographs, notes, and abstracts, to which the same principles apply.) Ordinarily a scientific paper is purported to be a contribution to knowledge, in the form of an article in a more or less reputable and scholarly periodical (usually called a "journal"), or perhaps in a multiauthored book.

So far as organization goes, scientific papers as a rule have a fairly homogeneous standard format. In reading them one proceeds from title to abstract to introduction, materials and methods, results, discussion, acknowledgments, and literature cited, with minor variations. Having the work organized in this way obviously saves the reader, as well as the author and editor, a lot of work. There are no surprises. One knows precisely where to put something and where to find it. The advantages of homogeneity are evident even in the list of works cited. Different publications have different ways of abbreviating titles of periodicals and for providing information about volume, date, and pages. Every time one writes for a given journal one has to learn what these conventions are, and adapt to them.

Enough has been said about this aspect of form. What about content? Consider first the advantages to saying the same thing, over and over again, in a series of scientific publications. There must be some advantage, for the practice is exceedingly common, and not just in the sciences, despite the general agreement that papers are supposed to report on original work that is not published elsewhere.

Minor differences do make for originality of a sort. Whether in doing the research or in writing it up, one can learn a few standard procedures or formulas, and then churn out papers in volume. Once one has learned to describe a species of mite, one is pretty well set up to describe yet another species of mite, or, if a bit more enterprising, a species of tick. Venturing into tick physiology might prove a bit more ambitious an undertaking, because it means shifting fields. But we should make an important distinction here. There is a real benefit to science whenever somebody describes a new species of animal or plant. Every species is different, and each needs a name in order that scientists shall be able to communicate about them. Describing the living world down to the last mite is perhaps not the best way to spend one's time, and purely descriptive work can degenerate into mere hod carrying, but at least the contents of the hods are made available to architects and builders. On the other hand repeating the same physiological experiment on different species may or may not be useful.

For many products, quantity is much easier to judge than quality. Hence the short-term reward system, especially in academia, leans heavily upon the quantity of publication. The quantity can be measured "objectively" in terms of the number of titles or pages. This creates forces that multiply the number of titles relative to the amount of subject matter. One effect is the tendency to try to get one's name on as many papers as possible. We shall come back to this maneuver later. Another is putting a single piece of research into as many papers as one can. The game is played somewhat as follows. First, publish an abstract of a talk delivered at a meeting, or perhaps a preliminary note. Then divide your work into a series of small papers rather than a single large one. Then reiterate what you have said in a "symposium" volume, a review article, and perhaps a book. With luck you can manage a few polemical articles and the sort of book review in which you discuss your own work rather than the book itself. Multiplying the number of titles has the additional advantage of increasing the number of pages. The same material has to be gone over more than once, or at least summarized and referred to. With the references we have yet another advantage, that of being able to cite one's own work.

Citing one's own work, unlike citing that of somebody else, does not add to anybody's reputation. It does, however, draw attention to the fact that such work exists. Furthermore, increasing the number of titles raises the probability that others will encounter one's work by chance. It is like the plants, such as orchids, that produce large numbers of very small seeds rather than a few big ones.

Probably the world would be better off with fewer titles, fewer words, and less redundancy. But who, pray tell, is going to police the authors? Surely not the authors themselves! They stand to benefit the most, except insofar as redundancy decreases output. Adding water to milk has always been easy. Nor should an editor be expected to take much responsibility, except in reducing the number of words per article. He is under pressure to publish as many titles as he can, and the more titles per issue the greater the probability that one of them will turn out to have been worth publishing.

The subscribers themselves may have no more objection to redundancy than the authors and editors do. Especially if one feels obliged to read what one cites, long papers are not the best thing to pad a bibliography with. In some ways a reader even benefits from the redundancy in an author's work. At an extreme, one can get away with reading one paper per author. So why bother to read more? Some diversity of content may justify reading more than one among a given author's productions, at least for a small audience and a competent author. However there are disadvantages to having so much diversity among one's publications that the potential readership finds it hard to predict what the content will be. A homogeneous series establishes a precedent and a tradition. It sets up the kind of reputation enjoyed by chains of hotels. People know that one writes about a given range of topics, and nothing else. Hence everybody knows what to read and what not to read, keeping reading to a minimum, and freeing academic man for the academic life.

The scientific paper has come to be treated as if it formed a corpuscular unit of scholarship, existing independently of similar units. One contribution, one paper. Such an assumption tends to deprive a work of its context. If it is unusual for a scientific paper to be read, it is even more unusual for somebody to read a scientific book. Rather it has become common practice to read "parts" of books. Treating a series of chapters as if they were, like a mere anthology, connected by nothing more than a title or a common theme, is apt to lead to serious misconceptions. The last paragraph in the penultimate chapter in my book on the economy of nature contains a widely quoted piece of hyperbole: "Scratch an 'altruist' and watch a 'hypocrite' bleed." Discussions of what purport to be my views generally overlook the next chapter, especially the last paragraph in the book, which depicts social behavior in somewhat more generous terms. Had my critics been willing to pay for more than a single page of photocopying, they might not have accused me of advocating what I was attacking.

Turning now to pedagogy, we have the question of whether it is economically expedient for a teacher to vary his educational product. We may begin with the undergraduate lecture course. Having taught such a course on invertebrate zoology at Berkeley for some years, I can bring some personal experience to bear upon this topic. Invertebrate zoology is an ancient and venerable branch of learning. Covering as it does all that is known about the overwhelming majority of animals, it has a vast literature to which an ambitious scholar might reasonably devote many years of study. What a pleasure it was, when the university could not devise better ways for me to spend my time, to read about my subject and prepare my lectures! To make up a good series of lectures from scratch requires an enormous amount of time, even when one has a good grasp of the subject. The second and subsequent deliveries are obviously going to involve less work in simply doing an adequate job, but the notes can always be improved and they generally have to be updated. An annual revision of one's notes can be a good learning experience. Giving basically the same lectures repeatedly has some advantages. One learns what topics are and are not suitable for the students. By giving particular attention to certain areas every year I found it possible to focus upon details and gradually improve both the course and my own knowledge of the subject.

Many teachers go so far as never to revise their lecture notes, and at Berkeley this was said to be true of one of the professors of botany. This expedient obviously saves a great deal of time for such activities as committee work, and even research. Going over the same lectures time and again would perhaps even enable one to commit every word, gesture, and gag to memory. However, notes when unrevised tend to get stale. The students find out that they need not attend the lectures if they have access to notes from a previous year. They find that the homogeneity extends to the examination questions as well. And the course has to emphasize those aspects of the subject that are not currently under investigation. Otherwise the course will become out of date, with unfortunate consequences for student and teacher alike. Nonetheless some students, especially premedical students, are happy with such homogeneity. They know precisely what the course will be like, and what they will have to do for a grade.

Next let us consider whether there should be any diversity among courses on the same topic. Should, say, two courses listed as "Invertebrate Zoology" by different teachers have anything in common besides the name? The case for standardization is best appreciated where a course forms a module in a curriculum, and where one course serves as a prerequisite for what comes next. The job is easier if the teacher can presuppose that the students have already learned certain materials. This is particularly the case with respect to basic principles and vocabulary. Much time gets wasted when whoever presents an advanced course has to provide remedial instruction on the fundamentals. So perhaps there ought to be a body of central material which everybody who takes a course on invertebrate zoology is expected to learn. The trouble comes with deciding what these materials are supposed to be. A course on invertebrate zoology can emphasize classification, or it can emphasize behavior, or ecology, or any of a number of other things. Therefore a course can deviate a great deal from what many of us would like to consider the norm.

Ideally the content of a course ought to be determined, at least in part, by the interests and needs of the students. It is problematic just how important this consideration turns out to be in practice. Academic positions do not exist merely in order to provide instruction. They also may be needed to give academic man something to do. Someone is hired and the undergraduate curriculum must be tailored so as to justify paying his salary. Often a teaching job will be given to someone who is not an expert in a given area, but who knows enough about it to be accepted as qualified to teach it. In this case we are not concerned with a specialist teaching a general course, but with one teaching in some coordinate area: not with an invertebrate zoologist teaching general biology, but with an animal behaviorist trying to teach anatomy. If he who offers a course outside his major area of specialization truly is interested in the subject, the problems will be minor. For example, if an anatomist were really motivated to upgrade his competence in physiology, he might have to work harder, but at least he would have good reason for applying himself. However, there is every temptation to convert a course on what really does not interest one into a course on what really does interest one. This is an alternative to getting rid of the responsibility itself. One might get somebody else to teach it. Another possibility is to teach it badly so that there will be less demand for it, and then ask that the course be discontinued.

Graduate schools have every reason to produce modular students, who are, after all, destined to become modular professors. This consideration raises the question of how much diversity is acceptable both in the raw materials being selected for graduate school and in the finished product being granted diplomas. There are obvious tradeoffs between adapting the grist to the mill and the mill to the grist. When there is a glut of students, the mill can grind upon what the millers deem appropriate. So long as there is an adequate supply of homogeneous grain, one is tempted merely to keep grinding away. But it would not be reasonable to leave maize rotting in the fields just because wheat is easier to mill. The market itself demands variety, and will pay for it. In times of scarcity, care is taken not to discard grain with the chaff.

Good grist for an academic mill means the sort of graduate student who will do all of the various things that are required of graduate students without giving much trouble. What counts is getting through, and an unusual mixture of talents is apt to clog the works. The requirements aim at a certain level of mediocrity in various accomplishments; and although a virtuoso performance in one area is always applauded, it makes little if any difference in compensating for inadequacy in another. Should anybody try to make exceptions, it will always be looked upon as a degradation of standards, and with good reasons. Remember that our mill grinds out diplomas, and only incidentally produces functioning scholars. The consumer is assured that the product meets certain specifications, not that it exceeds them in some capricious or unpredictable fashion. And applying such metaphors gets difficult when we consider that both the grain and the mills are resources, both dependent upon markets.

Of course the mill in question grinds out a range of products, inducing it to accommodate a range of inputs. Remember, however, that we are dealing with several productive subunits (departments) which may have to be more selective than the larger one (the university). The division of labor sets up a variety of subordinate institutions, each of which has its own economic structure.

We can understand the forces conducive to homogeneity by considering the productive unit that consists of a single professor and the students who work under his direct supervision ("in his laboratory"). The question to be asked here is: What are the advantages to having the students all work on the same kind of problem for their dissertation research, in much the same way, using the same basic approach, so that when they get their degrees they are very much alike in what they can and cannot do?

So far as production goes, the answers are easy to come up with. They are primarily means of reducing fixed costs. The fewer kinds of research one's students do, the less equipment one must buy, the less one has to know, and the less one has to read. If each student in successive years needs the same kind of attention, one knows what to expect. It is much easier to deal with a group of people who all behave in the same way—who think the same thoughts, know the same truths, and provide the same answer to any given question.

Homogeneity also has advantages with respect to marketing. When a department has a slot to fill, it shops in places where the module it seeks is being produced. Once one has established a precedent, and provided a few examples of one's wares, these attain a reputation and an image. The more predictable and readily identified is one's product, the more apt it is to attract customers. The more homogeneous it is the less guesswork and thinking will be involved in selecting it. If your students are known to be more or less what is wanted, the market will seek you out.

On the contrary, homogeneity tends to saturate the market. A single department can only use so many replicas of a given professor. And the total demand for a given kind of product will be less than infinite. One perhaps would rather not have one's students competing among themselves for limited resources of a given kind, and the problem is compounded by one's students' students. A certain amount of product diversification at once increases the extent of the market and mitigates the effects of competition within one's sector. Hence there is a tradeoff between economies of production and marketing on the one hand, and the demands of one's customers on the other. Just as automobile manufacturers produce more models when the existing demand for cars has largely been met, professors should be expected to produce more than one kind of student when competition for jobs is keen.

A satisfactory analysis of the academic job market has to deal with partial monopoly, and with imperfect competition. A professor who is in a good position to market his students is apt to enjoy a greater degree of control over the raw materials and the means of production, thus obviously reducing one cause of deviation from homogeneity. Although it is not easy for one professor to monopolize certification in a given subject altogether, oligopoly is an established fact of academic life. This of course restricts the autonomy of graduate students. As a consequence of not paying the piper, graduate students do not call the tune, but they are to some extent free agents in the choice of schools and professors. This naturally induces the faculty to form cartels and trusts. Until one has obtained one's doctorate it is almost impossible to opt out of academia without having to opt out of scholarship as well, and the situation does not improve much afterward. These days few possess the financial resources necessary to be private scholars, and private practice generally means sticking entirely to the applied sciences.

Modularity carried to excess in academia threatens to manifest itself as social and even political conformity. Letters to *The Wall Street Journal* often complain about the high proportion of liberals and even radicals among university professors. The solution proposed is usually the sort of quota system of the sort that conservatives oppose with respect to minority hiring in general. Anything but increasing salaries in order to attract conservatives away from business! A quota system would have consequences that anybody can predict. A host of professors would switch their registration to the Republican party, and continue to vote Democratic. Academic man has shown vastly more ingenuity in qualifying persons for membership in supposedly disadvantaged minorities.

But is there really a problem to be solved here? Everybody knows that different sectors of the economy and different ways of making a living attract people with characteristic attitudes and systems of values. Working in the public sector attracts people for whom earning a lot of money is less important than certain other things.

Since renouncing the academic world I have shifted my base of operations to a museum. The attitudes of people who work there differ considerably from those of the employees of a large corporation, but they make a great deal of economic sense for an institution that depends largely upon philanthropy for its support. Institutional loyalty is very strong. Although the employees find their work intrinsically satisfying, and take it very seriously, they also spend a lot of time socializing. Great emphasis is placed upon having good interpersonal relationships and being a "nice" person. The whole pattern indicates that good working conditions take a very high priority. In view of the extent to which the museum benefits from the contributions of volunteers, it is a most economically rational arrangement. Some of the people who work there full time are living off pensions. Some of the paid employees are women whose children are grown up, and who work largely in order to keep busy. And then there are those of us who live off fellowships, grants, and private income. It is very difficult to fire somebody who doesn't have a job.

Yet in spite of such qualifications, academic freedom is more than just an academic issue on campus. I remember being told by a professor at one of the campuses of the University of California that he would stop at nothing to make life difficult for the advocates of sociobiology, including blocking their advancement to tenure. Evidently he was unwilling to pay the price for a forthright and open recourse to the pen. Of course nonconformity, provided that it follows the established guidelines, is not just tolerated, but institutionalized. My remarks on this point were once quoted in an interview that I gave to a reporter from *The Deseret News:* "I gave up cigarettes when I left Salt Lake City, and pot when I reached Berkeley."

All this is very elementary economics, even though we rarely think about such matters from such a point of view. The basic principles of economics apply universally. Modularity characterizes all organisms, including ourselves, and not just in our goods and institutions, but in our minds and bodies as well. Perhaps modularity is most conspicuous among plants, in which each leaf appears to be built upon the same plan. Even the petals of flowers are modified leaves. The teeth in one's mouth, and the fingers of one's hands are all variations on a theme, and the parts vary according to the role each plays in the economy of the body. So too with ribs, vertebrae, indeed with literally every cell and chromosome. There are good reasons for this. Nature, mindlessly pursuing her craft over innumerable generations, preserving what works and discarding what does not, has produced marvels which no intellect is apt to duplicate. We, the products of such reiterated generation and selection, are able to contemplate and understand her actions. Yet we see that, destitute of foresight, she is no Divine Artificer, producing works of artistic perfection. Rather, she dumps consumer goods on a tasteless market. Body, mind, and institution are all parts of the same empire—and economics is a supremely imperial science.

Chapter 7

THE ACADEMIC
DIVISION OF LABOR

PRODUCT HETEROGENEITY LEADS US TO THE PROBLEMS OF SPECIALIZ-ation. To what extent ought the left hand to differ from the right? How wide a range of merchandise ought to be sold in a grocery store? What are the relative advantages for a physician in being a general practitioner or a urologist? Should a professor of chemistry know anything about psychology? To answer such questions we need to understand some fundamental, but much-neglected, aspects of economic theory. In particular the principle of the division of labor, one of the oldest and most venerable in economics, deserves our closest attention.

The division of labor was mentioned by Plato and Aristotle, but little was written about it until 1776, when Adam Smith, in *The Wealth of Nations*, made it one of the pillars of his system. For him the division of labor was the rationale for industrial organization, and its application the basis for economic progress. Subsequently economists have done remarkably little to improve upon, or develop, the theory.[64]

Adam Smith recognized three advantages to the division of labor. *First*, it increases dexterity through practice. *Second*, it saves time that might be dissipated by switching from one task to another. *Third*, it focuses the attention upon a particular activity, thereby leading to innovations and improvements in the means of production. Each of these deserves comment.

First, consider how dexterity is increased through practice. Obviously someone who has not spent enough time learning how to do a certain job will not do it rapidly or well. This is true of washing dishes, typing, or filling out income tax forms. If you have ever tried to put furniture together from disassembled kits, you have no doubt noticed that the first piece took more time than the second. Learning any skill may be considered an investment in time and effort. The fewer skills one learns, the less one has to invest in such learning. This affects one's wages as well as the cost of one's education. Investment in learning any skill is subject to diminishing returns: as one learns, there is less and less improvement per amount of time invested in practice. Even though one has not learned the skill perfectly, one may find that a greater return is realized through learning some other skill.

Second, we have the matter of time saved through not having to change from one task to another. Even when we switch from some task to a closely related one, such as from cooking to washing dishes, we may lose time by having to put away one set of tools and get out another. When a factory changes its product there may be a period in which new equipment is installed and the staff is retrained. This downtime, as it is called, has a cost additional to that of the new equipment and the training themselves. However, there can also be costs to not changing tasks. We may not be able to work at one task all day long, and even when we can our productivity may drop off. I find it difficult to write more than three or four hours a day. Hence I usually schedule my writing for the mornings, and devote the afternoons to something else, such as library or field work.

Third comes the attention that, according to Adam Smith, leads to progress through innovation. Those who produce or use a machine a great deal are particularly apt to think about how it is made and how it works. A long period of application to a given task may lead to experiments, deliberate or otherwise, that lead to something better. From such attention and self-interest it does seem likely that the flow of inventions will be augmented. In Adam Smith's day the inference seemed particularly reasonable. Much of the improvement that accompanied the agricultural and industrial revolutions in England resulted from the efforts of innovative craftsmen and their supervisors.

The notion that technological change is the major engine of progress is as valid in our day as it was in Adam Smith's. However, specialization to some extent militates against inventiveness, and this point has been made so often as to be a commonplace. To be sure, one enjoys a significant advantage with respect to opportunity for invention by focusing one's attention upon a narrow range of tasks. This, however, does not make it either a necessary or a sufficient condition. For one thing the attention must be focused in the right place. For another, there has to be an incentive.

That innovations do emerge in highly divided industries is well established. The fact that companies offer bonuses to creative workers shows that they are putting the incentives in the right place. Nonetheless it is known that workers often conceal such innovations from their supervisors and others, because they want the profits diverted to themselves. The division of labor allows the employee a certain monopoly, because he can prevent such flow of information, to the detriment of the firm and of the economy as a whole. Improvements in the product itself are a somewhat different matter. Here the division of labor seriously militates against improvement because it cuts off the flow of information between users and producers. This is one reason why the producers of certain goods, such as computers and copiers, are apt to service what they make. Their experience informs them of where improvements are desirable.

Another advantage to the division of labor is that it allows us to take advantage of diversity in talents and interests. Different physiques are suitable to professional jockeys and basketball players. If someone derives pleasure from a given line of work, he might as well do what he enjoys and let his neighbor do something else. A diverse economy tends to be more productive insofar as it provides opportunities for talents that otherwise might be wasted. Note, however, that the efficacy of this principle may depend upon proper attention being given to the economy as a whole. Nothing necessitates that the economy will provide a variety of occupations. Monopolies may limit the range of products, and local circumstances may force a given region to specialize on just a few products. There is a dearth of opportunity where a particular region specializes in agriculture or mining and imports everything else.

Yet another advantage to the division of labor was proposed by the

French sociologist Emile Durkheim.[65] As he saw it, the division of labor holds society together by creating a sense of mutual dependency among its diverse elements. Thus the baker feels grateful to the miller and to his customers by providing him with supplies and a market. He is pleased that he can call in a plumber or an electrician. Perhaps he appreciates the performance of the cook at a restaurant.

One might argue, however, that the division of labor has consequences opposite to the one suggested by Durkheim. Perhaps we would rather not be dependent upon plumbers and electricians, especially when these have a monopoly. Our relation to the cook is apt to be strained when other than purely discretionary income is involved. In the past few years we have seen a movement develop toward a return to self-sufficiency and the simple life. Many will take a considerable cut in income to live the life of an independent artisan. But even when we grant that the division of labor can produce social cohesion, we must categorically reject the notion of Durkheim that it exists *in order to* produce that effect. A medical student does not decide to become a urologist rather than a general practitioner in order to make society better off. An industrialist does not set up an assembly line in order to endow his employees with a kind of team spirit unless he believes that the existence of such a spirit will increase his profits. Everything flows from self-interest.

According to the Marxist view, the division of labor has an effect quite the opposite to that suggested by Durkheim, and a different mystical and ideological significance as well: It keeps the proletariat divided and reduces the proletarians' power. It may be true that having the various elements of society divided into small occupational factions militates against their uniting for common ends, and it may also be true that this consequence is used to control and exploit them; but this does not necessarily mean that labor is divided in order to control and exploit laborers. Such a teleological interpretation has to be accepted on the basis of paranoia or faith, and in the face of evidence to the contrary. There is no reason to think that labor is more often divided where such control would be advantageous to the persons in charge. Labor is divided among competing firms, and in purely cooperative, voluntary associations such as clubs. Indeed it is ubiquitous among organized beings. My pocketknife has a variety of blades. My whole gut is organized into a disassembly line, with mouth, esophagus, stomach, intestines, and anus all having their special offices.

In spite of such objections, the notions of Durkheim and the Marxists should not be lightly dismissed. They do contain a certain measure of truth. Given the division of labor instituted because of its economic advantages, there is an opportunity to manipulate it for social and political ends. One might expect it to be used this way in bureaucracies, and in dictatorships run according to the principle of divide and conquer. In many societies occupations have become more or less hereditary. An ancient Egyptian was required by law to follow the occupation of his father. We encounter somewhat the same thing in contemporary disputes over traditional sex roles. Some occupations have been thought appropriate only for one or the other sex. In many societies life has become so tenuous that a fixed place, however modest, has been seen as preferable to the risks associated with finding a new one.

In medieval society the various classes were supposed to have both rights and duties, and an important function to perform. Guilds were organized partly in order to assure a partial monopoly over crafts and trades. The academic world, indeed, was organized in the middle ages on the model of the guild, and still retains much of that original character.[66] A place in an economy is a resource, and he who possesses one will defend it against encroachments. Anything that fosters mobility will naturally be viewed as a threat.

Nineteenth-century economists had a rather poor understanding of what limits the extent to which labor can be divided. Indeed it was generally taken for granted that the more minutely labor could be subdivided the better. Improved understanding of such matters has largely been a development of the twentieth century. Adam Smith nonetheless did enunciate the principle that the division of labor is limited by the extent of the market. What he meant can be explained by means of a concrete example:

Suppose that you are a potter, and that the circumstances are such that your customers want to buy only ten pots per day. If you can produce no more than ten pots per day, then you will be kept busy all the time. If, however, there is a more extensive market—say for twenty pots a day—you might train an assistant to do part of the work. The assistant might prepare the clay, leaving you more time to throw the pots. Observe that we cannot apply a straightforward and simple arithmetic here. If the division of labor reduces the cost of the product, this consequence may in turn increase the extent of the market, perhaps leading to further opportunities for the division of labor. If pots become cheaper, more people may want to own them, and each person may buy more. A lower price should make it profitable to ship them over greater distances.

Furthermore, labor can be divided in various ways. Labor may be divided vertically, according to the stages of production. Thus one craftsman might throw the pots while another fires them. Or it could be divided horizontally, with several potters each concentrating upon a different kind of pot. Anything that increased the variety or the quality of the pots might increase demand and hence enlarge the market. Therefore different ways of dividing labor might be used if what mattered was lowering cost, raising quality, or increasing diversity.

As has already been pointed out, nineteenth-century thinkers saw no limit to the division of labor beyond the extent of the market. Hence they emphasized the importance of increasing the extent of the market by lowering the cost of carriage, by fostering international trade, or by other mechanisms. Progress was virtually equated with the division of labor. Herbert Spencer made the division of labor one of the bases for a vast evolutionary system which he called a "synthetic philosophy." He presupposed that more and more specialization was the same thing as progress, and enumerated instances of what he had in mind from chemistry, biology, and sociology, finally making it an ethical principle. These days most of us find Spencer's works dreadfully tedious reading. But his contemporaries found his scheme attractive, for it encouraged the belief that the world is fundamentally good, and getting better. In effect he made evolution into a secular religion, much as have certain sociobiologists of our own times. A close examination of his works reveals that Spencer enumerated only those facts that lent plausibility to his theory. Even in his day the data of biology and economics were adequate to show that specialization is not a universal trend. Nobody seems to have given much thought to reasons for combining labor or for being a generalist.

To this very day economists have done remarkably little to develop the theory of the division of labor beyond the contribution of Adam Smith. If you doubt this, merely examine a few elementary economics textbooks. Biologists have not done very well by the division of labor either. Part of the reason is that it is generally considered meritorious for academic man to be ignorant about various matters that supposedly do not affect professional performance. Therefore it is socially acceptable for intellectuals to know about cocktail party psychoanalysis rather than experimental psychology, and Marxist babble rather than marginal-utility theory. However, this has not always been the case, and the failure of communication between biology and economics is largely a twentieth-century phenomenon. Well into the nineteenth century political economy was discussed among the intellectual community as a whole.

Darwin, who founded the modern science of ecology in 1859, was profoundly influenced by economics, both directly through the writings of economists themselves, and indirectly from his main source of ecological theory early in his career, namely Lyell's *Principles of Geology*.[67] One of the most important events in the history of the world took place when Darwin read Malthus's *Essay on the Principle of Population*, a very influential work on economics. A favorable climate for interdisciplinary transfer continued well into the century. John Stuart Mill's *Principles of Political Economy* was widely read and discussed. Gradually the public image of economics became distorted by politics and academia. On the one hand works addressed to society in general degenerated into pseudoscience and superficiality. On the other hand principles that might have been transferred to biology became the province of academics with specialized technical interests and whose channels of communication were almost exclusively with the pecuniary sector of the intellectual economy. Only now is bio-economics beginning to reopen those channels of communication.[68]

We should be careful not to confuse the subject matter with the discipline. Which problems biologists and economists alike are supposed to work on depends mainly on tradition. Economists ordinarily do not possess the intellectual skills or general experience requisite for dealing with the division of labor. Neither do many biologists. One needs to understand how things work, or function, and how they are put together. Although an invertebrate zoologist is taught how an embryo develops, an economist usually is not taught how steel is made. He is taught how to use a certain kind of equilibrium theory, and how to manipulate equations. There is nothing like a laboratory course in the economics curriculum. As an anatomist I like to conceive of my science as primarily one dealing with organization; and my experience as an anatomist, solving real problems with real animals, was invaluable in my own efforts to understand the division of labor.

The first biologist to mention the division of labor was Aristotle, but he did not say much about it. Not until 1827 did the Belgian physiologist Henri Milne-Edwards explicitly discuss the topic and make anything of an impression upon biologists.[69] He explained his principle of the physiological division of labor by means of industrial analogies. Unfortunately he saw advantages, but not disadvantages, to this division of labor. The main role it played in his thinking was to provide a criterion for deciding how "high" or "low" an organism is supposed to be. Higher animals have functions concentrated in distinct organs. He did not otherwise specify when labor would be divided. Nor could he turn the principle to good use in solving problems. Hence when the principle was taken over by evolutionists, they too failed to develop it. It was assumed, for example, that hermaphroditism is primitive, and that separation of the sexes into male and female organisms is the advanced condition. This erroneous inference gained plausibility from the habit of regarding man as the most perfect of creatures. This in spite of the fact that simplifications in structure are commonplace in evolution. Spencer, in his *Principles of Biology*, made the physiological division of labor an example of progress. Darwin was seriously misled by it. He thought that the division of labor would increase the amount of life in the world, and for some time thought that this would account for organic diversity, or what he called the "divergence of character." Because the problem seemed to have been solved, it was some time before he discovered a principle of divergence that depended upon competition.

Other efforts to apply the division of labor to biology were equally unfortunate. Ernst Haeckel, Darwin's main popularizer in Germany, wrote an essay on the division of labor in colonial animals and insects.[70] He compared the soldier castes to officers! Nonetheless there has been a long tradition of studying the division of labor in insect societies. It has tended to be descriptive, with little effort to explain why labor gets divided the way it does, still less to generalize beyond the particular objects being considered.

A major oversight in both economics and biology has been the distinction between what I have called the "competitive" and the "cooperative" division of labor. Given an uncritically teleological outlook, one is apt to assume that everything in the universe is going to be "optimized" in all respects. We can easily see why Adam Smith, who was a Deist, and therefore believed that laws of nature had been ordained to that end, would expect the actions of individuals to lead to the welfare of the whole—provided, of course, that we do not interfere with the working of those laws. Hence *laissez-faire*, and what he called an "invisible hand," which optimizes all. Darwinism, which envisions the natural economy as operating through the competitive interaction among single productive units (organisms and families) implies that the whole will not be optimized, except as the incidental result of whatever favors the output of the parts. A failure to make this distinction between cooperative and competitive division of labor has been one reason for the enduring popularity of social Darwinism, the balance of nature, and other superstitions.

The cooperative division of labor occurs where the output of a productive unit as a whole is optimized, as in an organism, a factory, an ant society, or a socialist economy. The competitive division of labor occurs where the productive units maximize their own output by specializing, irrespective of what the effect on the whole might be, as in an oyster bank or a free-enterprise capitalist economy. Corporations or independent craftsmen here specialize so as to gain a competitive advantage over other such units. Within a corporation a craftsman will specialize or not in a way that fosters effective cooperation with other workers so as to make the corporation compete more effectively with other corporations. For example an employer might put a certain number of generalists on the payroll to cope with emergencies and bottlenecks. If a certain kind of specialist is very useful but only on rare occasions, he might be kept on the payroll even if he were not particularly efficient most of the time. Within a firm we might find both cooperative and competitive division of labor among the employees. This reflects the fact that above the level of the organism we rarely find a strictly cooperative unit. At the organismal level, the division of labor between pancreas and spleen is strictly cooperative. Hence it is often easier to understand the division of labor if we consider anatomical materials.

My own insights concerning the division of labor arose from purely zoological interests. For some years I studied the evolution of complex reproductive systems in a group of marine snails and slugs that had become hermaphroditic, with male and female parts occurring in the same animal. At the beginning of the evolutionary series there was

99

just a single duct in which various reproductive processes took place. Later the single duct became divided into three separate ducts: one for incoming sperm, one for outgoing sperm, and one for eggs. At the time it did not occur to me that this transformation exemplified the principle of the division of labor, though its advantages were clear.

Later in my research the question of why these and other organisms had become hermaphroditic in the first place increasingly attracted my attention. Hermaphroditism is the rule in flowering plants, and very common in many groups of animals, including not only snails, but such abundant creatures as earthworms and barnacles. Under some circumstances an animal is better off as a "simultaneous hermaphrodite," which is male and female at the same time. Then "he and she" can mate with any mature animal of the same species. In some cases hermaphrodites will even fertilize themselves, though they generally do so only as a last resort. As has been recognized for some time, this capacity can be very useful, especially in rare animals, in those which do not move around very easily, such as snails, and in attached ones, such as barnacles.

There is another kind of hermaphroditism, called "sequential hermaphroditism," in which a plant or animal changes from male to female, or from female to male, or even back and forth repeatedly. Many of these changes became intelligible when, in 1969, I proposed the "size-advantage model."[71] In one version of this model, originally applied to a few species of fish, the sex change is explained by the fact that the males fight, and the winners monopolize the females. Such competition exemplifies Darwin's "sexual selection," and explains many differences between the sexes. Since as a rule the bigger males win the fights, an effective way for such a fish to reproduce is to be a female until attaining a size sufficient to win the fights, then become a male. This hypothesis and variants of it have been found widely applicable to both animals and plants, and generalized so as to be an important aspect of what is called "sex-allocation theory."[72]

Organisms like ourselves, which have but one sex throughout life, may be said to have labor divided on a *spatial* basis, this time between organisms. The sequential hermaphrodites have labor divided on a *temporal* basis, between smaller and larger stages in the life cycle of a single organism. In simultaneous hermaphrodites, labor is combined rather than divided so far as the organism goes, but it may be divided spatially in the sense that different parts of the body have male or female parts. In any case, the division of labor puts the male and female functions into different places, or has them occur at different times, with the result that they do not interfere with one another. From this simple principle of noninterference, virtually everything necessary for a general theory of the division of labor may be derived.

Sex-switchers appear not to be doing as we might expect from the application of Adam Smith's second principle. In spite of the disadvantages of losing time, or of what is often called the cost of retooling, the fish do indeed change sex. Likewise it is not exactly to the point that having male and female organs in different parts of the body might somehow increase dexterity through practice. Nor would the separate sexes of jellyfishes and ferns seem to have much to do with inventiveness through attention. The extent of the market is not always applicable to such materials either.

Whether and how labor will be divided or combined depends on whether two (or more) activities interfere with each other, or, on the contrary, have some advantage when done together. Thus we may recognize both *conflicts* and *complementarities*.

Complementarity is implicit in the proverbial killing of two birds with one stone. Conflict is exemplified by the difficulty of throwing stones and skinning birds simultaneously. Perhaps an early agriculturist killed birds primarily to protect his crops, but in so doing he could also have acquired valuable food and perhaps even put the feathers to good use. The trick is to get as many benefits from a given activity as possible. We are all familiar with the phenomenon, even though not everybody has given it much thought: shopping on the way home from work is a commonplace.

Whether labor will be divided or combined depends not on efficacy in a mechanical sense, but on the net economic payoff. We have mentioned the cost of retooling, which is saved by not switching tasks. Such costs vary from one activity to another, as do the benefits from switching tasks. Sometimes the cost of retooling has to be paid if the product is to sell at all, for example, where fashion is important. Some activities combine very well with one another. For example if one is a student one needs to spend a lot of time studying. A job in which one's main duty is just to be on hand in case something needs to be done combines very well with studying. Babysitting and serving as a

101

night clerk in a hotel are examples. Such positions tend not to pay very well, simply because the employee has much time to use for himself. In addition to the cost of retooling there is the cost of tooling up in the first place. A plumber needs one set of tools, a carpenter another. To ply both trades one has to pay the fixed cost of both sets of tools—minus, to be sure, the savings that might be realized if a tool can be used for both. A jack of all trades has to make do with an inferior set of tools, tie capital up in underutilized plants, or perhaps rent or swap a great deal. One way or another the costs must be paid.

Now consider the intricate tradeoffs involved in the domestic economy of a common object: the Swiss army knife. I carry such a version of the traditional pocketknife with me most of the time, and find it particularly useful when traveling. Such knives are available to suit the needs and tastes of various purchasers. For example, mine has a corkscrew, something I would never wish to be without, but not a Phillips screwdriver, magnifying glass, saw, fish-scaler, or lathe. For want of an adequate generic term, let us call these elements "blades."

There are two reasons for increasing the number of blades. In the first place if there are two blades in the conventional sense, we have a spare. If the big one gets dull, the little one will do. However, it is perhaps more important that each is suited to a different range of tasks. The scissors differ greatly from the can opener. On my knife there are two screwdrivers, one large and one small. I suppose one could open wine bottles with a screwdriver, but that would be difficult and messy. The more tools one has the more jobs one can do, and the better one can do them. However, certain multipurpose blades work reasonably well, because the different functions do not interfere with each other. The bottle-opener and the can opener on my knife each have a screwdriver at the tip. As the number of blades increases, there are disadvantages which an economist would call "diseconomies of scale." The knife becomes more expensive, clumsier, and less portable. Diminishing returns set in, and at a certain point one decides that the addition of a shovel is not worth it. Probably the largest Swiss army knives are purchased as gifts and rarely used.

Fixed costs are very important in determining whether labor will be divided or combined. Remember that a professional toolkit must be purchased if one is to ply some trade. Substantial savings can be realized by reducing such fixed costs, and sometimes this can be accomplished by combining labor. The different medical specialties are a case in point. A dentist and a psychiatrist use quite different equipment. On the other hand a group of ophthalmologists or general practitioners may share certain items that they do not use all the time, and even quite different specialists may share hospitals or office space. Hence the advantages of group practice.

Analogous means of reducing fixed costs have been studied by biologists. If it is so good to be an hermaphrodite, why do so many animals have separate sexes? Part of the reason is that a compromise between male structure and female structure, or between male behavior and female behavior, does not function very effectively. Eggs and sperm might get in each other's way. Another reason is fixed costs. With separate sexes an animal does not have to invest by producing, maintaining, or transporting the organs of two sexes. Social units such as families create opportunities for cost sharing, analogous to those realized by physicians in group practice. In birds the mother and the father often take turns guarding the nest, much as physicians take turns being on call in case of emergencies.

Closely akin to maneuvers for reducing fixed costs is the "free ride" principle. Among animals in general, only the mother cares for the young. Males devote most of their reproductive time and effort to sex pure and simple. Paternal care as we know it in many birds and in our own species is a rare exception when the totality of creatures are taken into account. Among these exceptions is a group of marine animals called pycnogonids, distantly related to spiders, and somewhat resembling them in outward appearance. The females sit around and feed all the time. The males seek out the females, fertilize the eggs, and carry their developing offspring about, finally delivering them to an appropriate habitat. The males thus act as sort of living perambulators; but since they wander about in search of mates anyway, the cost is lower than it might be. By the same token, when businessmen travel, they may carry some of their paperwork with them, and get it done en route. Under such circumstances the ride itself is not quite free, for it does cost something to transport a group of baby pycnogonids or an attaché case.

The unity of biology and economics is also seen in the division of labor on a temporal basis. Both plants and animals tend to defer reproduction until they reach a certain size and age. A life history usually features growth, dispersal, and reproduction. In higher plants the general rule is for the juveniles and adults to remain in one place, dispersal being effected by dormant seeds. In a butterfly there are four distinct stages: egg, larva, pupa, and adult. The egg merely survives and develops. The larva (caterpillar) specializes in feeding and growth, though it has a limited capacity to move from place to place. The pupa does not feed or disperse—like the egg, it just develops and survives. The pupa is often referred to as a "resting" stage. Actually it is a retooling stage, necessitated by extensive remodeling (metamorphosis). Adult butterflies reproduce, and also disperse to new habitats, providing their offspring with transportation. Feeding may or may not occur in adults.

Among insects as a rule, dispersal is the function of the adults, which possess the organs necessary for flight. Among marine animals such as crabs and lobsters, it is rather the young stages that provide for dispersal. Transport by water is cheaper in small marine animals because they can keep afloat and avoid being detected by predators more readily than large animals can. Such facts indicate that there are no simple and general rules as to how labor will be divided. There are laws of nature applicable to all economic phenomena everywhere, but the particulars of evolutionary history and ecological circumstance must be supplied to explain and predict what will happen.

The modern assembly line exemplifies very well the spatial division of labor allowing for production on a continuous-flow basis. The various operations are carried out in sequence, and specialized tools and craftsmen are brought to bear upon the product at the appropriate time and place, without interference among the various activities, and without anyone spending much time changing tasks. As previously mentioned, the human gut, a disassembly line, exemplifies the same principles. Every animal that ingests food (and a fair number, such as tapeworms, do not) has to carry out a series of operations on it, in which the food is eaten, then broken down physically and chemically; the nutritious part is taken up, and the waste is discarded. In man, these operations are carried out on a continuous-flow basis, in different parts of the digestive system, and more or less simultaneously. However, there are many lowly creatures in which there is a sort of batch processing, during which the operations are carried out in the same organ, one after another. In sea anemones and flatworms, food is taken up and swallowed, then passed to the stomach, where it is broken down and absorbed. There is no intestine, and only one opening, which serves as both mouth and anus. As a result the animal has a very limited ability to eat, defecate, and otherwise carry out the various operations of food processing simultaneously.

The human mouth is equipped with parts used in the early stages of breaking food down mechanically. It does a few other things as well. Saliva contains some digestive enzymes which are responsible for chemical breakdown in initial stages. The various kinds of teeth exemplify the division of labor quite well. We have incisors at the front, used in cutting, and molars at the rear, used in grinding. In addition the human mouth forms part of the speech-producing apparatus. This connection is not physically necessary, and it has a few disadvantages. It is difficult to talk with one's mouth full. However, one can listen and chew at the same time, so those who are enjoying conversation during a leisurely meal are not greatly inconvenienced.

The origin of speech in man has not been purchased at the cost of new organs for producing sounds, though preexisting ones have been modified somewhat and of course the brain has been considerably reorganized. Thus the mouth is a good example of a part that does not have a single function. Such combination of labor is far from unique in the human body. The liver is a detoxifying organ. It also aids digestion and stores energy-rich chemicals. But perhaps the best example of an organ with more than one function is the human hand, the action of which is facilitated by a division of labor between forelimbs and hindlimbs. The hand, however, attains its greatest usefulness when supported by that even more remarkable organ, the human brain, the functions of which seem to have multiplied in proportion to the flourishing of the species.

Let us now consider how labor might be divided and combined for the benefit of scholarship. The basic principle could hardly be simpler: combine labor where there is complementarity, divide labor where there is conflict. We might as well illustrate the principle with one of the burning issues of our time: research and teaching. The two have long been combined, and it is curious that Adam Smith saw in this very union one possible limit to the division of labor. He pointed out that one of the best ways to master a subject is to deliver lectures on it over a period of years. It forces one to go over the same materials repeatedly, paying close attention to the fundamentals. But neither he nor anybody else to my knowledge seems to have carried this train of reasoning very far. Everybody knows that professors do research, but their reasons for doing so are not the sort of thing to which most people give a great deal of thought.

If teaching provides a good learning experience, research does even better. A productive scholar is forced to grapple with exemplary problems, thereby gaining a deeper and more concrete understanding of the subject. Much is to be said, however, for a combination of both teaching and research. One cannot feasibly hope to do research on everything. An hour spent preparing a lecture is doubly valuable if it means reading materials one must read for research purposes anyway. Resources such as books and microscopes can be used for both. Able students can provide intellectual companionship and stimulation, and when they themselves begin to participate in research, they become junior colleagues and collaborators.

One expects a productive scholar to be an enthusiast with respect to his studies. It stands to reason that teaching will be better carried out by someone who is interested in his subject. The same may be said for learning. The benefits of research in education are best seen when students are able to begin their scientific careers in the laboratory as undergraduates. Time and again such experience has been decisive in the choice of a vocation. A young person who is doing research is no passive receptacle for textbooks and lectures, but has entered the world of productive scholarship.

When teacher and student work together at research they are apt to form a happy community. The point was brought home to me most forcefully during some of the worst periods at Berkeley. The student newspaper reported that the happiest graduate students were enrolled in the sciences, such as organic chemistry. The most dissatisfied were in the humanities, especially French. The Philistines who commented upon these matters were at a loss to explain why the cold, objective sciences were outperforming the warm, subjective humanities. They might have reconsidered their basic premises. Scientists have a vested interest in good teaching. Their students form part of the team engaged in research, and teaching is recognized as a valuable means of communication. In the humanities teaching is a way of making a living, or incidentally a means of indoctrinating the young into one's political beliefs. Or whatever. Naturally we must not see the difference here as absolute. Not all scholars are scientists, and many of the reasons for teaching well or poorly apply to everybody.

Not just any combination of teaching, research, and administration will prove effective. The experience might be interesting, but the economic benefits would be few, if someone were to teach chemistry, do research on historical linguistics, and also chair a music department. One's various activities may or may not lend one another mutual support.

Administrative chores contribute very little to what goes on in either the classroom or the laboratory. A professor in a contemporary university devotes an incredible number of hours to mere housekeeping and trivial meetings. Much of this time is devoted not to furthering his own career, but to passing judgment on the performance of others. Examinations are bad enough, but days on end can be devoted to writing letters of recommendation, evaluating prospective students and job applicants, and deciding who gets advanced to tenure. Hence for the senior staff there is little opportunity to spend time in the laboratory or the field, and much is delegated to subordinates. Add to this the fact that chores are apt to be scheduled at some inconvenient place or time. Trains of thought are interrupted by telephones and by meetings scheduled every other hour. Yet everybody seems to discuss such matters as if the problem were created by a conflict between teaching and research. Again, it is not research that keeps professors out of the classroom, but paperwork.

Those who are no longer able to do research commonly go into administration. If they have simply run out of ideas and have nothing of a scholarly nature to contribute, but still are interested in the life of the intellect, all well and good. The show must go on, and someone experienced at research possesses at least some of the qualities needed for running it. Such a temporal division in a career has much to recommend it in principle, but it creates problems because of the way it affects how decisions are made. Administration is particularly attractive to those who really are not interested in scholarly affairs at all. As everyone tends to run things according to his own interest, an order of priorities is established such that the running of an institution becomes its purpose. Even the most benevolent of administrators, when not involved in research, will be cut off from certain sources of information

107

necessary in order to do his job properly. Among the most important of these is the grapevine, best accessible to those who actually have something to contribute to it. Nobody wants to talk to somebody whose only topic of conversation is the janitorial aspect of life. Hence a dedicated and enlightened administrator will try to keep his hand in at scholarship, even if the cost is high and the return in terms of productivity is low. For equally good reasons he might teach an occasional course. But economic reality being what it is, deans tend to go to meetings where teaching is discussed in the abstract, where research is discussed in terms of the overhead it will bring, and where the participants can connive for more luxurious managerial perquisites.

The interplay between teaching, research, and administration helps us to see how conflicts and complementarities affect the division and combination of labor. Given this background, let us now return to the principles sketched out earlier, beginning with Adam Smith's observation that the division of labor increases dexterity through practice. It takes a certain investment of time and effort to develop a given level of competence. One cannot learn everything perfectly, nor is it even worth the effort. We can master a few skills, or learn many well enough to get by. Thus we derive the proverbial expression of being a jack-of-all-trades but master of none—which stands in peculiar disharmony with the ideal of the Renaissance man. Of course some things ought to be done perfectly or not at all. Brain surgery is a good example. Bathing is not.

The acquisition of a skill is subject to economic threshold effects. If one will only have to read one paper in Chinese during one's entire career, it is better to hire a translator than to learn the language. Really, however, it is more enlightening to look upon the acquisition of a skill in terms of diminishing returns upon the time and effort invested in learning it. Let us take a closer look at foreign languages. We shall consider here only the ordinary scholarly uses of foreign languages, such as reading the literature in a field such as optics or paleontology, and ignore the cultural byproducts and the advantages for recreational travel. For disciplines in which language plays a central role, such as comparative literature or linguistics, the basic principles would still apply, but a more elaborate treatment would be needed.

Once one has learned some basics of grammar and vocabulary, there is no particular point at which one's ability to use a foreign language becomes adequate or not. Rather, with patient study, one's vocabulary increases, one uses the dictionary less and less, and one gets more out of the text per unit of time devoted to reading. As one masters the language, however, the benefits drop off. With a little knowledge, one can get the gist of the text, and with a solid reading knowledge, one can use the language for the ordinary scholarly purposes. In other words, one does not have to be able to speak or write the language to have ready access to the scholarly literature. In the early stages of learning, a new word is a valuable acquisition, for it cuts down on time spent using the dictionary. Later on, however, the new words encountered occur less frequently in the text, and one's return on learning each word would be said to diminish. At a certain point the effort needed to learn the word exactly balances the inconvenience of looking it up, so that it is indifferent whether one learns it or not.

Where the balance occurs—the indifference point—is analogous to the "margin of cultivation" in agriculture, where investment exactly equals return, and there is no profit. Such considerations are fundamental to marginal utility theory, which seeks to determine the balance among possible choices. Generally this is done in terms of monetary decision making, but there is nothing that necessitates doing so. When one's knowledge of a language is sufficient that one's time could be better spent doing something else, one will cease to invest the effort necessary to improve one's skill at it. Consider how one might apportion one's effort between learning two foreign languages. French and German have traditionally been required for the Ph.D. in American universities, so we might as well use them for the example. Assume (unrealistically) that the French and German literatures are equally worth knowing. If one knows just a few words of French, and many words of German, one's investment in time and effort to learn a French word will give a much higher return than would learning a German one. Hence one ought to work to improve one's French, until one reaches that last, marginal word, at which point it becomes indifferent what one should do. If learning French is easier than learning German, one perhaps ought to spend more time learning German, for although the cost of learning German will be higher, so will be the return. This assumes, however, and rather unrealistically, that one cannot substitute anything for knowledge of the German literature. Actually one can read more in French or English, spend more time in the laboratory, or debase one's scholarship. The last option is very popular in American academic circles, to the point that language requirements have been eased. As I once remarked at a Berkeley faculty meeting, "Our students are illiterate enough as it is in English; why expect them to be illiterate in German and French?"

In choosing which skills to acquire, economic man should prefer those which are cheap to come by and which offer a high rate of return. But how does one know what the rate of return on a given skill or product will be? If one is a scientist, one is involved in a particularly uncertain enterprise, especially with respect to the long term. Should a given skill happen to become less valuable, people will invest less in its acquisition. In a free market, the number of people entering a certain profession should decline when it becomes less rewarding. However, there is a serious problem involving opportunity costs for those who are already committed to a given line of specialized production. Somebody has to pay the cost of retooling, or the specialist will have to be consigned to the junkyard. In academia this generally means becoming an administrator.

Consider what happens when the important and interesting problems in a given area of study are solved. Under such circumstances one might continue to work on the less significant problems that may happen to remain. Otherwise, the only option besides getting out of research altogether is shifting fields. The ease with which this can be done represents the cost of retooling. The greater one's intrinsic versatility, the lower such costs will be. Certain parts of an intellectual's toolkit are applicable to a wide variety of tasks. In changing projects one may have to improve one's French or learn some more mathematics. It seems unlikely, however, that anybody would have to unlearn German or calculus.

The particulars with respect to factual details of a given discipline may have some applicability to another one. This is certainly the case when a biologist shifts from living animals to fossils. But we need not restrict ourselves to content and principles. Anyone who has developed the capacity for devising ingenious experiments has a skill that is invaluable in all of the natural sciences. Creativity does not become obsolete.

We have found ourselves dealing with Adam Smith's second explanation for the division of labor. It saves time that would be used in shifting tasks. As we have seen, this is but one aspect of the cost of retooling in general. Adam Smith's explanation presupposes that two tasks cannot be carried out just as well simultaneously. It also suggests that one has to switch back and forth repeatedly. But a temporal division of labor, in which one devotes different parts of the day, seasons of the year, or even phases in one's career, to different activities involves few such changes and they may be well worth the cost. In one's daily routine, a shift in tasks may be desirable: back and forth from physical to intellectual work, or between jobs that tire different sets of muscles.

One should not get the impression that we deal with a kind of factory that turns out a series of homogeneous units that stand entirely by themselves and do not constitute a larger whole. This comparison might perhaps be apt for the works of some, but by no means all, novelists and painters. Each work inhabits its own cosmos, and we need not consider the others to appreciate it. Likewise a botanist might spend a whole career in describing one species of fern after another, or an organic chemist in synthesizing and purifying one steroid derivative after another, with all being united merely by the fact that these objects were new to science. But not every scientist works in that way. Indeed, our botanist's descriptions might be preparatory to a new classification of the ferns, in which perhaps some important generalization about evolution would be central. There is a connection between Darwin's book *On the Origin of Species* and his *The Expression of the Emotions*, just as there is a connection between Newton's physics and his mathematics. A scientist's whole career, if it be thus of one piece, is a single performance, and only intelligible as such.

Therefore if one is a scientist one must not envision one's life as producing an indefinite number of bricks, but rather as constructing a monument to one's creative prowess. A shift in tasks may inhere in the work to be done, just as the foundations must be laid before setting up the pillars. When young it is reasonable to exploit one's skill as an experimentalist, and to gather materials which ultimately may take their place in some larger synthesis. But we must not assume that the whole emerges automatically from the parts. An architect has to do more than just assemble materials. Even though the plans can be altered or developed as one goes along, there has to be some conception of the entire task at hand. Otherwise we get nothing but a dunghill in stone.

Let us now consider the third of Adam Smith's explanations for the division of labor. It supposedly focuses attention upon a given task, thereby furthering the inventiveness that boosts productivity. We have already observed that in science novelty is not just something conducive to productivity; it is the product itself. So we really have two questions. The first is the question of how specialization improves the technical means of scholarly production; the second is whether specialization produces new kinds of scholarship.

An anatomist may rely heavily on a microscope, and this attention might well lead to better ways for making slides or other minute anatomical preparations. But would a narrow focus lead him to discover new organs, or to discover something previously unknown about the same organ? As an anatomist who has in fact discovered an organ, I can say with some confidence that close attention to detail is a necessary condition, but not a sufficient one, for such discovery. One has to know where to look, and one is more apt to find a good lead by approaching the problem with a variety of techniques than with just one. Close attention to detail may be crucial in making discoveries when it results in finding anomalies that otherwise might pass unnoticed. Up to a certain point a specialist is apt to be in a particularly good position to notice that something unusual is going on. A discrepancy may be overlooked when observation is casual. But he who focuses only upon the immediate task is ill equipped to place his work in a larger context. So a fact that ought to evoke a serious reconsideration of theory may pass as not even worthy of mention.

Darwin, in the years following the publication of *The Origin of Species,* brought out three books on the pollination and reproduction of plants. His findings profoundly impressed botanists, and gave rise to an enormous literature on floral biology. Before Darwin, flowers existed mainly to beautify the landscape and allow botanists to identify plants. The wealth of descriptive material makes it easy to overlook how Darwin's research was stimulated by his evolutionary theorizing and intended to develop and illustrate it.

However narrow one's focus, then, one ought to compare what one has found with the general stock of knowledge. One should attempt to do so on a broad scale. Major intellectual innovations often come from outside a discipline. Pasteur worked on chemistry before he turned to microbiology. Darwin spent many years working on geology.

Molecular biology was founded by people with strong backgrounds in the physical sciences.

Interdisciplinary transfer being so important, one might expect scientists to devote considerable effort to looking for resources to import into their own fields, and to exporting their own product beyond the normal disciplinary boundaries. But they seem not to do as much as might be reasonable, and some interesting possibilities come to mind. We might consider this a problem in what bioeconomists call "optimal foraging strategy." An innovation is but one of many resources that a scholarly entrepreneur must gather, and he will experience diminishing returns upon efforts to innovate. He has a problem to solve, and wishes to solve it with the minimum amount of effort. This provides two basic considerations. First he will want to minimize search time. Second, he will not try to come up with the best solution, but rather will accept the first one that seems to work adequately at the time—in other words, he will not optimize, but satisfice. The usual procedure is to plug in some hypothesis or other stock response which is usually found to be acceptable by practitioners of the discipline. Perhaps some *ad hoc* hypothesis may be necessary to explain away minor discrepancies; otherwise one may have to cast around for an alternative. It is cheapest to forage upon nearby and familiar ground, and once in possession of what seems to do the job, one hardly will waste time going farther afield. The only obvious limitation to this consideration is that one's immediate bailiwick may have been picked clean. Animals will often continue to feed upon a given kind of prey when it has become scarce, even when a better one is more common. Such is the economic force of habit, and we may expect scholars to do likewise.

In routine scholarship there is very little need for creativity. One can do without it, merely by engaging in what verges upon plagiarism. Furthermore entire careers have been made on the basis of a single contribution. Hence there is less demand for innovative thinking than one might think. The cost further limits the supply. The innovator has to forage on alien ground, with uncertain returns. He also has to develop the very capacity to innovate. Creative thinking in science may depend to a considerable extent upon genetic endowment, but it is a skill that has to be cultivated. Be this as it may, entrepreneurs are very well paid, and a few scientists are indeed willing to put up a little venture capital, or even a lot of it. Rather than look upon scientific change from the point of view of whether "normal" or "revolutionary" science is being done, we might better consider how the state of the market rewards or militates against creativity. Attention to detail is a good thing—provided it is attention to the right details by the right people. It does not automatically generate novelty.

Chapter 8

THE DIVISION OF LABOR IS LIMITED BY ALL SORTS OF THINGS

HAVING COMPLETED OUR DISCUSSION OF ADAM SMITH'S THREE advantages to the division of labor, let us now consider some other explanations for its existence, beginning with the notion that it allows the economy to take advantage of individual differences in talent and taste. From the outset we must be careful not to confound the cause of such division of labor with its fortuitous consequences. Employers do not divide labor within their firms in order to provide job opportunities for a range of employees. They accept diversity as a fact of life, and utilize the available resources in the most effective way. In building houses we utilize a variety of materials, including wood, concrete, brick, and stone. Our ability to use both brick and stone perhaps lowers the cost of houses or improves their quality, but nobody will build a stone house as a make-work project for that kind of material.

Therefore the free market will not arrange itself so as to prevent talent from going to waste. Nonetheless great benefits result from having people do what they do best and what they enjoy doing most. People have to be motivated to work, and not all the rewards of one's occupation are pecuniary. For most of us the mere fact that one does a job well itself yields a certain amount of psychic income. Especially in scholarship, enthusiasm for the subject makes all the difference between success and failure. Thus it stands to reason that putting a scientist to work on projects that do not interest him will detract from performance and waste resources, whatever the motives for doing so. And if one wishes to invest resources in science, one should find out what the interests and enthusiasms are, and work with, not against, them.

Providing a diversity of products does assure that certain kinds of talents will not be wasted. Ideally one ought to find out what resources are available and make the best use of them. A scholar planning a career has strong incentives to do well in this respect. A choice of projects suitable to one's talents and interests does not have to be imposed from without. Any sensible decision about such matters will take full cognizance of unusual combinations of tastes and abilities. Anatomy has gained much from the contributions of those with a talent for drawing and geometry. D'Arcy Wentworth Thompson's remarkable book, *On Growth and Form*, owes its unique qualities and much of its excellence to the author's gifts for mathematics, natural history, and elegant writing. The work surely did not suffer from having been written by a fine classical scholar, the translator of Aristotle's *History of Animals*. It is difficult, however, to find a place for persons with unusual combinations of talents and interests, and in the modern academic world the cost of doing so can be prohibitive.

Little need be said for the moment about the sociological explanations for the division of labor. Ideally there ought to be a harmony among the various branches of learning. Like the members of an orchestra, all should work together toward a common end, appreciate one another's contributions, and together enjoy the rewards for a good performance. They should not attempt to drown out one another's notes, nor decide by fisticuffs who shall wield the baton. Scientists, however, do not form one vast orchestra, but play solo, or in trios and quartets, and as individuals and as groups they compete and get along with one another just as musicians do. Sociology is important, but it does not explain the division of labor. Economics does.

Adam Smith maintained that the division of labor is limited by the extent of the market. Such limits may readily be seen in the scholarly journals. These have multiplied and become subdivided in proportion to the magnitude of the industry. Some biology journals have undergone a sort of "vegetative reproduction" into botanical and zoological sections with different readerships and different editors. The existence of a specialized journal is contingent upon there being enough articles to fill it, and enough subscribers to keep it going.

As a second example, consider scholarly meetings and conventions. If there are only a few people delivering papers, the sessions may have to deal with a broad range of topics. But with many in attendance the group can be split into sessions on different topics that run concurrently. There are some interesting tradeoffs here, however. One can organize larger sessions, giving fewer presentations. In that case those who speak will benefit from having a larger audience, but the rest will not be heard. And if they can't speak, they find it difficult to justify attending the meeting at all. (Actually it is a grotesque perversion of reality to act as if people went to meetings to attend talks, but the U.S. Internal Revenue Service once made attending them a requirement for a tax deduction!)

So too with academic departments. It is difficult to organize a department with less than one member, and many of those that do have just one member exist as a means of handling difficult personalities. Among the economies of scale enjoyed by large museums, laboratories, and universities is the ability to support highly specialized groups of scholars. If there is to be what is called "interaction," there must be at least two participants, better half a dozen. So far as the life of the intellect goes, such people can operate as an independent, autonomous, or even quite isolated, unit within the whole. They benefit, of course, from the economies of scale that result from sharing equipment, administrative support, libraries, and other resources with groups of the same kind. Although they might "interact" on an intellectual basis with other groups within the institution, they need not do so. However, the mere fact that the intellectual division of labor can be carried to a certain point does not tell us how such division of labor is affected by diminishing returns in general.

Somewhat different considerations determine how far labor is divided when it is a matter of the competitive division of labor on the one hand, and the cooperative division of labor on the other. Competition is most intense and most destructive between producers of more or less the same commodity. This is a fundamental principle in bioeconomics, and the basis of much thought on competition among species ever since Darwin founded the science of ecology. To have a large number of scholars working on more or less the same problem may give it more attention, and the incubus of rivalry may hasten progress. However, it results in much waste of time through duplication. Nor is this the least of the evils. Two laboratories with the same mission will conceal their trade secrets. In so doing they will deny the scientific community the benefits of their discoveries in order to maximize personal gain. They may resort to spying, sabotage, and deceit. These and other results of their competition will have to be subtracted from any benefits.

Such destructive tendencies might be mitigated by having would-be competitors work on different projects. There would be additional benefits to this strategy. It would help keep opportunities from being missed. It would not only increase the quantity of areas being investigated, but would also tend to focus diverse talents where they would do the most good. In many branches of knowledge it is considered good manners to find out what others are doing and work on some aspect of research that others are not studying. If nobody else is working on a given problem, or if nobody is approaching it in the same way, one also enjoys the benefits of a monopoly. Unfortunately the intellectual marketplace may emphasize the demand side rather than the supply side, letting opportunities go begging because certain areas are in vogue.

The relative advantages to combining labor are what really sets—or at least ideally ought to set—the limits to the division of labor. In designing an optimal policy, one should consider what particular combinations are apt to be complementary, or neutral, or lead to conflict, and act accordingly.

The combination of specialist and generalist in a scientist's approach has much to recommend it. A specialist benefits if he is at least something of a generalist in two distinct ways. In the first place he can bring a larger number and wider range of resources to bear upon his work. These resources can be facts, arguments, theories, or ways of thinking. In the second place, his contribution may have value for people working in other areas. There are distinct advantages to knowing both one's sources of supply and one's potential markets. In general scientists are aware of the need to be enough of a generalist to have access to the obvious resources. However, it does not seem likely that such opportunities are being exploited as well as they might. Where to begin looking for useful imports may be far from obvious, and they might come from quite unexpected quarters. The other aspect, being able to see the relevance of one's own work for others, would seem to pose even greater difficulties. A discovery of general significance may fail to be recognized as such by its discoverer and therefore not be communicated effectively. The traditional explanation for the neglect of Mendel's discovery of the basic laws of heredity has been that his work was overlooked or unappreciated by others. Perhaps more satisfactory is the newer interpretation, that Mendel himself did not realize what he had accomplished, because he was working on a different kind of problem. [73]

However broad one's interests may be, one gains an immense advantage through mastering some particular branch of knowledge. Such mastery is hardly to be acquired without engaging in some kind of original research, and that means focusing upon a problem narrow enough to be manageable. To learn how to do research one has to work on a problem in the concrete, and not on what might be called "the problem" in the abstract. There is no substitute for having to evaluate dubious theory in the light of perhaps equally dubious fact. The resources thus acquired, especially the mastery of one's own intellect, are readily transported into other contexts. So too in a lesser degree are the theories and the facts. Thus it is not so much a tradeoff between being a jack-of-all-trades and master of none, as a nontradeoff with respect to being a master of one trade and a jack of many. Perhaps the best way to be a generalist in a specialist economy is to be narrow in a wide variety of fields.

Some areas of learning provide a more commanding position over knowledge as a whole than others do. They give one a greater opportunity to work on larger and more diverse problems, and are particularly conducive to synthesis. Among the many attractions of evolutionary biology is that it occupies so central a place in modern thought. All sorts of things evolve and have histories. Thus via paleontology, genetics, sociobiology, and bioeconomics, evolutionary biology can serve as a kind of bridge connecting the physical sciences with the social ones. Other disciplines are equally strategic. The study of language, for example, helps connect logic, psychology, anthropology, and comparative literature.

Another major complementarity results from the union of theory with practice. By this I do not mean that scientists ought to work on applied problems, any more than artists should be expected to paint billboards. Rather, knowledge should not be cultivated by two kinds of scholars, one concerned only for generalities, the other only for particulars. Aristotle may or may not have been right when he said that knowledge is of universals. It remains the case that knowledge is acquired through particulars. Aristotle himself argued that "practical wisdom" depends upon knowing individual things, and there is nothing more practical than the practice of scientific investigation. One does a particular experiment, not "the" experiment. Knowledge has to be *about* something.

The same is true of the humanities as well. There is no necessary connection between the ability to write good literature and the ability to perform well as a literary critic. Nonetheless many eminent authors have written outstanding critical essays, and it stands to reason that a critic will do the job better after trying his hand at writing a few poems or stories. Indeed, an ill-written critical essay would be poor credentials for its author. Furthermore, literary critics are at least readers of the works themselves. They do not limit themselves to hypothetical novels or verse.

These days only a few philosophers maintain strong links with the empirical sciences. Much "philosophy of science" has little if any connection with what goes on in the laboratory. So too with the history of science, especially the sort that emphasizes societal influences. This situation may seem a bit odd, but it makes a great deal of sense as a consequence of how academic departments have to be organized and practitioners have to be trained. Philosophers and historians have their bases of economic power and influence in philosophy and history departments, and this inevitably determines what they will be required to believe. Having connections with science departments would perhaps aid their research, but it is cheaper to avoid the kind of research that would be aided by such connections. It is very costly for an academic philosopher or historian to learn science well enough to understand the real thing. The cost can be reduced considerably by studying imagined science on the one hand, or the circumstances under which science exists on the other.

There are various ways of combining labor so as to produce effective complementarity. Economists who have studied diversified firms distinguish between what they call *horizontal integration* and *vertical integration*. In a vertically integrated firm, the successive stages of production are combined. Thus a restaurateur might integrate vertically by purchasing a farm that would supply him with fresh produce. This kind of integration is generally explained in terms of assuring the firm of a reliable supply of materials and a demand for the product. Less obvious perhaps is that a knowledge of the technology used at one stage in production may be useful at some other stage of production. Earlier in this book it was mentioned that instrument manufacturers often market and service their own products. The knowledge so gained tells them what their customers want and how the product might be improved. They get somewhat of a free ride with respect to marketing research and the costs of developing their products.

Horizontal integration involves acquiring a number of productive units of a given kind. A restaurateur might integrate horizontally by buying another restaurant. He might want to enlarge the scale of his operations the better to make use of his managerial skills or to reduce such fixed costs as that of bookkeeping. Or it might pay to gain the advantages of modularity by having several similar restaurants in different localities, or local ones that differ somewhat in menu and decor. In either case the reason for having two restaurants rather than one probably means that a balance has been struck between economies and diseconomies of scale. There is an optimal size for a restaurant. A restaurateur might gain more customers by having two rather different French restaurants, perhaps one of them specializing in seafood. He would probably not get very good results by having two restaurants if one were French and the other Chinese.

The same basic principles apply to the integration of knowledge. Sometimes different members in a team of scientists will do the work in the library, in the laboratory, and at the writing desk. But when labor is thus vertically divided, the persons contributing to each stage of production are apt to understand the other stages rather superficially, and a horizontal integration may be more efficient. Vertical integration is very common among those who combine pure and applied research. Somebody who mastered an experimental technique or the use of some instrument such as an electron microscope might be said to integrate horizontally if he applied it to a wider variety of problems.

There is another sense in which integration might be said to be horizontal or vertical. This occurs where the objects known are themselves naturally related to one another both vertically and horizontally. Biology provides an excellent example. The subject is divided vertically in terms of the taxonomic groups, such as botany and zoology. It is also divided horizontally according to the integrational levels: molecular, cellular, organismal, and populational.

The rationale for integrating vertically (from one level to another) in this second sense is fairly easy to understand. A great deal can be learned about an object by taking it apart. One can also learn a great deal by seeing how objects relate to one another in the context of some larger whole. Anatomy, basically the study of organs and their organization, derives much benefit from work on smaller units such as cells and tissues. It also provides useful materials for ecology, since it reveals how organisms make their living. Both teaching and research often emphasize what lower levels imply for higher ones. The reason is not that there is any intrinsic merit to "reductionism," but that it is easier for us to think analytically than synthetically.

Horizontal integration (again in the second sense) has a somewhat different advantage. Some problems are more conveniently studied with plants, others with animals. The differences provide opportunities for doing better experimental work and allowing a broader range of materials for comparison. If one wants to understand how organisms are affected by an attached mode of existence, one should look not only at plants, in which this is quite unexceptional, but at such unconventional animals as barnacles and sponges. Such opportunities are apt to be missed, however, unless one actively seeks them out. This demands a certain expenditure, and not everybody is willing or even able to make it.

Horizontal and vertical integration are not in every way compatible. Indeed, it can be very difficult to accomplish both without a certain loss of content. One can be a general physiologist, or a general botanist, but in practice one becomes either a plant physiologist or an animal physiologist. A great deal of effort has to be devoted to learning the particulars of each group of organisms, or of the objects ranked at each level in the integrational hierarchy, so that being a generalist requires prohibitive costs.

Much confusion results because of conflicts between vertical and horizontal organization within institutions. When I was at Berkeley some of the division into departments was vertical—there were departments of botany, zoology, and entomology. But the Department of Zoology was partly subdivided horizontally, into cellular, organismal, and populational zoology, with vertical components incoherently superimposed—vertebrate and invertebrate zoology. This was partly a matter of metaphysics, partly politics, partly administrative convenience. Life itself is not organized along departmental lines and a zoologist like me has good reason for studying both molecules and organisms. Subsequently Berkeley has begun to abolish vertical departments altogether, and to judge from what has happened at Stanford and elsewhere, one motive may have been to destroy systematic biology.

Add to this the fact that it may be advantageous to combine labor neither horizontally nor vertically, but upon some other basis. One might be a paleobiologist, worse still a paleoecologist, or even a marine biologist. It would be rather like our restaurateur opening not another French restaurant but a French bookstore. Even if a given combination is effectual from the point of view of production, it may not succeed well enough from the point of marketing. A discovery about marine animals may not attract the attention of terrestrial botanists right away. My own work on sex-switches immediately became the basis for much research by ichthyologists, but it was a decade before the same theory was applied to plants. Such experience is commonplace.

The economic situation for botany and zoology does not differ much from that in other branches of imaginative literature. For any of a wide variety of reasons, a novelist might wish to diversify his product horizontally. He might not have enough good plots. Or his readers might not wish to read more than just a few novels by the same hand. Or his materials might better go into a short story or a play. There might be any number of reasons for turning to verse, or nonfiction. An author's success is largely the result of developing a good reputation. One work attracts attention to the others, so that a series of novels will develop a clientele and generate demand. We enjoy one novel, and perhaps go back for more. Yet we may feel that we have read enough novels for the moment, and turn to another genre. Perhaps we look for a book on travel, and find one by our favorite novelist. The elusive general reader has some appetite for variety, and this encourages authors to diversify. Scientists are in a somewhat different position with respect to their readers. The literature is generally not written in order to be read, though some of it is, and to that portion the same considerations should apply.

A novelist might engage in vertical integration by becoming not just author, but editor, or publisher, or perhaps even bookseller. A certain amount of experience in publishing would no doubt give many authors some valuable skills, and editing another's work can be a valuable exercise. On the whole, however, author and editor should not be the same person, and this combination generally arises out of pecuniary necessity rather than artistic motives. The obvious exceptions are not hard to enumerate. Some authors can only write an occasional piece, and might as well devote part of their time to something else. An author of a play might very well participate in its production, as Shakespeare did. In this case the author makes a substantive contribution to both stages of production. But all too often such combination relegates authors to a sort of hackwork they rightly may feel is degrading. In selecting a publisher watch out for editors who are frustrated writers. They can make the author's life miserable by trying to tell him what to say.

Early in his career an author may find it hard to make a living at his chosen profession. Only a few are lucky enough to find their early works a financial success, and even the more successful ones may need to supplement their incomes. The best solution would be inherited wealth, or a good patron, perhaps a sinecure. For most people such a solution is not available, so let us consider other options. A writer needs something to write about, and early life might well be devoted to gathering materials. A job that does not consume all of one's time, yet provides a wealth of experience has much to recommend it. Anthony Trollope worked for many years in the post office, and spent a great deal of his life traveling around as an inspector and surveyor. This brought him into contact with all sorts of people in various parts of the world, with beneficial effects for his novels. But we must add that he forced himself to rise early and to work hard at the writing desk every day. Not every occupation holds out this possibility. One might get so overworked or distracted as to find no time or energy left for writing. One might go into journalism or hackwork, but these activities may teach one bad habits, and may even detract from efforts to form one's own style.

Joseph Conrad's novels profited greatly from his early years at sea, so it seems reasonable that a writer might seriously consider working at something far removed from literature. However the market of late holds out the possibility of an academic career. Someone who aspires to be a writer can earn his bread as a professor of English, teaching others how to read and write. The drawback is that the experience yields little to write about other than the literary and academic world, primarily the latter, and not much of it at that. There is indeed a certain market for novels about the academic and scholarly worlds. C. P. Snow, for example, has written some good ones, but they enjoy much of their interest from having been written by a scientist. The market for novels about goings-on among professors of English is particularly apt to become saturated.

To this we must add that years of work are necessary to master the trivia that qualify one for the Ph.D., even if one is allowed to submit a novel as a dissertation. Little of the effort and expense will have much benefit for one's artistic needs. Indeed, my father dropped out of the doctoral program at Berkeley, precisely because it was ruining his ability to write poetry, and his experience was anything but unique. But such considerations should not deter aspiring novelists from going to a university and taking classes in literature. That is a good thing for most people. However, there can be too much of a good thing, and courses in literature, like so much else, are subject to diminishing returns, and other areas of study might be more appropriate. When John Steinbeck was at Stanford, he devoted most of his attention to marine biology. *Cannery Row* and *Sea of Cortez* are not about the English Department. They are about life.

Unlike a scientist, a novelist gains very little from engaging in pedagogy. A physiologist might find that he needs data on more animals than he has time to study himself, and might farm various groups of them out to graduate students, who would become his collaborators, perhaps eventually forming a school. But what would a novelist do? Would he have graduate students write some of the chapters? Would he provide them with plots? The students would stand to gain equally little. At most they would get some helpful criticism, but the major role would be just certification—providing a union card for just one more academic writer. So we can only expect that a serious novelist would regard every act of assistance to his students as a waste of his time, in terms of furthering his literary career. He might like the students' company, enjoy teaching, and do the job well from a sense of duty. But that is utterly irrelevant. His physiologist colleague would have precisely those motives too. For some people teaching is a vocation as well as a mere job, but this is true irrespective of what they teach. The students' writing might be of high quality, and every novelist ought to read good literature. But it is hardly likely that what a student writes will be the sort of first-rate work on which the novelist should spend his time. And this again contrasts with the physiologist and his students, for even though the students' work might not be downright outstanding, it still might provide the physiologist with facts he really needs. He would have every inducement to having the work done as well as possible. The novelist would benefit as much as the students from reading literary classics, and to this extent there would be a fruitful combination of labor. But such complementarities are much less extensive than they are in the sciences.

On the whole then it is best for a novelist to avoid pedagogy as a major source of income. This is not to say that writers should avoid the campus altogether. It is a good place for them to visit, in order to read and discuss their works, and to gain some contact with the world of learning. I only argue that the principle of diminishing returns implies that they will soon have enjoyed too much of a good thing. Furthermore, what applies to novelists and poets does not necessarily apply to the whole English Department. It is quite different with literary history and criticism, in which the teacher may have more of a vested interest in the prosperity of the student.

Let us now turn to the prospects for combining various branches of learning into what may be called "hybrid" fields. In general these are apt to flourish where there exists some obvious advantage to moving intellectual resources across the boundaries of conventional disciplines. In some cases this occurs where the boundaries are narrow and even artificial—witness biochemistry. So too there may be some particularly useful resource for what on the face of it at least are quite separate areas: biophysics and psycholinguistics. Some hybrid disciplines are united primarily by techniques or gadgets. Microbiologists deal with a quite heterogeneous melange of creatures that have little more than size in common. Or there is a common environment, as in oceanography and marine biology.

Such interdisciplinary commerce may be studied from the point of view of the cost of carriage, as well as the value of the commodity. One might even analogize it to foreign trade. Some disciplines exist partly because such commerce is possible. Again, biochemistry is a good example. The commerce is facilitated by the existence of a common language. Paleontologists and neontologists have a fair dialogue going at present, in spite of paleontology having been mainly linked to geology, often serving as little more than the "handmaiden of stratigraphy." The two share a common classification system for all organisms, whether living or extinct, and the anatomical nomenclature is virtually the same. Hence at least in certain areas there can be productive dialogues intelligible to both sides, though perhaps with less real understanding than might be desired.

All too often, however, the only thing that gets transported from one branch of learning to another is jargon. The founders of new disciplines often try to create the appearance that something important has happened by inventing a new vocabulary. This was particularly true of ecology and animal sociology.

The practitioners of a new hybrid discipline often have to choose between continuing to operate within a traditional area while branching out into the new one, or else becoming specialists of a new kind. Theoretically they might become masters of both ancestral disciplines, but this is difficult. If the hybrid discipline has important resources and techniques peculiar to itself, then there is some reason to specialize in it. On the other hand one gains another advantage through possessing expertise in an area outside of the hybrid discipline, but highly relevant to it. One can become an exporter of traditional goods, perhaps quite valuable ones, without knowing much about the market for which they are destined. The discipline itself benefits from retaining the strengths of those that gave rise to it. When a discipline cuts itself off from its sources of supply it may gain something through redirecting its efforts along different lines. However it risks combining the weaknesses of two disciplines rather than their strengths. The history of science, for example, is apt to make up for its lack of scientific rigor by bringing in the subjectivity of the social sciences.

One good reason for not becoming a mere specialist in some hybrid discipline is that one loses certain kinds of complementarity. When one studies the literature of a subject for the purpose of advancing that subject itself, the knowledge so gained may be put to good use on the history or the philosophy of that subject, and the knowledge can flow in both directions. To some extent the objections to such combination are legitimate. The fields may not be particularly complementary. Historical research focuses upon a different literature than does a timely review of a subject, though this is a matter of proportion and emphasis. It might be argued that someone who actually does research in some branch of knowledge is apt to have some unfortunate biases. He may put too much emphasis upon what seems important at the present day, or introduce anachronisms, or adopt a partisan viewpoint. It is often forgotten that every scholar has his point of view. The ones who claim to have no difficulties with such matters are hypocrites or fools. Although there are ways around such difficulties, one of these is certainly *not* to reduce the number of perspectives, and put everything in the hands of a small group of professionals. This is precisely what professionals want, and helps to explain why professional historians of science have lately written so much about the professionalization of science. Therefore a scientist who works on history ought to know something about history, and an historian who works on science ought to know something about science. But neither should be expected to know all the trivia of both.

This brings us to one of the most fundamental truths about knowledge, and to the key to understanding the advantages of generalizing. What counts is not the trivia of a subject, but the fundamentals; in other words the basic principles. It is these that need to be most deeply appreciated and most widely disseminated throughout the learned world. This point is not so obvious as it might seem, for we readily confound the fundamental with the general—the principles with their implications—the roots with the harvest. The fact that all vertebrates have backbones is more general than the fact that all mammals have hair. But neither of these truths embodies any fundamental principle of biology. They are simply useful summaries of important contingencies, well worth knowing for the same reason that it helps if we own a telephone directory. The fundamental truth here is rather that all the creatures of the earth are united by bonds of common descent. Only when the taxonomic hierarchy stands in clear relation to the underlying evolutionary nexus does it provide anything properly called knowledge. Biology as properly understood offers not just a body of fact and theory, but significant ways of thinking: historical thinking, functional thinking, economic and environmental thinking. Understanding biology means knowing how to think about life.

Having devoted many years to the study of biology, I am convinced that one does not need to know a great deal about it to be a good biologist. The reason it usually takes so long is the amount of time devoted to peripheral materials and inessentials. The details one picks up in a biological education are merely illustrative, and albeit something of the sort may be indispensable, the choice of examples is merely a matter of convenience. Rather than the details of any system of classification, one needs to know how the objects are classified, why they are classified that way, and how to use the system to do research. The principles of anatomy, which explain how the parts are organized into systems, are not numerous, and can be understood by reference to a few good examples. Evolutionary theory is a vast and difficult subject. However, the really crucial acquisition is being able to think about change as a consequence of one organism outreproducing another. Beyond that one needs some practice applying the principles to individual cases until one can use them adeptly. Of course a truly erudite biologist will know a great deal more, but that is a different matter.

Biology is by no means exceptional in this respect. Organic chemistry used to be a most ponderous subject that had to be dealt with largely by brute force of memory, but the textbooks were shortened by explaining the data in terms of mechanism. In general, therefore, it would seem that the basic principles are fairly well accessible, and need not be the monopoly of specialists. Sometimes, however, the fundamental principles are neglected, and even the specialists may not really understand them. Asked to advise a publisher, I read about a dozen of the biology textbooks used in elementary courses in universities. Most of them provided an erroneous definition of the word "species." I do not mean that they provided one of which I do not approve, but rather they misinterpreted one of which I do approve. Lately I wanted to find out how economists use the word "competition," and thought I might begin with three dictionaries of economics intended for the use of students. Not one even had an entry!

Such neglect of fundamental vocabulary is perfectly intelligible. Ordinarily we do not define our terms clearly from the time we begin to use them. Rather we hear a word and use it. So long as no objection gets raised we are satisfied. A student learns to impress his elders by using technical terms, and receives just as much credit whether or not he knows what they mean. At a certain stage we may reflect upon the real significance of our vocabulary. However the temptation to cut corners is always with us. We do not bother to reflect upon the meaning of terms until struck with some real problem in our discourse. This makes sense economically, for we do not wish to invest in semantic research unless it is going to give us some return. It is mere pedantry to quibble about words, and a cheap and easy way to divert attention from what the words designate.

As with words, so with theories. We cut corners. The economic optimum is to understand a theory just well enough to solve the problem at hand, and no better. If the problem is merely getting out a paper, we may require but a very modest understanding of the theory. What counts is merely giving the *appearance* of understanding the theory, though of course the real thing will have just that effect. We may be satisfied when we possess just an elementary version of a theory, one that has been simplified and perhaps distorted a bit, but nonetheless will allow us to get by. Herbert Spencer's expression "survival of the fittest" beautifully exemplifies such distortion. Natural selection works through differential reproduction, not mere survival. It is, as Darwin put it, "the preservation of favored races in the struggle for life," but even the term "races" here should be replaced by "individuals, including organisms." Since reproducing when dead is not exactly easy, survival does indeed contribute to fitness. Therefore, in many cases, one gets along well enough by thinking about selection in terms of differential mortality. The trouble comes when the simplified version utterly fails.

An alternative to understanding the principles is to have a series of mechanical rules. We are familiar with this in the form of "schoolmarm English," which gets learned in high school and should get unlearned in college. There is also a lot of schoolmarm experimental design. In certain kinds of research it is desirable that the person who gathers the data not know what hypothesis is being tested. This prevents various kinds of bias, such as a desire to please the experimenter. But there are advantages to having the data gathered by somebody who knows what he is doing. A knowledgeable informant is apt to be more careful, observe more accurately, and see to it that the experimenter gets precisely the sort of information that is requested. A proper decision about such matters depends upon understanding the principles of experimental design, not mindlessly applying whatever rule one was taught in graduate school.

Economizing with respect to mastering the principles is especially pernicious where a scientist stands to gain the most, namely under unfamiliar circumstances, and where there is an opportunity for innovation. If our job is merely to apply a theory in a routine fashion, we need hardly understand it all. But if we seek to develop the theory— to apply it to new problems, to improve it, or even to replace it, we need a sound grasp of the principles. We can know that our understanding suffices to give an acceptable solution to some problem, but we cannot know in advance whether a better understanding would give a better solution. Often a meticulous reconsideration of the fundamentals will reveal that there are better ways of doing things, but only if one has larger goals. Ptolemaic astronomy still works well enough for navigation. Biologists can still use nonevolutionary classification systems, if all they want to do is keep their shell collections in order.

Genius does not obey the rules, it ordains them. The rules in science are not fixed. They are subject to revision and improvement. Any innovation is apt to cast all the received wisdom into disrepute. New rules must be created, old ones reconsidered. This task can be carried out effectively only if the rationale of such rules be understood. It is no accident that the classics of scientific literature remain worth reading long after they have been superseded by more up-to-date treatments. Inventing a theory is apt to involve close attention to principles, and the understanding thereby gained may lead to a wealth of insight. Indeed the classics may be the only places where the principles are well propounded, and later authors may corrupt and distort them as much as they improve and develop them. So we derive much more than antiquarian entertainment when we turn to the writings of Einstein, Darwin, or Adam Smith.

Chapter 9

THE COSTS AND BENEFITS OF CHEATING

UNDER WHAT CONDITIONS SHOULD A SCIENTIST ENGAGE IN UNETHI-
cal practices? From a moral point of view, the obvious answer is
"never," and it is widely believed that scientists are peculiarly immune
to corruption. The fact that pure science at least has few lawsuits,
formal codes of ethics, or regulatory agencies, suggests that there is no
serious problem here. Applied science is an aspect of business, of
course, and we expect it to need more supervision. But are scientists
really as virtuous as their ideals might suggest? Is there something
about science that makes crime not pay?

In this discussion "unethical" will for the most part describe
improper dealings with consumers of scientific products, especially
with other scientists. We are concerned primarily with what we generally call "theft" and "fraud." Plagiarism, for instance, is considered as
much a crime in science as it is in literature. Theories are inventions,
and one can steal credit for a discovery much as one can steal a
microscope. Fraud may consist of lying about the data in order to get
one's work accepted. Sabotage may take the form of preventing a rival
from publishing a paper or getting a job or a grant. Unfair labor

practices are many, with the most obvious example being putting one's name on an underling's publication when it ought not to be there.

It should be observed at the outset that not everybody welcomes a discussion of these matters. In presenting talks to academic audiences I have been accused of corrupting the youth—a charge that has also been leveled against people like Socrates, Jesus, and Machiavelli. Some people assume that those who discuss the more sordid aspects of human behavior approve of them. Perhaps they fear that others would sin more often, if only the ubiquity of sin were better known. Or they may believe that lying is a good way to control the behavior of their inferiors. Maybe they are afraid that their own behavior might become suspect—that they may begin to doubt themselves. A hypocrite is most successful when sincere.

For most people dwelling upon such unpleasant matters can be depressing, especially when little can be done about them. My own experience has been that although it was painful to come to grips with the problems, with understanding has come not just hope that things might get better, but a solid conviction that they are not as bad as they sometimes seem.

There is a considerable literature on fraud in science, but virtually all of it is journalistic, and of the yellowish variety at that. And a great deal has been written from a moralistic point of view. The less said about such materials the better.[74] This analysis rather draws upon the work of sociologists and philosophers of science who have attended to such matters, and adds an economic aspect to the discussion.[75]

Anticipating what will be said in a later chapter, we may note that much of the fraud that has lately been exposed has occurred in medical research. This makes perfectly good sense from an economic point of view. Much medical research is done in response to the public's well-intended but unrealistic demands for products that honest scientists would never pretend they are likely to provide. Therefore applied medical research attracts the sort of person who is willing to make a living by giving the appearance of supplying the public with what it wants.

According to one traditional view, scientists are honest because of their idealism and love of truth. Much evidence supports this contention, the only question being how adequate it is. According to the more sophisticated view that has emerged from modern sociology of science, the scientific community has a vested interest in the right conduct of its members. If credit is not given to those who truly deserve it, then nobody would be motivated to do research. Furthermore, scientists use other scientists' work in their own research. A paper that records inaccurate measurements is as bad as an instrument that gives erroneous readings. Hence not only is bad research not rewarded, it is penalized. Outright cheating leads to ostracism and oblivion. Again, this seems perfectly reasonable, and no doubt represents a large measure of the truth. But the way things really work out in practice is somewhat more complicated, and the economic aspects deserve more attention.

A scientist values his reputation for the same basic reasons that a merchant does. He has much to gain by providing a product of high quality year in and year out. His customers are very discriminating, and any defect in his work will soon become apparent. If the goods are not satisfactory, it will surely become a matter of common knowledge. If his was an honest mistake, or an unavoidable accident, the customers will remain loyal, provided of course that he does what he can to rectify matters. But given one instance of fraud, the customer loses all confidence, and may even want a refund for everything furnished before.

Suppose I were to publish a paper that incorporates another scientist's data. Later it is found out that my conclusions were wrong. Everybody then wonders whose fault it was. If the data I used from somebody else's publication turn out to be fraudulent, or even the result of incompetence, I might be just a little bit annoyed. Or perhaps beside myself with indignation and wrath. It is not simply a matter of passing the buck. Nor is it unique to science. In football, the quarterback is supposed to pass the ball to the very best of his ability, and it is not just the receiver who feels let down if he doesn't try hard enough.

But there is also an inducement to give an appearance of quality. In science, as in everything else, one tries to place oneself in the most favorable light possible. When applying for a job, one tries to make a good impression. One bathes, dresses neatly, and arrives for one's interview on time. One accentuates strengths and conceals weaknesses. This is not being hypocritical, but doing precisely what everybody expects one to do. In virtually any line of work an ability to make a good impression is a valuable skill. An applicant who did not know at least that would be rejected as an ignoramus, and one who did not care would be rejected as not sufficiently motivated.

So too in scientific publication. It is easier to get a paper past the editor if it is neatly typed, well written, and does not contain a lot of spelling errors. Likewise it makes sense to accentuate the positive aspects of one's contribution and to appear as clever and erudite as possible. Although one ought not to ignore or gloss over the shortcomings of one's work, it makes no sense to dwell upon them at length. How far one should carry the ornamental aspects of scientific writing is problematic. Producing scientific writing of high literary quality takes a great deal of time and effort, not to mention talent, that might be better invested elsewhere. In writing, as in cooking, there are places for different kinds of performance. A fish poached in water can be quite tasty. One might wish, however, to add some wine or a pinch of herbs to the bouillon. A fine sauce won't hurt, even if the diners hardly feel it necessary. But one must never lose sight of the basic principle that there is no substitute for good ingredients. Take a cow patty, cover it with hollandaise, garnish it with truffles, serve it on a silver platter, and still it will not be a culinary success.

It has been said that scientists always protect their own interests by being constantly on guard against what might turn out to be sloppy or even dishonest work. This is certainly a valid point, but it has to be qualified in certain important respects. One of these is what may be called the "emperor's new clothes situation," which tends to make me believe that there is considerable merit to the social constructionist view of science. Sometimes a scientist gets into a position of generally recognized authority, so that not only do his views get accepted uncritically, but even facts that conflict with them get discounted. Such a personage can do a great deal of harm, even if driven by the purest of motives. Error is not corrected until something unusual happens that overcomes the inertial resistance to change.

A good example from invertebrate zoology is that of the late Sir Maurice Yonge, of Glasgow University. In an earlier chapter I related how a student of mine once found a style in the gut of a snail. It was anomalous, because the snail was a carnivore, and, according to Yonge and his school, a carnivore would have enzymes that would digest the style. Really, the argument makes little sense, not the least reason being that by the same token carnivores should digest their own guts, but they do not. Yonge also claimed that the style dissolves under the influence of acid in the gut. His data, however, showed it dissolving, but not in the range of acidity of the gut itself. His work in general was full of holes. My attention was first drawn to the problem by Yonge's statements about molluscan evolution that made no sense. His procedure was, in fact, to think up a plausible explanation for what he saw, adduce evidence that provided no real support, and casually dismiss evidence to the contrary.

Yonge made his reputation as the leader of an expedition to the Great Barrier Reef in 1928 and 1929. He obtained brilliant experimental results, showing that corals do not depend upon sunlight for their growth, as had seemed reasonable from the existence of microscopic plants in their tissues. It turns out, however, that the growth of coral reefs does indeed depend upon sunlight and the contribution of the symbionts. Yonge discarded his data on the corals that failed to grow in sunlight. This held up the study of coral growth for many years. But Yonge was a powerful figure in the British scientific establishment, and it was considered bad manners and risky policy to criticize his views.

While still a graduate student I read George Gaylord Simpson's *Principles of Animal Taxonomy*. I assumed that the parts I could not understand were due to my lack of background and experience. Soon thereafter I reread the same work, and it began to fall to pieces. I began to call attention to Simpson's errors, and this perhaps explains his hostility to my work on Darwin. But it was a long time before I was willing to come right out and say in print that Simpson's philosophy of taxonomy was one long series of blunders from beginning to end. Simpson, after all, had received credit for the paleontological aspect of the synthetic theory. A more critical attitude toward Simpson's work has lately become fashionable, and it is hard to say what the ultimate verdict will be. A couple of my friends despise Simpson because they were assigned his works for reading as undergraduates, and suffered because they could not make sense out of them.

Bertrand Russell reacted in much the same way toward Hegel. He remarks: "When I was young, most teachers of philosophy in British and American universities were Hegelians, so that, until I read Hegel, I supposed there must be some truth in his system; I was cured, however, by discovering that everything he said on the philosophy of mathematics was plain nonsense."[76] I am inclined to agree with Russell's judgment, and so do many others, but that is not the point. Watch out for situations in which someone's intellectual credentials are taken for granted.

There is a fair number of well-documented cases of outright fraud in the scientific literature. Occasionally people report on imaginary experiments or provide bogus data. The temptations for doing so are not difficult to understand. It saves work. One does not have to do the experiments, and the sort of data one needs might not readily be obtained. The danger, of course, is that one may be caught. The uncertainty that affects scientific research creates a serious problem for would-be cheaters. If somebody does an experiment that seems to give clear support for an hypothesis, and that hypothesis is then decisively refuted, people are going to ask what happened. Not only will the work in question become suspect, but other work by the same scientist will be questioned as well. He who is going to engage in fraud, therefore, should do it on behalf of an hypothesis that is true, or at least one that is hard to refute.

A good scientist is a professional skeptic: he knows that any hypothesis, however plausible, might prove wrong. Therefore the bad scientists are the ones most apt to play the charlatan. A dogmatist may be tempted to cheat because he knows that he is right. For him, to gather data that check out all the possible alternatives and give them a fair hearing would be a waste of time. Hence a fraudulent experiment will provide a grounds for conviction that would have been arrived at anyway, without all the work.

One of the most notorious cases of fraud in science was the Piltdown hoax, in which a bogus fossil was produced from the skull of a man and the jaw of an ape. [77] The hoax was discovered largely because the bogus materials could not be fitted in with real fossils that later accumulated. The same is true of the bogus specimens used by Kammarer in support of Lamarckian evolutionary theories. In neither case do we know precisely why these frauds were perpetrated, nor do we know for sure who was responsible. But it may be that persons with good intentions were simply trying to gain acceptance for what they believed to be the truth. If so, they were the good intentions with which the road to Hell is paved. Good scientists never lie.

If outright fraud is uncommon, bias—often unconscious—is rampant. Stephen Jay Gould provides some excellent examples of data fudging on the part of racists—whom he abhors. [78] So do I, but it isn't just racists and other villains who behave in this manner. Gould himself has attempted to resurrect the views propounded by Richard

Goldschmidt in the 1930s and 1940s about evolution occurring through "saltations" or "leaps"—so-called "hopeful monsters." His colleague Ernst Mayr has asked in print, and with an obvious sense of indignation, why Gould completely ignored the evidence which Mayr had amassed against Goldschmidt's views.[79] The situation is even more complicated than that. Charles Darwin addressed the issue of saltation at great length in a book on the relationship between embryology and evolution, published in 1868, entitled *The Variation of Animals and Plants under Domestication*.[80] Gould must have known about the existence of Darwin's book, because in 1969 he reviewed my book on Darwin, which devotes a chapter to it. However, Darwin's book is not even mentioned in Gould's book *Ontogeny and Phylogeny*, even though it is obviously germane.[81] Goldschmidt must also have known of Darwin's work, though he fails to mention it in the text, and Gould likewise does not cite it in his introduction to the reissue of Goldschmidt's book.[82] And, as Richard Dawkins among others has pointed out, Gould's comparison of Goldschmidt's saltationism with his own notions about punctuated equilibria was a gross misrepresentation.[83] What is going on here is quite straightforward. People are trying to sell a given point of view. Those who know how to evaluate the product are not the same as those to whom it is being marketed. Hence there is no incentive for a clear and forthright discussion of the issues.

That kind of bias is ubiquitous to the point that it is not considered unethical, perhaps not even reprehensible. Everybody distorts things just a little bit at least, and everybody else knows it. But we do find ourselves in a sort of gray area. And soon enough we find ourselves faced with practices that are downright shady, and not apt to be excused on the basis of mere human frailty. One trick is to throw away the data that contradict the hypothesis. A similar maneuver is to conduct perfectly valid research, but derive false conclusions from it. Or one can do a series of experiments that do not really test the hypothesis. Even more flagrant is to publish data that clearly refute the hypothesis, but assert that they support it.

There are various ways to avoid detection of submarginal performance, ones that make sense in view of the simple economic circumstance that it takes a lot of work to assess the validity and quality of a contribution. One trick is obscure writing—anything that will make one's work hard to follow. A lot of esoteric jargon helps, especially if one's critics are apt to be in some other discipline. Or one could use a lot of mathematics, especially the sort that is not part of conventional education in one's field. Another possibility is to write a huge monograph, with page after page of tables, charts, descriptions, and all the other trappings of empiricism. The overwhelming majority of readers will have to take the author's word for it, and rely mainly on the summary rather than checking every detail. One's tracks can be further concealed by publishing the premises in one paper, the conclusions in another, and perhaps the connecting argument in a third. Better put the different parts in different journals, and ones not likely to be found in a single library.

To show how this works I draw upon one of my own experiences with a traditional topic in evolutionary biology called "Bergmann's rule." Some groups of animals display a geographical trend, with animals of larger size occurring near the poles, smaller ones nearer the equator. This fact has been explained on the basis of a very simple physiological principle. A large body loses heat less rapidly than a small one does, because it has more mass relative to its surface area. Consider how tea in a cup cools faster than tea in a pot. The large animals would therefore save on energy in cooler climates. This explanation is intellectually satisfying, and the sort of thing that makes good material for undergraduate lectures and textbooks. However, the data that bear upon the geography of size in animals make one wonder whether the traditional explanation is sufficient. For one thing, such trends occur in small, cold-blooded animals, and these do not have a heat-conservation problem. For another, the trends sometimes go the wrong way, animals getting smaller, not larger, near the poles.

It occurred to me that perhaps what was really important was the food supply, which also varies geographically, and I produced some evidence on behalf of this hypothesis. My manuscript was reviewed by Mayr, who was a good critic, partly because of his immense erudition, partly because I was attacking views he had defended at considerable length in his publications. He told me about a paper on fossil elephants which showed that as the climate got colder the animals got larger. I went to the library and consulted the original publication. But although the text asserted that as the climate got colder the animals got larger, an analysis of the raw data showed that as the climate got colder the animals got smaller!

It is interesting to consider why such discrepancies have been glossed over and ignored, and why there has been so much resistance to criticism here. The reason is that Bergmann's rule had an important place in the canonical literature of the evolutionary biology of the 1930s and 1940s. It provided evidence that animals within species are minutely adapted to their local circumstances. At present we have much better evidence, including that of Kettelwell on industrial melanism in moths. But that is a more recent development, and Mayr evidently perceived my attack on Bergmann's rule as "breaking ranks," as it were. And the crucial role of the traditional explanation in arguing for evolutionary thinking in general, evidently militates against our giving a fair hearing to what may be better evolutionary explanations of the same body of facts.

Where exactly to draw the line between "managing the truth" and outright lying is not easy to decide. Although lying is considered reprehensible, it is not against the law, except for special cases such as perjury and slander. Stealing, including plagiarism, is another matter. But once again, we have some difficulty deciding where to draw the line between plagiarism and certain other things. Copying somebody else's work word for word is obviously a flagrant case of plagiarism. To avoid detection, the plagiarist ought to change the names, the details of language and style, perhaps expand certain sections and delete others, in short make all sorts of changes that cover up the resemblances to the original. But that is precisely why those who can do the job well are not apt to plagiarize. If one is going to go to all that trouble, and if the result is acceptable to the reader, one might just as well write an original work. A good writer has no reason for plagiarizing. Furthermore, the quality of the work plagiarized is directly proportional to the probability of detection, all else being equal, of course. Nobody would copy *Hamlet* word for word and get away with publishing it under his own name. On top of this, the more one's plagiarism succeeded, the more it would be exposed to a variety of readers, and the greater would be the probability of its detection. Likewise, the more one does it, the more apt one is to be caught. And once caught, one is not likely to go undetected if one tries it again.

With such disincentives, one might wonder why there is any flagrant plagiarism at all, either in literature or in science. The answer is that plagiarists are not seeking the kind of rewards that appeal to good writers or good scientists, who want to get credit for what really is their own work. A real novelist or scientist hopes, however unrealistically, that his publications will be so successful that they will be studied in minute detail by a vast and discriminating audience.

We should be able to predict to some extent the sort of person who will steal a piece of literary or scientific property and what they will steal. In the first place a kind of psychopathology may be involved. A certain kind of mentality delights in getting away with dishonest acts. A lot of plagiarism has been carried out in prisons. Second, the work plagiarized will be of low quality, or else of moderate quality but apt to be inaccessible to the people who might detect the plagiarism. Third, the work will be the kind that is prepared for citation alone, and not to be read. Finally, the plagiarist's goals will be to obtain the status of authorship for motives different from those of the artist or scholar. Thus a habitual criminal discovers a new area in which to exercise his talents. Or some nobody wants the other residents of Void, Nebraska to confer upon him the status of an author. An untalented soul wants to become a teacher or an administrator, and needs that degree. Or just a couple of papers will be enough to make tenure.

Getting out a series of perfectly legitimate scientific papers is so easy that anybody with a reasonable amount of time and a modicum of brains can do it without cheating at all. Why spend two days stealing something when it can be earned in one? Furthermore, it makes no sense to become a criminal when there are countless opportunities to do what is immoral, but not illegal, or at least what is not likely to be punished if found out.

The borderline between scholarship and plagiarism is rather indefinite. Everybody knows this, and a bit of fudging is indulged as merely normal cupidity—like excessive optimism as to what counts as a deduction on one's income tax. So too it is very difficult for a scholar to distinguish between his own original contributions and the results of his reading. Add to this the temptation to give oneself the benefit of the doubt in such matters, and one of those gray areas opens up. By playing down the originality of one's predecessors and exaggerating one's own, a work may appear to be far less derivative than it really is. Given the subjectivity of any decision as to what constitutes novelty or importance, any charge of misconduct will have to be largely a matter of opinion, and it will be uncharitable not to give people the benefit of the doubt. Furthermore, one's readers are not apt to know much about the sources upon which one has drawn, so these can be duly cited anyway. It is not likely that one's sources will be checked out, still less likely that anybody will complain if they are.

Another possibility is to ignore one's sources, leaving them out of the bibliography altogether. One can plead that one has been unaware of them, or just forgot. Such fallibility, if freely admitted, will tend to damage one's reputation for scholarship, but then again, nobody is perfect. A related problem arises with the priority of those who happen not to have been used as sources. If someone has already made a discovery, he should get the credit, even when someone else has arrived at the same results independently. A responsible scholar is expected to survey the literature and give credit where credit is due. The trouble is that there are no fixed standards for this aspect of scholarship, and it is hard to say what constitutes irresponsible behavior with respect to it. One cannot be expected to read everything, and the less one reads the more time one can spend in the laboratory and at the writing desk. It is easy to economize in a self-interested fashion, saving time on scholarship in a way that just happens to give one undeserved credit.

Giving credit to those to whom it is due is thus not necessarily expedient. But whether it is due or not, there is a strong incentive for giving it to anyone who is involved in editing the journals in which one publishes, to anyone who is in a position to block one's professional advancement, and to anyone who might be a useful supporter. Similar considerations apply to deciding from whom credit may be withheld with impunity. For example, one may be able to get away with ignoring the foreign literature. A Norwegian biologist, the late Professor Sunniva Vader, once remarked to me that Scandinavians were puzzled by the fact that Americans so often republish Scandinavian work. I suggested that it had something to do with the language barrier, but she reminded me of what I knew perfectly well in the first place, namely that Scandinavians publish everything of interest to the international scientific community in English. Their journals, furthermore, are perfectly accessible. Be this as it may, the language barrier does give a scientist something of an excuse for plundering across national borders. By the same token it is very easy to ignore work in other disciplines. Psychologists are expected to read and cite one body of literature, zoologists working on animal behavior another.

So much for piracy. Let us now consider grave robbing. One inducement to a scholarly career is that one's contribution is more enduring than one's body. Good works, beyond the mere satisfaction of doing them, are monuments to one's virtue. Actions that deprive the dead of credit for their good works are disincentives to virtue on the part of the living. Only the living can discharge the responsibility of honoring the dead. But it is easy to find an excuse for ignoring the old literature. We are supposed to be modern, after all, and keeping up with the latest journals is work enough as it is.

Unpublished materials are also vulnerable. A scientist's contribution is apt to circulate in the form of rumors, conversations, lectures, theses, and manuscripts before it appears in print. This is as it should be. If errors are screened out, misunderstandings are forestalled, objections are answered in advance, and the presentation is improved, then the author as well as his readers will benefit. A conscientious scholar, therefore, will seek the advice of other conscientious scholars before submitting a work for publication. Such assistance is acknowledged in print. In addition to expressions of gratitude, however, and in addition to any favors given in return, the reader has access to a privileged document and all the advantages and responsibilities which this entails. Knowing of somebody's work before it is published can be most advantageous, since it means not just keeping up with the literature, but actually getting ahead of it. If due acknowledgment to such sources be given, there is no ethical problem, but the opportunities for mischief are obvious.

With respect to talks, conversations, and unpublished manuscripts, an author has at least some ability to keep his work out of the hands of the unscrupulous. This is much more difficult with respect to the anonymous reviewing of papers submitted for publication and of grant proposals. In fact, the reviewing process is not strictly anonymous, as was pointed out earlier. David Hull has urged upon me the point that it usually is not particularly difficult to figure out who a reviewer is, and my own experience fully confirms his insight. He reasons that only a few people are apt to be sent a paper on a given topic. Other information may further narrow things down, such as a characteristic style of writing or argumentation. The reviewer may have access to information that others do not. Furthermore, people tend to blab. When a paper of mine was sent to the journal *Malacologia*, someone casually remarked to me that it had been sent to Henning Lemche of Copenhagen. This confirmed my suspicion, because the review said that I had misinterpreted one of Lemche's theories, and only he would have been likely to say that. I might add that the late Dr. Lemche's review was quite helpful, and that he had no obvious reason for wanting to remain anonymous.

The reviewing process creates opportunities for sabotage as well as espionage. A skillful use of it can prevent one's competitors from publishing, or at least prevent them from publishing in an optimal place. In theory it cannot block publication altogether, because, where there is a free press, an author can always publish his own journal or book. Indeed, some journals have been founded in the hope of instituting more academic freedom. However, it costs a great deal to found and edit a scientific journal. Even to submit a paper to another journal takes more than just a few cents for postage. And a delay may be enough to give one's rival a valuable competitive edge, and a crucial one where priority is involved.

Although the rights of scholars are to some extent protected by freedom of the press, there is no such limitation with respect to governmental patronage. In certain branches of learning doing research without grant support is exceedingly difficult, and in almost all a grant helps a great deal. Reviewers of grant proposals are in a very good position to engage in espionage and sabotage. Granting agencies have little incentive to protect the applicant. This induces reviewers to abuse their power and applicants to take countermeasures. One such measure is to apply for funds to support work that has already been done, but has not yet been published.

If one devoted all of one's time to sabotaging the work of others, one would have no time for one's own. This creates a disincentive for the best workers to review grant proposals. Reading them does have some of the benefits that reading manuscripts does, but a busy scholar would probably better devote his time to reading manuscripts for friends.

A few other opportunities for borderline plagiarism deserve mention. A lot of material appears in student reports and research papers, and in unpublished master's theses and doctoral dissertations. These are not an official part of the scientific literature, and one is not expected to treat them as such. However, if one has used them, one is supposed to acknowledge that fact—just as one is expected to cite unpublished manuscripts. This stricture is not always obeyed, partly because detection is not very likely. Once a discovery is mentioned in the literature, the literature itself will be cited, even if it credits unpublished material. The use of unpublished theses and the like is risky, because the quality is apt to be low. Use of bogus material in the hope of getting academic credit is much less risky than publishing it, for the simple reason that detection is less probable.

Student and teacher commonly work together as a sort of team. To some measure they might well share a certain amount of credit—and blame—as might any other pair of collaborators. If the two really work together and produce a joint contribution to knowledge, then they might equally well be joint authors on the resulting publications. The ethics of this relationship, however, are not fixed, and vary from culture to culture and field to field. A student has good reason for publishing with his teacher. Not the least is that the teacher will be motivated to provide more help. Also the name and reputation of the teacher will increase the amount of attention that the publication receives.

It is esteemed an act of generosity for a teacher to avoid such coauthorship, since the student will have less credit, and may need it to advance professionally. Furthermore, joint publication means not just joint credit, but joint responsibility. A coauthor's bad work might damage one's reputation. Coauthorship also creates opportunities for buck passing. When there is more than one author, who contributed what may be far from obvious. This may make little difference to readers whose interests are purely intellectual. It does make a great deal of difference when people are applying for jobs or being considered for tenure. *Curricula vitarum* consisting of only coauthored papers are treated as the products of intellectual parasitism. In certain areas of research collaboration is essential and joint authorship is routine. Naturally such areas attract the sort of person who could not do well on his own, as well as those who are good team players.

In recent years there has been a tendency in some fields to increase the number of authors per publication. Part of the reason is that larger teams are involved, but there is also the sort of circumstance that has led to grade inflation. It is easier to give in to demands for putting a name on a paper or for raising a grade than it is to say "no." Lately I have done a lot of work in a molecular biology laboratory, and

146

have been much amused by the postdoctoral fellows' accounts of how the other postdoctoral fellows connive to get their names on papers. One trick is to volunteer just a little assistance on every project going on in the laboratory. We systematists mostly publish with one or perhaps two authors, so I have had to learn a whole new set of rules. Because species names include the name of the describer, multiple authorship here would be a gross inconvenience. And long lists of authors' names make bibliographical work more burdensome.

It is not unusual for somebody in a position of power to put his name on work by a subordinate without having contributed anything scientifically. More about this sort of thing will be said in the next chapter. At this point we merely note that there are very good reasons for not abusing students, and these are more than just matters of honor and morality. Happy subordinates do a better job. They also tend to reciprocate. Once they leave, they may be dependent on their former supervisors for letters of recommendation and other services, but they are much more difficult to control. If they become powers in their own right, they are in a good position to get even.

But obtaining justice when plundered by an academic robber baron may be difficult. Very early in his career the Russian embryologist Eli Metchnikoff (1846–1916) discovered some remarkable facts about the sex lives of certain nematode worms. Within the same species there was a generation that lived as parasites inside the bodies of insects and was hermaphroditic, but their free-living offspring had separate sexes. Metchnikoff informed Professor Leuckart of Giessen about his findings, hoping to obtain assistance, but Leuckart published Metchnikoff's work as his own. Metchnikoff attempted to enlist the assistance of other zoologists in pressing a claim for priority, but they would not cooperate. The affair has become notorious only because Metchnikoff's wife discussed it in his biography.[84] Scientists are reluctant to do battle with somebody firmly entrenched in the academic power structure, especially when they have nothing to gain and much to lose.

This brings us to such topics as revenge, scandal-management, and whistle-blowing. Consider what happens when somebody "rats" on one of his colleagues. Here, academic social behavior is largely dominated by two principles: "Don't rock the boat," and "Honor among thieves."

147

We must understand that when somebody joins the faculty of a major university, he has not sold his soul to the establishment, but rather has become an integral part of that establishment itself. A reasonable and self-interested academic wants to avoid the evil consequences of flagrant abuses, but also fears getting caught himself, and abuses are built into the system. If the rules are bent a little from time to time, it is largely because those rules are imperfect. Everybody knows that. There are some abuses that obviously cannot be ignored, such as misappropriating funds for strictly personal use. By this I mean something like taking one's wife to a meeting and pretending that one took a graduate student in order to charge a vacation trip to a grant. If that sort of thing happens everybody's perquisites are threatened, even ones that are by no means unreasonable—such as an honest little junket, in which one has a good time, but does in fact get lots of work done. A few years ago somebody asked me why I was doing research in Yucatan, and I replied that I like to dive in warm water.

Fear of scandal at once helps to keep people more or less pure and militates against their taking action with regard to the misconduct of others. Academic life is supposed to be tranquil. One is not supposed to create trouble for one's colleagues. Making abuses generally known is apt to be viewed as airing dirty linen in public. It is therefore customary to pretend that corruption does not exist. Hence there is a strong disincentive to taking any real corrective action before the problem gets out of hand.

A whistle-blower is apt to be someone not deeply involved in the academic power structure. Perhaps he is young, perhaps something of an outsider. He is also likely to be someone who has been aggrieved by him upon whom the whistle is blown. The whistle will probably not be blown until the situation has gone far beyond the generally accepted limits. And the whistle-blower suffers dearly for doing what is, in truth, a great service to society. If an investigation results, one cannot readily predict how far it will proceed. Scandal might involve friends, or even oneself. Those little peccadilloes might be turned into mortal sins. The malefactor may ride out the scandal, and whether he does or not he may try to get even with those who do not support him. He may turn upon his colleagues and point out that they are far from pure themselves, and they of course will blame not themselves but the whistle-blower. And the whistle-blower must also face the wrath of unindictable co-conspirators, coauthors, friends, wives, mistresses, and anybody else who happens to suffer. Once, of course, the whistle has been sounded loud and clear, and once it is obvious that a coverup is not going to work, everybody gets into the action in order to salvage whatever is left of his credibility and reputation.

Chapter 10

SOME TOOLS OF MARKETING

NO ENTREPRENEUR CAN TURN A PROFIT SIMPLY BY MANUFACTURING goods. The goods must be sold, and sold at more than cost, and this means marketing them. But the various stages of production and marketing can be combined or divided. A novelist, for example, turns manuscripts over to a publisher, who then both manufactures and markets the finished book. The novelist has to persuade the publisher to accept the work, and is apt to hire an agent for that purpose. In general the agent receives a certain percentage of the royalties. It seems unlikely that any author would give someone a portion of the royalties as a mere largesse, so there must be some benefit from the agent's services. Agents may in fact possess a certain monopoly over the market, but the competition among them for good manuscripts implies that more is involved.

Agents may be looked upon as middlemen. They try to get the contract that will be most profitable for the author, and as an incentive they get a percentage of the royalties rather than a flat fee. Since agents devote all their time to such activities, they enjoy economies of scale and the benefits of special expertise. They know the publishers, and they know what the publishers want. They know how to negotiate.

Having a number of clients at any given time, they do not have to market just one book, or just one kind of book. An author can approach a publisher directly, and publishers do in fact solicit manuscripts. Although this eliminates the agent as middleman, the cost to author and publisher of submitting and soliciting manuscripts may be higher. Having book salesmen solicit manuscripts from academic writers is a common way of reducing such costs by means of the combination of labor. For the author there is a definite tradeoff between time spent marketing and time spent writing. If an author is very prolific, he may not have much time available for anything but writing, and not every author considers the pecuniary rewards the sole determinant of how to spend his time. The act of writing may itself be a source of pleasure, or what economists sometimes call psychic income, even for hacks.

The author may join forces with the publisher to market the finished book. This may mean autograph parties at bookstores and appearances on television talk shows. It may mean seeking the kind of publicity upon which the motion picture industry thrives. Again, a certain balance has to be struck between time devoted to such activities and getting another book ready for publication.

The author's and publisher's interests may or may not coincide. The author of a scientific book, for example, should think twice before submitting a manuscript to a university press. On the positive side it may be said that the people who work for these institutions can be quite agreeable, and often do a fine production job. They specialize in turning out a product of high quality in small runs for a select audience. Yet they are not always interested in selling books, or in getting them onto the market within a reasonable time. They often let a manuscript sit around rather than immediately sending it out for review. They have little incentive for taking decisive action. For a scientist, delay in publication is apt to mean loss of priority and other depreciation of the product. This helps to explain why scientists prefer to publish in journals even when these have backlogs, and to assume that books generally contain little that is new.

Those of us who do write books on science appreciate a good performance from our publishers, and reciprocate by recommending them to other authors. With respect to this book, my choice was strongly affected by such advice. The incentives are there, but they might work better.

The same basic principles apply throughout the economy of the intellect, and the marketing aspect of science can readily be seen as many variations upon a common theme. It is not enough for a scientist to make a discovery. He is expected to take an insight and develop it, showing its utility in research. At the very least, he must publish. He also is expected to show why the discovery is important. Sometimes this can be accomplished merely by presenting an intelligible account of what has been done. Watson and Crick did not have to belabor the implications when they announced their discovery of the structure of the genetic material. The problem was notorious to their colleagues, and the solution held out all sorts of opportunities for further research. Their predecessor, Mendel, failed to attract significant attention during his own lifetime, even though in retrospect he appears to have pulled off an even more impressive intellectual *tour de force* in discovering the fundamental laws of heredity itself. He failed to say that he had discovered what he now gets credit for, and the most plausible reason is that he did not realize what others would ultimately make of his discovery.

A theory will not go over very well simply because it is true. It must somehow relate to the existing, or perhaps developing, corpus of knowledge. One way or another, a case has to be made for its being useful in practice, in the sense of helping to solve problems of one kind or another. Someone who invents an hypothesis is expected to test it, and a failure to follow up in this respect may be taken to indicate that the inventor does not consider it very important. A scientist who is primarily a theoretician may not have the experimental apparatus and skills that might be needed to develop his contribution. In that case he ought to make it clear what sort of empirical research needs to be done, and make sure that the proper experimentalists know about it. Successful theoreticians often enjoy a lot of prestige. Their product has to be good enough to interest others, not just themselves.

In spite of these considerations, a scientist may reasonably specialize with respect to the various stages of production and distribution of goods and services. Even if he does not become a pure theoretician, experimentalist, or whatever, a decision has to be made as to how time shall be allocated. Such decisions are influenced by considerations of talent and opportunity. Those whose gifts are for different stages of production may strike quite different balances.

Although the greatest prestige rightly goes to those who make discoveries and design and execute experiments, no small amount of credit is due to those who make a discovery known to the scholarly community, and even to the general public. Uniformitarian geology benefited greatly from Playfair's *Illustrations of the Huttonian Theory of the Earth*. Lyell's *Principles of Geology*—which was more than just a textbook—and Darwin's *Journal of Researches* were instrumental in the same basic way. This was in addition to the presentation of much new and original material.

Darwin's writings on evolution were more or less intelligible to the general reader, but they were written for scholars. His supporter Thomas Henry Huxley wrote more popular books such as *Man's Place in Nature*, as well as essays and textbooks for nonscientists. He did so partly because he had to support a large family on a professor's salary. Huxley applied the same high standards to his popular works that he did to his technical ones. These days many academic authors are doing quite the opposite: letting the vulgarizer's bad habits affect their scholarly writings.

We must not neglect the complementarities that result from being personally involved in all the stages of production. Darwin pointed out that he was a good observer because he was a good theoretician. Theory tells the observer where to look, and it tells the experimentalists what manipulations need to be performed. Darwin taught himself to be a good geologist by doing geological research in the field. His advice to scientific voyagers is well worth quoting:

"But let his aim be higher: by making sectional diagrams as accurately as possible of every district which he visits (nor let him suppose that accuracy is a quality to be acquired at will), by collecting for his own use, and carefully examining numerous rock-specimens, and by acquiring the habit of patiently seeking the cause of everything which meets his eye, and by comparing it with all that he has himself seen or read of, he will, even if without any previous knowledge, in a short time infallibly become a good geologist, and as certainly will he enjoy the high satisfaction of contributing to the perfection of the history of this wonderful world."[85]

Likewise, experience in the laboratory, field, museum, and library tells one where the opportunities lie for devising new and significant theories. Nor should we overlook the benefits for theory and experiment from time spent at the writing desk. The very exercise of organizing one's thoughts and putting a reasoned exposition down on paper imposes a certain discipline that is hard to gain otherwise. The demands of writing can be a great stimulus for creativity, for a wide range of abilities have to be mobilized. Very likely those scientists who enjoy writing gain more than just a larger quantity of authorship. Much the same may be said for presenting lectures and for other forms of scholarly communication.

We should not assume that a scientist who develops or markets another scientist's theory is a middleman pure and simple. In commerce middlemen provide a wide range of important services, including storing, transporting, and delivering goods. But a scientist who markets somebody else's theory can add something of value to the commodity itself. A book or a review article can be a mere compilation, like the telephone book, or it can be a real synthesis with an important creative aspect. Yet a marine biologist whom I know personally had difficulty in getting tenure at a second-rate university because one senior colleague insisted that a chapter in a treatise on his subject ought not to be counted as a publication. I suspect that this was more of an excuse than the real reason.

Everywhere scarcity determines price. Creativity is in particularly short supply. He who possesses little of it might well be tempted to build a whole career on just one idea. When I was at Stanford, precisely such a maneuver was urged upon us graduate students by one of the more influential professors. He is now a moderately successful administrator at another institution. By a simple extension of the same basic principle, one might build a career upon salesmanship and virtually nothing else.

A common technique is the "media event" in which a discovery is announced at a time and place where it is assured of receiving a lot of publicity. Under such circumstances it is easy to make exaggerated claims of originality and significance. A related maneuver is the *success de scandale* ploy. Perhaps one launches an attack on generally accepted views; since criticism is an accepted part of scientific discourse, this is not considered intrinsically reprehensible. However, such efforts will not sustain themselves unless something meritorious is offered, and in the long run matters will be judged on the basis of the legitimate scientific issues.

A competent scholar, or even an experienced layman, should be

155

able to tell a legitimate critic from someone who is merely out to gain notoriety. The legitimate critic identifies the substantive issues and argues the case on its merits. There may be problems of a conceptual nature, or perhaps certain anomalous facts. One may not be convinced by what such a critic says, but one comes away feeling that one understands the issues better. Not so with the mere controversialist, whose performance is apt to leave one frustrated, confused, or perhaps just annoyed. He evades the issues. He talks too fast. He plays to the gallery. He tries to score by winning points with the audience, rather than by changing anybody's mind. In short, he engages in a debate rather than a discussion—like the politician he is, rather than the scholar he pretends to be.

A theory can be marketed solely on the basis of its novelty, apart from any other consideration of its scientific merit. Novelty is fashionable in both scholarly and consumer goods. But a theory is not like a hat, to be worn for the season and discarded once it has ceased to amuse. A scientist is both a producer and a consumer of capital goods, and does not want to produce for markets which no longer exist. So merely being fashionable will not take the place of making a solid contribution. Once novelty begins to wear off, consumers will look to the quality of the product. But such considerations have much less weight with those who are administering some academic institution, and for whom appearances may be the only issue. And since such persons may be intellectual Edsels themselves, their judgment may leave something to be desired.

Changing fashions in research, however reasonably motivated, can have unfortunate effects upon productivity. It is expensive to retool, and wasteful to abandon a plant that could turn out a good product with little cost of maintenance. If scholars changed their interests and methodologies only when there was obviously a better paradigm at hand there would be no problem. There would be obsolescent fields of inquiry with no demand for their products. It was most appropriate to replace the geocentric theory of the universe and the phlogiston theory of combustion with their modern alternatives. A good theory drives its inferior competitors out of the market.

Theories are not the only scientific goods that compete—areas of investigation and even whole branches of knowledge compete too. This competition is imperfect and may or may not result in one product replacing another. The airplane has not replaced the automobile. A new field of investigation, simply because it is new, offers many opportunities, both apparent and real. If the rewards for changing fields are great enough, the old one may be abandoned altogether. The result can be unfortunate in some respects, as when the automobile supplants public transportation.

In theory there ought to be a kind of balance struck, dependent upon supply and demand. However, the appeal of "modernity" can lead to a kind of "slash and burn" exploitation of new trends, in which a sequence of new fields is intensively cultivated and then abandoned. Fads are likely to give rise to a cyclical economy of the intellect, with undersupply in a given discipline leading to a debasement of the quality of its practitioners through the inevitable tendency of vacuums to attract the kind of people who fill them. Supply overshoots demand, leading to a glut. Artificial stimuli are applied to keep the boom going. When the collapse comes, the plant may have to be kept going through pedagogical make-work projects, or even be abandoned.

Fads militate against an optimal division of labor. They create a market for a limited range of talent at a given time, and lead to neglect of valuable sectors of the economy. Nobody is equally talented at everything, and talent cannot be produced to order. The versatility of genius has its limits. It is unlikely that Newton could have produced a first-rate play, and even less likely that Shakespeare could have invented calculus. Even where talents of a certain kind can be cultivated, their supply tends to be very inelastic. The supply cannot be increased fast enough to keep pace with the changing demands generated by rapid changes in fashion.

Before the stock market was regulated, it was common practice for groups of speculators to create a market for a stock by selling it back and forth to one another, giving the impression that something of real value was changing hands and driving up the price. By a similar maneuver, a group of academic operators can give a factitious appearance of value to their products. This can be accomplished by holding a lot of meetings, founding journals, and anything else that will generate a lot of paper. Holding meetings is fairly easy, provided that somebody is willing to attend them. Meetings provide the sort of product that granting agencies and the like can hold up as concrete accomplishments. If the meetings are held in pleasant places, those who are invited can fairly readily be induced to generate some manuscript in exchange for transportation and expenses. There is then a strong inducement to publish materials of marginal quality and to duplicate what has already appeared elsewhere. Publishing in the form of a "symposium" volume allows one to circumvent the usual reviewing process. If the members of the discipline or movement in question form their own societies, with their own journals, they can determine what is publishable. Most importantly, perhaps, they can cite one another's publications. This is taken by outsiders as evidence that the publications in question are worth citing.

This brings us to the economics of citation. A work is cited every time it is mentioned in another work—usually in a list of references at the end of a paper, or perhaps in a footnote. There are some problems here, because a work might be mentioned often in a few papers, or occasionally in many, giving a misleading impression of how important it was. The number of citations can be increased by breaking a paper up into several smaller ones. It should be more or less obvious that sheer number of citations does not necessarily reflect the quality of a paper. Indeed, a paper might be held up as a bad example, and infamy confounded with fame. In spite of such drawbacks, the frequency of citation, like the number of titles, has come to be used in assessing the quality of a scientist's contribution. This has given rise to the *Scientific Citation Index*, which tells who cited whom and when, but not why. Having been thrown, together with the amount of grant money a scientist has, into the witch's brew of evaluative techniques, citation frequency creates an incentive for having one's work cited as many times as possible.

The reasons why anybody's work is cited at all are far less clear than one might think. Much of what has been said about this matter looks suspiciously like folklore. That citation is primarily a means for awarding credit is largely taken for granted. When a scientist publishes, he is supposed to read the literature and cite those among his predecessors who have made the contributions upon which his own rest. Thus, if he has tested someone else's theory, he gives credit to her for the theory; for not to mention her work would be tantamount to claiming that it was he, not she, who deserves that credit. She would rightly consider him a thief, and might seek revenge, or at least an apology. Plausibility thus supports the view that one reason for citation is to give credit. That does not mean, however, that giving credit is the only reason for citation. Nor does it mean that such credit is given to the person who really deserves it.

Citation provides the reader with various kinds of useful information. What is the problem? Who has worked on it? What have they done? Citing publications means that the readers can go to particular works for more information, and this need not have anything to do with apportioning credit. The reader might want to know more about some peripheral topic, and would appreciate being told what the good reference works are. This is particularly important for a more general audience. In many cases publications are cited merely to justify a premise, to explain how a word is being used, or to avoid repeating what has already been said elsewhere.

Citation also helps to establish the author's credibility. If the author shows that he knows what literature is relevant, the reader will tend to get the impression that the author is erudite and competent, and this may well be the case. There are some complications here; not the least is that form may be substituted for content. The mere fact that one has cited a paper does not necessarily mean that one has read it. To cite a work that one has not read is considered misconduct, but nothing compels one to read it with understanding. Citing a large number of references is one way to pad a paper, but that may involve actually going to the library.

Citation tells the reader where the author got his information. This allows a certain amount of buck passing should any source of information prove unreliable. Although scientists are expected to be critical of their sources, they are not expected to be prophets. Merely by examining what an author cites, one can infer all sorts of things: his field, what "school" he belongs to, who his collaborators are, what languages he reads—the list could go on and on. This makes it somewhat easier to evaluate his work. I once ran across a citation to a book by a German named Zimmerman entitled *Die Coelomtheorie*. The origin of the coelom, or secondary body cavity, is an important topic for us invertebrate zoologists, and I wondered how I had overlooked a whole book on it. Then it dawned upon me that in 1965 a German botanist named Walter Zimmermann had published a book entitled *Die Telomtheorie!* Perhaps the author of the paper in question had instructed his assistant to festoon the work with impressive-looking references, and failed to check up on the results.

In 1911, 1913, and 1924, a zoologist named Adolf Naef published a long discussion, in German, on the comparative anatomy of mollusks. These papers are often cited with the same wrong dates, at least to judge from: (1) the copies I have examined, and (2) Naefs citations of these works. Sometimes one of these papers is cited, not just with the wrong date, but with the title translated into French. This practice may have something to do with a French malacologist named Alice Pruvot-Fol having translated the title in her list of references. Generally one should be careful about accusing anybody of misconduct under such circumstances. Bibliographic apparatus has a nasty way of breaking down. A paper might be cited from memory under circumstances in which the original was not available, and the author's copying a secondary source would hardly indicate not having read it. When I copy a title out of somebody's list of references I try to check the original very carefully. I once went so far as to pay somebody to go to the library and recheck all the citations in one of my book manuscripts. Even so a few proofreading errors inevitably get through. There are also serious problems with respect to actual dates of publication. I once was accused of misciting a book by Darwin, when in fact I had correctly cited a different edition.

The fact that a work has been cited does not mean that it has been praised, only that it has received a certain amount of attention. Therefore it is possible to be cited by such maneuvers as getting involved in polemical exchanges. A related stratagem is to publish the kind of work that is apt to draw a critical response from colleagues. Or by concentrating on volume one may hope that chance alone will get one's name in print. The honorific terms for those who employ these stratagems are "provocative," "innovative," and "prolific." The pejorative ones are "contentious," "speculative," and "redundant."

An economic view of citation helps us to understand what Robert K. Merton has called the "Matthew effect."[86] He bases the term on a passage in the Bible (Matthew 13:12): "For whosoever hath to him shall be given, and he shall have abundance: but whosoever hath not, from him shall be taken away even that he hath."

Eminent scientists tend to get credit for what their less eminent colleagues have done. For one thing, eminent people tend to receive a lot of attention. Once they become eminent, people tend to read and cite their works. Furthermore, it is easier to remember a well-known name than an obscure one, and this biases the sample. If somebody's name is identified with a given area of research, then that person's name will be more likely to get attached to contributions in that area. The mere fact of eminence provides a cheap substitute for inquiring as to the basis upon which that eminence rests. The main reason why a scholar gets an honorary degree is that somebody else has already given him an honorary degree. (Another important reason is that the recipient does not get paid for the lecture delivered when the honorary degree is awarded.)

Another aspect of the Matthew effect has to do with the institutional affiliations of the eminent. The leading scholars tend to be associated with the leading universities. Consumers take this as a sign of endorsement. Therefore they decide what to read partly on the basis of where it was produced. As has often been pointed out, the reputation of an institution may outlive any substantive excellence upon which that reputation was originally based. And the quality of a university varies greatly from one department to another. Nonetheless scholars try to associate their names with those of prestigious institutions. By the same token, one way to become a prestigious institution is to hire big names. The effects on salary differentials are all too obvious, those on the real relationship between prestige and quality perhaps a bit less so. A "good" undergraduate degree means a "good" graduate degree, and in turn a job at a "good" university. This obviously militates against vertical mobility, either upward or downward, but to what extent is hard to say.

Citations may indeed be used as a means of giving credit, but that does not tell us to whom credit should be given. The person to whom a scientist wants to give the most credit is obviously himself. In fact self-citation is exceedingly common, and for obvious reasons it is not considered a measure of anybody's contribution. Citing the work of some prestigious figure may lend an aura of respectability to one's own work. In biology Darwin is of course the culture-hero of the whole field, and citing The Origin of Species makes a good impression. There are some lesser figures, and even some anti-heroes, such as Lamarck. German biologists are apt to cite Goethe and Kant, Russians Marx and Engels.

A different strategy is called for when citing one's contemporaries. Here it is a matter of doing unto others as you would have them do unto you, provided that they are really likely to do so—and doing unto others as you would not have them do unto you, provided that they are not in a position to get even. It makes sense to cite those who will reciprocate by citing one's work in return. This in addition to the obvious cut that must be bestowed upon those who control such amenities as jobs and access to the journals. In general this means citing the most prolific authors, particularly those who will be the most prolific in the future. There will tend to be a strong correlation between past and present productivity. Furthermore, past productivity generally correlates with present academic power and influence.

Conversely, it is hardly worth the effort to cite authors who are no longer active, or those who work in another field. One's professional rivals are another matter. If one does not cite them, they may try to get even. Therefore one has a very difficult problem of deciding who is in a position to even the score. At any rate, one hesitates to begrudge them more credit than one has to.

The same general principles apply to destructive criticisms and pejorative citations, although one must bear in mind that it is better to be attacked in print than not to be cited at all. A pejorative criticism is most effective where the author criticized is in no position to reply, unless the rationale is to generate a polemical exchange. It may indeed be possible to set things up so that both parties benefit from such a controversy. After all it increases the number of papers and citations. The return here is greatest to both parties if they are in different fields, because both can win in the eyes of their colleagues.

One can get into serious trouble if one miscalculates when giving or withholding credit. Fortunes are apt to change, and it may not be easy to assess who is in a position to advance or impede one's interests. It is perhaps better not to abuse somebody who, although not powerful himself, may have numerous or powerful friends. Indeed, one might even multiply the number of citations, putting in a good word, or at least an indifferent one, for everybody who might appreciate seeing his name in print. Carried to its logical conclusion, of course, that means virtually the entire population of the globe.

Applying for grants may be treated as a kind of marketing—of skills and other resources in order to obtain capital. Writing a grant proposal is in some respects like writing a scientific paper. Indeed, one way to economize is to use the same manuscript for both purposes. However, there are some important differences. Not the least is that one is attempting to please the bureaucrats who run the granting agency, who, in turn, have to please other bureaucrats as well as politicians. One also has to please those who serve as peer reviewers. It is somewhat like getting a scientific paper through the editorial hurdles, but here the similarity ends. The proposal will be used as a resource by bureaucrats, but not by the scientific community as a whole. Only a few scientists will see it. Publications based on the grant will only be tenuously related to it.

The scientists who evaluate the proposal will no doubt be favorably impressed if it contains some original and exciting ideas and well-planned experiments. It also helps to have a good record for productivity and quality. But what counts most is making a good immediate impression. Consequently one tries to appear trendy. An impressive-sounding title is very important, because that is all that will be seen by many of those who have to be impressed. The very anonymity of reviewers makes it somewhat difficult to know whom to please. Therefore the appropriate tactic is to please everybody and offend nobody. This is sometimes difficult because reviewers can be very creative in finding fault with a proposal. In one of my recent proposals, for example, I was rather vague about which particular species I was going to study, partly because it is not easy to predict which representatives of a given order, family, or genus will be readily available, and partly because initial results would affect what came next. To satisfy the granting agency I had to make up a list of animals that I might use, because one reviewer felt that such information ought to have been provided.

A great deal of work goes into writing grant proposals. When one considers that only a small portion are funded, it is obvious that much of this effort is wasted. The problem is compounded because grant proposals may have to be revised extensively to meet the requirements of the agency with respect to budget and other details, in addition to purely scientific matters. Often getting support results largely from persistence in rewriting and resubmitting proposals.

The granting agencies have little if any incentive for economizing upon the time expended by the applicants. Consequently it is not unusual for a scientist to spend all of his "research" time writing proposals and administering grants. The agencies also have very little incentive to ease the burden upon the scientists who participate in peer review. There seems to be a tacit understanding that such activity helps make one part of the old boy network. The only scientist I know to have openly rebelled against the system is Professor Nicholas Holland of the University of California, San Diego. He kept submitting grant proposals to the National Institutes of Health, and they kept turning them down. They also kept sending him proposals for review. One day he sent them a letter saying "You don't send me any more grant proposals, and I won't send you any more grant proposals." This action freed up an immense amount of time, not only for research that led to many fine publications, but for service as editor of a scholarly journal.

Reviewing grant proposals, serving on panels, and editing scholarly journals are ways of providing services to the power structure in exchange for influence. One can get a lot of mileage out of being a joiner, attending meetings, and otherwise doing things that have little relationship to the quality of one's scientific work, but that do facilitate marketing, not only of the product, but of the producer.

The producer is rewarded in the prestige economy by obtaining certain tokens. In England, of course, there is knighthood, which saves the government a lot of money. Knighthood seems to be given more as a reward for governmental service than for scientific accomplishment, but not everybody notices that. Everywhere there are such things as honorary societies, awards, and prizes. There are some obvious diseconomies here. Much prestige attaches to a degree from, or a faculty position at, what are esteemed the best universities. Yet such institutions may not be the best places for doing a particular kind of research. We marine biologists sometimes have to trade prestige for a chance to be near the coast. Grants in aid of research obviously serve as tokens of prestige, not only for the scientist, but for the scientist's institution. This creates an incentive for seeking grants for the prestige in a way that conflicts with the priorities of research.

Prizes are one way of rewarding people for good work. They have the advantage over grants insofar as success is more easily evaluated than promise. There are problems insofar as the rewards can serve as capital as well as remuneration. Therefore there is some advantage to having some prizes and other honors reserved for younger scientists. Also, there are diminishing returns as the size of the prize goes up. Probably having two persons share a prize does not mean each benefits half as much.

In 1986 James Buchanan received the Nobel Prize in economics for his work on public choice theory. Many economists have felt that he should have shared the prize with his collaborator, Gordon Tullock. I am told that Buchanan invested a lot of effort in obtaining the right connections, whereas Tullock did not. Tullock has done some fine work on bioeconomics and other rather unconventional topics, and the time for doing so must have come from somewhere.

Chapter 11

THE IDEOLOGIES OF
MONOPOLISTIC COMPETITION

MARKETING TECHNIQUES SUCH AS THOSE DISCUSSED IN THE PREVIOUS chapter lead naturally to a broad range of "extrascientific" matters, such as the methodology, history, philosophy, sociology, and politics of science. The matter of "ideology" in science has become very topical of late. We are presented with a thesis, or at least with a tacit assumption, that much of what scientists do is determined by values of a political or socioeconomic character. The question we must ask is not whether such is the case, for that is obvious. Rather, we must consider the larger picture of how the system actually works, and from that find out what roles politics and such really play in the life of the intellect. The system is indeed political, and supremely economic as well, albeit not in the way that many would have us think.

In particular, we must clearly distinguish between the kind of economic ideology that enters into the diatribe of Marxist professors on the one hand, and the effort to develop a legitimate economics of scientific behavior on the other. Marxism was invented partly by modifying pre-Darwinian economics, which presupposed that there is a teleological order in Nature, and that everything was tending toward some preordained goal. Marxism got rid of a certain kind of idealism, but retained the teleology, and therefore denied the most fundamental truth about evolution. The dialectic was an effort to translate a sort of divine conversation into materialistic terms, with everything the outcome of economic and social interactions. "Ideology" has meant the derivation of human beings' beliefs from their position in the socioeconomic system. We supposedly believe what we believe because we are bourgeois, or whatever, rather than because of the legitimate scientific evidence. Marxists, of course, would have us believe what is conducive to the interests of Marxists—getting the millennial state realized. And, as Marxists see it, anything we believe that runs contrary to notions of how things ought to be is the consequence of economic circumstances preventing our right thinking.

We surely do tend to derive much of our opinions and values from those around us, and our opinions and values do have a close connection with the means of production. People are taught to do that which keeps the local economy going, and with good reason. But to turn this into a monolithic explanation for human behavior creates a travesty. We have a physical environment, and discoveries about science affect social thinking—they are not merely affected by it. For good biological and economic reasons, we resist the tendency of society to dictate our beliefs and opinions. We try to preserve our own lives, and those of our children, and such interests may put us at odds with those of what is called "society." Any competent biologist ought to see at once that Marxist economics do not correspond to objective reality.

Furthermore, ideology is a weapon that can be turned against the person who wields it. When something is labeled an "ideology," the epithet is always a pejorative one, and it never seems to occur to Marxists that they are open to precisely the same charges. If everybody else's science is nothing more than a manifestation of economic forces, what about one's own? If bourgeois liberals are doing bad science, what about everybody else—without any exception whatsoever? Why not attribute the scientific behavior of Marxist professors to economic motives—perhaps of the basest, most pecuniary kind? Or even a desire to make what passes for an honest living?

One of the leading biological apologists for Marxism has been Richard C. Lewontin, of Harvard University, who, together with his colleague Richard Levins, has written a most revealing book on how ideology is supposed to affect the thinking of biologists.[87] I well remember a meeting on "the evolutionary synthesis" at the American

Academy of Arts and Sciences, in Boston. The meeting was on the history of biology, but Lewontin delivered a talk on the future of evolutionary biology, which understandably was not published in the volume of contributions.[88] Futurology has never seemed a particularly respectable branch of objective natural science to me, and I disagreed with his general outlook. So I told him that I did not like his metaphysics. He responded "I have no metaphysics!" Honest, he really did. It was part of the official discussion, and was recorded on tape. Naturally I replied "That's your metaphysics." Our discussion went downhill from there.

A few years later Lewontin delivered one of the Tanner Lectures at the University of Utah. It was all about sociobiology, and he might have said something interesting or new. However he did little but charge his opponents, rightly I think, with ideological bias. At the question period I asked him to tell us what his own ideology was, and the response was not at all bad, at least in comparison to the lecture. In 1974 both Lewontin and I had published books in which we attacked sociobiology.[89] That was a full year before Wilson's book on that topic evoked a storm of controversy. Both Lewontin and I recognized the ideological bias, but I detected it in all authors, irrespective of their political persuasions.

Levins and Lewontin acknowledge that ideology may indeed be a problem for themselves, but their actions reveal little if any union of theory with practice. Their fine chapter on the "commoditization of science" blames the ills of science on the capitalist system, and rightly so. But they are insensitive to the relationships between their ideology and their own bourgeois values. They fail to see that their academic Marxism is a cottage industry, and that their colleagues view them as purveyors of snake oil.

Science is better treated as a free-enterprise economy in which ideological diatribe is just one way of coming out ahead in cutthroat competition. In science the competition is not so much between facts and theories as it is between problems and the techniques for solving them. And success in such competition may mean not solving a problem but getting that problem solved in a manner that will give one the most credit. This gives rise to what we may call "internal ideologies" of science—in contradistinction to such "external" ones as Marxism and capitalism.

Remember that a scientist deals with problems and makes his

169

reputation by solving them. Ideally, the sole criterion of excellence is success, and credit is given to he who solves the problem. But let us not be naive. A scientist has a vested interest in his problem-solving apparatus. (Call that a paradigm or whatever you please.) Theories obviously compete. But so do the means of developing them. If someone using one approach refutes a theory advocated by someone using another approach, the approaches themselves are proportionately strengthened and weakened. Such competition can tend toward efficient allocation of techniques and other resources. But some of its effects are deleterious. A variety of problems may need a variety of techniques, and what works for one problem may not work for another. Nobody would throw away a screwdriver simply because a wrench did the trick for a given task. We may have a group of specialists, analogous to some with screwdrivers, others with wrenches, and all looking for work. If the screwdrivers will not do a certain job well, those who wield them will try to persuade everybody that the job cannot be done, or that it is not worth doing.

Let us examine the strategy of such ideological combat. It has a form, but let us not call it a logic. Basically the trick is to find some feature of one's own approach that makes it look good, and conclude that since that feature is lacking in the competition's approach, their approach is not good. The premises here can be just as suspect as the logic, but remember that we are not concerned with valid inference anyway. Consider, to begin, *quantification*. Science is supposed to be quantitative. Therefore, one bends over backward to appear more quantitative than the competition. Put numbers on everything. It matters little whether these really designate quantities of anything or are just placeholders like the page numbers in a book, or arbitrary codes like telephone numbers. Figures can be made up out of whole cloth if one feels like it. After all, if one is going to guess, one might as well guess quantitatively.

Another exceedingly useful weapon is *experimentalism*. If you do experiments and the competition does not, treat this as an advantage. It does not matter whether your experiments cast any light on the questions being asked. Indeed, one's goal should be to argue that the only questions that are answerable are the ones amenable to an experimental approach—particularly one's own kind of experimental approach. Such a posture has been especially popular among psychologists who study the White Rat. One counterstratagem here is to argue that there are some really interesting questions which we cannot deal with experimentally. The only way to study the evolution of behavior among rodents is to compare various different rodents. The trouble with this maneuver is that the opposition will simply reiterate the argument.

Experimentalism can be more effectually opposed by *naturalism*. A white rat or a college sophomore in the laboratory does not necessarily behave in what is called a "natural" fashion. Rats are not adapted to life in mazes. College sophomores love to "psych out" the experimenter. Therefore we obviously need to understand what organisms do in their ordinary environments. In fact we can do experiments in the field, and although these may be harder to interpret than ones done in the laboratory, they often give important results. Experimental work of this sort has been remarkably successful of late in ecology and social psychology.

Statistics is a most notorious ideological weapon, and one that has often been abused. On the one hand it can be used to make one's work more "objective." On the other hand, it can be used merely to give that appearance, or to obfuscate, or even to lie. In some branches of learning one is not supposed to use what are called "anecdotal" data. A single observation, even if it provides a serious challenge to received opinion, is thrown out of court. Consequently, rare anomalies might be screened out, perhaps even some rather common ones as well. In some disciplines, such as molecular biology, the use of statistics is viewed with suspicion. It is taken as indicative of bad experimental design. A good experiment, after all, is supposed to be simple, straightforward, and decisive. The more complicated one's apparatus, and the more convoluted one's reasoning, the greater the incertitude that surrounds the results.

Molecular biologists these days prefer to use *modernity* as a basis for justifying their lives. Prestige goes to the scientist who gets the most slops at the public trough, and who uses the often very expensive "state of the art" technology. Therefore a great deal of cost-ineffective work is being done with laborsaving devices. I note only a few curiosities about the sort of molecular study in which I have engaged. My collaborators inform me that the upcoming maneuver will be to gather great masses of descriptive data from a single organism. Nobody seems to have asked whether, given limited resources, one might not want a smaller amount of data from a wider variety of organisms. The animals studied have been chosen with little concern for their providing answers to important questions. The usual laboratory animals are used, and that is it. By the time somebody who does know what animals to study gets involved, the technology is out of date and the work is much less likely to be supported.

We might view *rationalism* and *empiricism* as strategical alternatives in ideological conflicts. Science invents theories and tests them by gathering data, and both of these activities are indispensable. The theories are useless if they do not relate to the real world, and the "brute facts" do not mean anything until they are linked up to some kind of generalization. The trouble is that one can market a theory without much reference to its explanatory utility. It might be attractive merely as an object for the exercise of theoreticians' skills. Now, the world is not set up so as to make life convenient for theoreticians, and they may find it expedient to introduce certain simplifying assumptions. In some cases these are perfectly legitimate. Physicists ignore friction when dealing with the pure theory of gravitational attraction. On the other hand they do not ignore friction when dealing with either the real or even hypothetical instances in which friction occurs. Covert oversimplification is much more apt to lead to error when biologists invent theories that ignore variation—for example, by supposing that all organisms are of the same age or the same sex. One way to justify surrealism in theoretical work is to claim that one works on "models," rather than "theories." Models in this sense do not pretend to correspond to objective reality.

If, on the other hand, one's research generates a lot of data, then one can claim to be a rigorous, inductive empiricist. If one lacks the ability to come up with a good theory, and *a fortiori* if one wouldn't know what to do with such a theory if one did, it behooves one to debunk theory in general, and claim that the safe road to truth lies in the patient and unbiased accumulation of facts. If one's facts bear upon a certain theory, then that theory nonetheless needs to be treated as important. Any other area of investigation has to be dismissed as mere speculation, perhaps the sort of thing that is "untestable" in a quasi-Popperian sense. Where Popper really said that theories are scientific only if in principle it is possible to refute them, we are handed the assertion that a given theory is, in practice, difficult to test.

The internal ideologies of paleontology are a case in point. It is expedient for some practitioners of that discipline to have it believed that only fossils can give us "direct" evidence about evolutionary history. This obviously gives them a monopoly over all sorts of topics. Those of us who do know something about paleontology are a bit skeptical. After all, a great deal of imaginative reconstruction goes into the interpretation of fossil remains, and this is not at all a bad thing. Of late a vocal faction among paleontologists has been arguing that paleontologists have to interpret their specimens in basically the same way that neontologists do. The main difference is that paleontological materials are badly preserved and largely incomplete. The issue here is not whether paleontology is or is not germane to evolutionary research. Rather, as with genetics and everything else, few have bothered to consider precisely what the various lines of evidence contribute, and anybody can take advantage of the general ignorance. Creationists do that routinely.

It is indeed a good thing to quantify, to experiment, to do field work, to use statistics and other gadgetry, to theorize, and to gather data. We are dealing here, however, with the notorious *argumentum ad auditores*—with playing to the galleries. Any fool can tell you that it is a good thing for science to be quantitative or experimental. But it requires a great deal of hard work and erudition to tell a good experiment from a bad one. The various maneuvers we have been considering have a straightforward economic rationale. It is cheaper to learn a rule than to master the principles that justify the rule and tell us how to use it properly. And applying the principles to any particular case again may require an enormous amount of work. So everybody has to rely to some extent upon superficial criteria of judgment, and anybody can take advantage of he who does.

In the long run we all pay for misjudgments that arise in such ideological controversy. The difficulties are compounded when judgment is passed by the scientific community rather than by individual scholars. The only persons fit to pass judgment are those who must know the truth if they are properly to conduct their own research. If the galleries are packed with persons who profit from using an ideological ploy such as experimentalism, there is a grave danger that they will support the kind of science that fits their unenlightened self-interest. And if they are packed with mere onlookers, or worse still with politicians, administrators, professors, and the general public, we can hardly expect more than an effort to justify oneself before fools.

The history and philosophy of science play important roles in ideological controversy. These are a bit more difficult to understand than straightforward abuses of methodological rules of thumb, for history and philosophy are legitimate branches of scholarship, and every educated person ought to know something about them. Beyond mere general intellectual culture, there are perfectly good reasons why a scientist might turn to philosophy, and these have mostly to do with the utility of philosophy in helping to solve problems. Like mathematics and telescopes, logic is a useful tool. There is every reason to learn how to distinguish between substantive scientific issues on the one hand, and merely verbal disputes on the other. A great deal of progress has in fact been made through cleaning up the vocabulary and not using terms equivocally. And much good has resulted from realizing that many issues are, properly speaking, "metaphysical."

In biology, the word "gene" now refers, not to a single kind of corpuscular unit, but to a variety of hereditary determinants, for which various names are available for those who need them. By the same token, we realize that the corpuscularity of genes was a mere assumption, and that we must not presuppose that they are "atomic," or that each of them controls a single "character." That these matters are important is clear from the fact that we keep falling into the same old mistakes. On the other hand, Bacon rightly observed that "It is the first distemper of learning, when men discuss words, and not matter." Verbal disputes are a fine way to obfuscate, to divert attention from the task at hand, and to create factitious arguments for one's views. Because philosophy is difficult, it is readily abused. Consequently philosophy has gained a somewhat tarnished reputation among scientists. As a result, bad science is sheltered from the sort of criticism that good philosophy might provide.

Bad philosophy in science is best recognized by its tendency to become divorced from efforts to solve real scientific problems. If you want to do good research, become a philosophical scientist. If you want to opt out of research, one way is to become a philosopher of science. Many have. A good example is Hans Driesch (1867–1941), who started out as a fine experimental embryologist. He got involved in vitalistic thinking, and became a philosopher. Perhaps that was just as

174

well, but his contribution to philosophy is now considered trivial, at least compared to his experimental work.

Scientists who no longer have anything to contribute in the laboratory often turn to philosophy, and the result is not always pleasing. Even worse are those who fail to make it in the laboratory, and try again at the writing desk. If one wants to do philosophy late in life, one had better get started when young. Perhaps the worst reason for turning to philosophy is to justify a piece of research that didn't go over very well—or a whole program of research, or even an entire career. If one's work is sound, it probably does not require much special pleading.

Such strictures do not apply if there are legitimate philosophical questions that emerge in the course of research. These can be the basis for a sound contribution, especially when the philosophical implications of a scientist's work extend beyond his immediate field—perhaps outside science itself, to the broader realms of intellectual culture. If philosophy continues to be an important aspect of a long and productive career in the laboratory, there is no need to question its legitimacy.

Philosophy often gets used as a weapon in ideological conflict. Here the combatants are apt to seize upon anything that promises to put down the opposition. We should not expect much foresight to be exercised—no careful evaluation of the philosophical doctrines being invoked prior to their use. Rather, the combatants behave like the Three Stooges in a slapstick film, picking up whatever philosophical pie happens to be handy and letting fly, heedless of what might be thrown back. Philosophical terms like "deduction," and "*a priori*" are used without consulting the dictionary. The philosophical doctrines invoked are often travesties of the original, and grossly misinterpreted. Everybody seems to be able to dredge up some crude version of nominalism that turns every object in the universe into an "abstraction," whatever that is supposed to mean.

A few years ago it was fashionable to take Percy Bridgeman's philosophy seriously and make everybody's work nonoperational except one's own. These days one cites Popper and everybody else's hypothesis immediately becomes untestable. In the nineteenth century it was a "Baconianism" that had little to do with Bacon. At various times it has been a "Kantianism" that would have appalled Kant. Forget about consistency here. If you bring in the law of contradiction, some philosopher must have denied its validity. If you want to abolish intellectual standards altogether, just invoke Feyerabend's adage that "Anything goes." Nobody feels embarrassed about having one philosophy for the laboratory, another for the writing desk—or one for attacking the opposition, another for self-justification. The goal here is not to be right, but to rally the troops, and put down one's rivals. And this is to be accomplished in the cheapest and easiest possible way.

The history of science has the same dual character as the philosophy of science. Historical investigation has a legitimate function in scientific research. There is every good reason for delving into the old literature. The classics often provide standards of excellence that deserve to be emulated. They also provide examples of unfortunate mistakes that ought not to be repeated. Sometimes problems of current interest turn out to have been solved long ago. Or the solutions that have come down to us may not bear critical examination. Sometimes finding out the difference between fact and tradition is impossible without doing a lot of work in the library. In anatomy and geology, the old literature contains a wealth of useful data that no sensible researcher would ignore. In systematic biology the names of groups of organisms are fixed by certain rules, and in consequence the only way to discover the acceptable names is to go back to the publications in which those names were originally proposed.

Scientists may also want to satisfy their curiosity about the old masters, to give them credit for their accomplishments, and to participate in an enterprise that has flourished, and may continue to flourish, over a long series of generations. The desire to obtain a certain approximation to immortality through research provides an incentive to do good work. And hope that one's work will be evaluated in a good light by future generations—equipped as they ought to be with a greater wealth of experience—encourages scientists to work toward long-term goals.

The great scientists of the past make fine heroes. For examples of hard work, self-discipline, courage, and devotion to higher goals, one need not look further than scientists on their best behavior. A certain kind of hero-worship is a good thing for science. People need to be motivated to do the very best they can, and heroes can be very useful in that respect. They give us standards. When everybody is trying to raise himself, we all benefit. But consider what happens when the mean becomes the ideal, and everybody behaves as if he could raise himself by lowering others. Such base motives have given rise to much of the literature that seeks to tear down the reputations of the great in the name of "humanizing" them. Jealousy and its products find a ready market these days.

Nonetheless, good historians of science have tended to demythologize the past and to debunk legends. In so doing they have provided us with a better understanding of the role of myth and legend in science. Edifying tales are indeed told for the "benefit" of the young. The story of little George Washington and the cherry tree was evidently made up out of whole cloth. The fairy tale about Charles Darwin discovering evolution on the Galapagos was created by pedagogues and textbook writers who embellished what really happened. [90] The tale still gets told, and it will be very difficult to get it out of the texts. But we do the same in all branches of knowledge. In invertebrate zoology we have the old story about starfish opening oysters by holding onto the shell and exerting a pull over many hours, to which the oyster ultimately succumbs. Like the tale of the hare and the tortoise, it is edifying, and students like to hear it, but it isn't true. Starfish can evert their stomachs through a very narrow slit, and they eat clams even when experimenters bind the valves together with wire.

The history of science as told by the *dramatis personae* is presented so as to make a favorable impression. Founders and followers alike tell the tale so as to further the interest of the school. Frank Sulloway, in a very detailed study, showed how Freud manipulated "history" so as to further a legend that would make it easier to market his views. [91] He smeared his friends. He burned his early papers. He lied about how he made his discoveries. The reasons for such behavior are perfectly intelligible: it was expedient for Freud to conceal the fact that his work had historical roots in evolutionary biology.

If scientists do not habitually lie about how they made their discoveries, at least we can observe that "managing the truth" is common practice. Darwin pretended, in his writings, and even in his correspondence when practicing delicate diplomacy, that he patiently accumulated facts and avoided speculation. He did indeed accumulate facts, and he seems to have taken an inordinately long period before communicating his results. He did not publish theory without massive empirical support. But the documents clearly show that the facts were collected with theory in mind, and that his was a speculative intellect as

177

well as a critical one. The imagination received short shrift because Darwin feared that it would prejudice the reception of his views. However, all this has long been an open secret. On June 6, 1863 Darwin wrote a letter advising John Scott to let theory be his guide, but not to publish theory until his reputation was well established, for fear of losing credibility.

Debunking the misconceptions that result from such hypocrisy is not to be confused with the calumny of the jealous. As Sulloway points out, we see Freud as more of a politician than we had conceived him, but nonetheless his accomplishment still seem heroic. As to Darwin, he comes across looking better, not worse, as the myths are replaced by reconstructions of what really happened based upon a vast amount of hard evidence. We are impressed all the more with the immense labor required to gather and process all those data, and we now realize that he was an even better theoretician than his earlier reputation suggested. Indeed, my original idea for reading all of Darwin's works and writing a book about them, was that I couldn't believe that somebody as simple-minded as that could possibly have discovered anything, especially natural selection. One result was to rediscover some fine contributions that had been overlooked. Another was the discovery that his various books were not on isolated topics, but rather treated aspects of one grand system. The more we find out the truth about Darwin, the more we admire the real man for what he really did.

You see, good scientists have strong egos. It takes an enormous amount of willpower to impose upon oneself the kind of discipline that is necessary to work toward long-term goals. A proud person will try to model himself upon some truly outstanding example. He wants to be great, not just famous. Such pride must not be confused with vanity or narcissism. A narcissistic person does not even want to be famous— just a celebrity. The narcissist's goal is not intrinsic worth, but relative status at most. So it stands to reason that scientists will esteem their heroes, and heroism itself.

But the history of science can become little more than a tool for winning arguments. It can be used to justify one's approach to problem solving. One tries to make it appear that one's approach has been particularly fruitful. One points to the heroes of one's faction in glow-ing colors, and smears the heroes of one's competitors. If some great figure from the past held the sort of views one approves of, one invokes that figure's authority. If not, one seeks to destroy his reputation. The results can be comical, or pathetic, or disgusting at times, and anybody seriously interested in knowing what really happened had better go back and read the originals.

There seem to be two schools of thought with respect to William Harvey's work on the circulation of the blood. One is the traditional view that it was quantitative, therefore good. The other is that it was not quantitative after all, and therefore not good. My own reading of the text suggests that it is not a good example of quantification, but that it is a good example of experimental—and also comparative—methodology.[92] Assemblers of selections from Harvey's works intended for students edit out the material on the comparative anatomy and embryology that do not fit the quantificationist or experimentalist ideologies. Abridgements are the curse of scholarship in all branches of knowledge, because they are so readily turned into a vehicle for lies.

From time to time I have tried to put in a good word for Ernst Haeckel (1834–1919), of "ontogeny recapitulates phylogeny" fame. He seems to have received a bad press. This annoyed an evolutionary embryologist, the late Sir Gavin de Beer, and an historian of biology, Frederick Churchill (who subsequently has modified his views). I used to be puzzled about Haeckel's reputation, and thought that it had something to do with his habits of offending people's religious sensibilities and mixing science with politics. That is all quite true, but something more subtle is involved. Commentary on Haeckel has been written by two factions within biology. On the one hand we have students of evolution, especially students of evolutionary history like myself. We tend to try to salvage whatever of Haeckel's work we can, in spite of many blemishes. Haeckel had a fine imagination, but often got carried away by his enthusiasms, and was not always very critical.

On the other hand we have students of experimental embryology, many of whom treat systematists as competitors. In the nineteenth century, comparative anatomy and comparative embryology were of fundamental importance in turning biology into an historical science. This research gave rise to a lot of opportunities for research on what was called "developmental mechanics," and other kinds of nonhistorical biology. The market for biologists having become saturated, a competitive situation came into being in which it was more expedient to discredit the competition than to enlarge the biological enterprise.

Therefore embryology became infused with an experimentalist ideology, and the experimentalists tried to give the impression that comparative anatomy and comparative embryology were not legitimate sciences. It is hard to say what the cause and effect relationship was here, but many of the experimental embryologists who flourished at the turn of the century were strongly opposed to Darwinism. This had the effect of delegitimizing the conceptual rationale of systematics. The usual claims that evolutionary history is unknowable appeared. Another symptom was the effort to make Haeckel into a villain. Later generations of experimentalists, including De Beer and Jane Oppenheimer, wrote about such matters, and reiterated and expanded upon what their faction had asserted. [93]

One might hope that professional historians would be able to recognize this "Whig history," but such is not the case with the textbooks of William Coleman and Garland Allen. [94] It is too rich a source of material for their Marxist approach to pedagogy. Once upon a time there was a wicked ogre named Haeckel, who kept a beautiful maiden named Modern Biology locked up in a castle called Morphology. Along came a handsome prince named the "young experimentalist." He killed the ogre and together they set up a people's republic and lived happily ever after. Here again the facts that have conveniently been suppressed turn out to be very interesting. For one thing, the experimentalists were largely Haeckel's own students. For another, the experiments they did were modeled upon experiments that Haeckel did on the development of an obscure group of marine coelenterates called siphonophores. [95] Haeckel's monograph was awarded a prize, and must have been widely known, especially to his students. Here we find good evidence that experimental embryology evolved out of comparative embryology. But of course if one believes in a dialectical interpretation of history, then it must have been thesis, antithesis, and synthesis. The revolutionary interpretation of the history of science fits the Marxist ideology all too well.

Far be it from me to claim that the history of science is nothing more than an ideological ink blot, into which are read all the follies of professors. What one gets out of the documents depends upon one's motives. If one really wants to make original discoveries about the history of neuroanatomy, one has good reasons for finding out what really happened; just as if one really wants to make original discoveries about the structure of the nervous system, one has good reasons for accuracy in tracing the course of a nerve. If one wants to learn from the classics how to perform better in the laboratory, one may have a different set of priorities, but one has good reasons for rightly interpreting the text. And if reading the old literature is basically motivated by a desire to do a thorough job of mastering one's subject, then at least one has the same good reason for understanding the science of the past that one does for understanding the science of the present, namely to contribute to the science of the future. If, on the other hand, one's goal is to win converts to one's version of Marxism or Christianity, to get a job in a history department, or to discredit one's professional rivals, one has a different kind of incentive. Perhaps certain persons with degrees in history will claim that thanks to their high professional standards ideology is a problem for everybody but themselves. Treat them like somebody who stands up in church and brags about how humble he is.

A great deal of harm is done because scientists get embroiled in ideological disputes and academic power struggles without first thinking matters through. They often take positions that are detrimental to science, especially in the long run, and often detrimental to themselves as well.

Consider, for example, what is called "reductionism." On the face of it, the question is whether, say, biology can be "reduced" to chemistry, or "fully explained" in terms of it, or whatever. People are notoriously vague about what that is supposed to mean, and for the present discussion it doesn't matter very much. There are, of course, some interesting philosophical questions that people ask in this connection. Are wholes more than their parts? How much knowledge is obtained by taking things apart on the one hand, or putting them together on the other? Are there different kinds of laws for different sciences? But let us not deceive ourselves. The real issue is economic, often even crassly pecuniary. It is not whether biology can be reduced to chemistry, but whether biologists should be replaced by chemists. The reductionist program is really an effort to further the interests of certain academic factions, and the metaphysics is largely window dressing. One is supposed to start with the parts and work up. The bricks have to be manufactured before we start work on the cathedral. Ergo, we put the brickmakers in charge and don't hire an architect. In pedagogy, so the reasoning goes, we must proceed from the most basic to the least basic. Hence teach about bricks first, then rooms, then houses. . . . All this makes little sense in terms of how people do research, or how people learn. Perhaps the best place to start learning is with whatever is most familiar, then work up or down depending upon what is economically effective in learning, not what is supposed to be metaphysically most important. But good teaching is not the economic rationale here.

The standard response under such circumstances is to invent an alternative "philosophy"—one that is perhaps just as bad from an intellectual point of view, but nonetheless one that will do the trick. Anti-reductionism seeks to establish the "autonomy" of biology. It minimizes the amount that can be learned by taking things apart. It claims that organisms and biology are somehow different from molecules and chemistry. It stresses the historical, the functional, and the adaptive aspects of biology, and claims that different kinds of philosophy are needed for living and nonliving objects.

At the time I launched my scientific career, reductionist approaches were flourishing. Ecology had not yet become a household word, and molecular biology was a new and very exciting field. When I was a postdoctoral fellow at Harvard my sponsor, Ernst Mayr, was the Director of the Museum of Comparative Zoology. He was in a desperate struggle to save our kind of biology from yet another effort at "modernizing." Like the other grand old men of evolutionary biology, including Simpson, Dobzhansky, and Stebbins, he found it expedient to claim that biology was somehow different from the physical sciences—different in more than just the sense that organisms are alive. Dobzhansky wrote a paper in which he contrasted the "Cartesian" or "reductionist" approach with the "Darwinian" or "compositionalist" approach.[96] The trouble is that Darwin's experimental work on behavior was about as Cartesian as anybody's. The Cartesian view he did reject, unlike his friend T. H. Huxley, was the notion that animals are "automata." As Darwin saw it, organisms play an active role in dealing with their environments. But this says nothing about the adequacy of studying animals from the point of view of their components.

I learned to avoid discussing such matters with Mayr, and argued about them bitterly with Stebbins. My problem was that I knew too much. I had been interested in chemistry from childhood, and had taken a lot of courses in physiology as a student. As an anatomist I saw

nothing either methodologically objectionable or metaphysically ultimate about taking things apart. That was just one way to figure out how
they work. The same could be said about looking at organisms in order
to understand species. Knowledge being unitary, it made no sense to
have one philosophy for galaxies, another for organisms. In my successful search for the laws of nature that govern reproduction, I was much
impressed by the parallel between the laws that govern the occurrence
of hermaphroditism and the perfect gas laws. As density goes up,
certain things change in a predictable way. But Mayr and many other
biologists have repeatedly claimed that there are no laws in biology,
even though they use them routinely in their own research! They don't
call them laws, but they function the same way that laws do in the
physical sciences. The irony here is that the putative absence of laws in
biology has been taken as grounds for claiming that biology is an
inferior kind of science—or perhaps even not a science at all. Had
people acted more like philosophers and scientists, and less like academic politicians, we might have understood such matters far earlier.

Whether or not factions attempt to destroy each other, and
whether or not they succeed, depends upon the competitive situation.
The productive units in the intellectual and academic economies are
not in "perfect" competition. They produce a diversity of products, and
enjoy at least a partial monopoly over various segments of the market.
They also stand to each other as suppliers and customers. The basic
structure of academia is that of an unregulated, capitalistic economy,
in which the division of labor is mainly competitive rather than cooperative, except that within institutions cooperative arrangements are by
no means uncommon. The natural economy provides a very good
model, with its competition within and between groups, its predator–
prey relationships, and symbioses like parasitism and mutualism.

Ecological theory tells us that competition within species is more
intense than competition across species boundaries. Stags fighting for
the opportunity to mate are not competing at all with rabbits, because
they belong to different reproductive communities. They might compete with rabbits for food, but the kind of plants that deer and rabbits
eat overlap very little. The competition is more nearly perfect, and
more intense, between deer of different species, still more so between
deer of the same species, than it is between deer and rabbits.

The situation has plenty of analogues in the political economy.

There is intense competition between airlines, less between airlines and bus companies, still less between airlines and hotels. The greater the degree to which one product can be substituted for another, the greater the intensity of competition. So an airline is better off getting rid of another airline, than getting rid of a bus company, which might actually help supply it with customers.

By a straightforward extension of the same basic principles, if one kind of biology can take the place of another kind of biology, then one of them is likely to drive the other off the market, or, as ecologists would say, competitive exclusion is apt to occur. But product diversification limits the incentive to drive one's competitors out of business. An airline might reasonably drive all of the other airlines out of business, but it should not destroy ground transportation altogether, and it should not destroy the resorts to which it carries passengers who would otherwise stay home. The various subunits of any industry have at least some interest in one another's welfare.

Therefore academics will try to destroy those branches of learning that reduce their own prosperity, and preserve those from which they derive a benefit. Given the complexity of the intellectual economy, a complex balance among advantages and disadvantages is to be expected. For example, it may be good to enjoy a monopoly on animal behavior in a zoology department. An animal behaviorist might well try to keep his department from hiring another animal behaviorist to keep control over that area. He would surely be disinclined to go along with the department hiring an animal behaviorist of a competing faction.

In some ways, however, having another animal behaviorist on the staff might be a good thing. They could cooperate in research and teaching. By joining forces they might gain a certain kind of academic power. They might even fill the whole department with animal behaviorists. Whether such a monopoly results depends upon the situation. A stable balance of power may or may not arise, and this may depend upon the number of factions. If there are three factions, two of them might join forces to wipe the other out, but then again they might combine only to prevent one of them from becoming dominant. If there are two factions, people may switch their support from one to the other for the very reason that they do not want a monopoly to arise.

If competitive exclusion does occur, it tends to reduce the general range of product diversity, hence to decrease the breadth of research and teaching that goes on within the institution. However, there are forces that oppose this tendency. The more biologists on campus, the more clout they have with the administration. Diversifying its activities might be a way to justify hiring more biologists.

One way to justify hiring more biologists would be to offer a wider variety of courses and graduate programs, attracting a larger number of students. To some extent students have discretion over what they will study and where. This is good for the students, insofar as the competition sometimes improves the performance of the faculty. However, this aspect of the free enterprise system reduces the ability of the faculty to exploit the students. Therefore they proceed much as if they were colonial powers. For example, they make courses prerequisites for other courses or requirements for a degree. This is, indeed, one of the major reasons why requirements exist. However, students tend to opt out of majors because of such requirements, and there will be diminishing returns as more and more such courses are added to a program. There may even be a perfectly legitimate reason for instruction in a given field. If this be so, there is always the problem of whether to hire somebody who is really interested in the subject or use it as an excuse to hire somebody who is not.

What economists call "product diversification" Darwin called the "divergence of character" and modern biologists call "adaptive radiation." As was pointed out earlier, producing a different product reduces some of the adverse effects of competition. This in addition to taking advantage of economic opportunities (or "empty niches" as biologists put it). If two academics occupy different places in the economy they should be indifferent to each other as competitors. In ecology a harmless associate, in distinction to a harmful parasite or a helpful mutualist, is called a "commensal" (literally a "messmate"). The natural economy probably contains few real commensals, for whenever two organisms live in close association with one another the effects are not apt to be completely neutral. But insects that eat the feces of grazing animals are perhaps legitimate examples.

It seems unlikely that the various factions in academia coexist because they all stand to each others as coprophages to their suppliers. In part they coexist because they are successful monopolists. But also they are mutualists that aid one another, and parasites that exploit their

185

hosts without destroying them. A physiologist probably would not want to abolish the chemistry department. He needs it not only for advice and collaboration in research, but also for pedagogical reasons. The history department is another question. The lack of product substitutability means he probably could not get rid of it entirely, though he could affect its budget. Other sciences might be a different matter. To some extent a balance will be struck through the interaction of mutual interests conflicting with competitive forces.

One might also look upon academic factions as occupying something analogous to what biologists call a "territory." They obtain control over a resource and defend it from competitors. In its ordinary, nonmetaphorical sense, a territory is a spatial entity. Birds, for example, will often have an area where they breed, nest, and maybe feed, and will fight interlopers, especially ones of the same species and sex. What is called "home range" differs from territory in that it is not defended, being simply the place where an animal habitually goes. In this sense the home I own would be part of my territory, but the park where I walk is just home range. In many firms salesmen are allocated exclusive territories in order to produce a cooperative division of labor. But they also engage in practices that keep competitors out of a given region.

The limits of a territory are affected by economic forces in a relatively straightforward way. As territory size increases, the cost of defending it goes up and the return on territory size goes down. A balance is struck. Home range is limited only by the cost of transportation. When an animal encroaches upon another's territory, the defender will threaten, then if that does not suffice, it may fight. An animal defending a territory is apt to defeat an interloper, evidently because, having more to lose than the interloper stands to gain, it has a greater inclination to engage in risky combat. So adjustments in territorial boundaries are apt to occur mainly in areas that are of least value to the defender. The occupant of the territory stands to lose more because the effective use of a territory depends in part upon having invested a certain amount of capital—in knowing its resources if nothing else. That capital can neither be transported nor transferred to a new owner.

In academia the straightforward, nonmetaphorical analogue of a territory is found primarily when the members of the staff fight to

186

establish hegemony over office and laboratory space. Professors don't like to move their belongings from one place to another just to make life more convenient for their colleagues. Their personal messes become so disorganized that they cannot find a thing. And, of course, they want plenty of space to spread out in.

What really ought to interest us, however, is analogous behavior with respect to areas of research and teaching, which is territorial only in a metaphorical sense, but which has much the same character. In systematic biology, experts tend to divide the world up into geographical and other areas and give the practitioners a certain monopoly. This tends to mitigate some of the effects of competition. They try to find out who is classifying what organisms where, and to avoid duplication of effort. There is so much work to be done in systematics that dividing it up will not leave anybody at a loss for something to do. So the competition is for work that will give a high return with respect to prestige or other amenities. Furthermore systematists have other incentives for avoiding territorial disputes. For example, they collect specimens. These are valuable resources, but not equally useful to everybody. So they trade them, and send them out on loan. If somebody tries to make a strictly competitive game out of such an enterprise, he may lose the goodwill and cooperation of his colleagues. That can be an exceedingly valuable resource. There are a lot of petty squabbles among systematic biologists, as is the case with human beings in general. But the real fights have to do with academic ideologies—competition between "schools" and the like.

A group of specialists may act like a guild, or other monopolistic organization, that attempts to control a given sector of the intellectual economy. It does so by determining who will be allowed to work in the field, what problems may be studied, what approaches are deemed appropriate, and what solutions are deemed legitimate.

The territorial character of such behavior becomes evident when the system is closed off from outsiders and the field is defended as an economic unit, with a vested interest in monopoly over both intellectual resources and monetary ones. The discipline becomes professionalized, with institutions set up so as to maintain loyalty and solidarity within the group. Professional societies and academic departments become hard bases of operation. Access to the field is restricted to those who possess the official credentials, which are of a kind that competitors cannot readily acquire. This means, obviously, a doctorate in that particular field. The product is made to diverge as much as possible from the competing ones, and to fill a distinctive place in the market. A group of problems, approaches, and solutions becomes the property of the profession, which expands or contracts according to how readily control over the area can be maintained. Some approaches and problems are either favored or rejected because of a need to make the field autonomous. Perhaps a topic peculiar to the discipline becomes its focus, its rallying point, and the basis of its disciplinary integrity.

All this effort to fortify and defend an academic specialism naturally gives rise to internal ideologies appropriate to the needs of the faction. Biologists and social scientists alike need to have certain beliefs about the relative importance of "nature and nurture" in human behavior. This is irrespective of the merits of the case, and, more importantly, in addition to the political bigotry with which the various factions rightly and wrongly accuse their opponents.

One result of such territorialism is that each field becomes ever more specialized, inward-looking, and isolated from the rest of the intellectual economy. Communication between disciplines comes to be avoided as a matter of policy. Each develops a language intelligible only to insiders. Problems become increasingly technical, and their solution contributes less and less that might interest an outsider. The field becomes autonomous in the sense that only a professional acting in the interests of the profession plays any role in evaluating the product. Theories thus become immune to any but internal criticism. The profession ceases to recruit immigrants from other fields, relying, instead, upon those cast in the mold of its own pedagogical machinery. So it all becomes academic in the worst sense of that word—divorced from real life, especially the life of the mind.

Perhaps the most unfortunate example is contemporary philosophy. It has become "scholastic" in a most pejorative sense. At certain times, philosophy has been a major concern of every educated person. It meant a certain kind of activity, involving a search for wisdom and an effort to experience and make out the larger connections among things. It was esteemed the most general kind of knowledge. Late in the nineteenth century it still played this role in the intellectual economy. The leading philosophers addressed the great social, religious, aesthetic, and scientific issues of the day, and addressed a wide, non-specialist audience. At least some of them provided what were considered meaningful answers to important questions.

Gradually, however, philosophy became a profession, and, as Bruce Kuklick puts it, a "mere job."[97] Where once the term "philosopher" had some connection with wisdom, now it means nothing more than somebody who occupies a position in a philosophy department. Even logic, that noble instrument of reason and discourse, has ceased to be used that way. It has become a jargon, and a means of obfuscation, a language of pedantry, not scholarship. But worse than that, it has created a way of dealing with problems that treats the world as if it were structured in a way that is conveniently dealt with by a logician's professional toolkit. So all the questions that philosophers are allowed to ask must have to do with language, and not the things with which discourse itself is concerned.

In transporting goods across disciplinary boundaries, the cost of carriage can be high. But it seems to me that the real problem is with artificial barriers to free trade. By inhibiting the movement of talent and its products across the boundaries of disciplines, academia gains prosperity at the expense of scholarship. It is a burdensome tax which, indirectly at least, the whole of civilization must bear, and from which it receives no services in return. *Laissez passer.*

Chapter 12

THE COSTS OF
SERVING MAMMON

THE ECONOMIES OF KNOWLEDGE AND OF VIRTUE ARE LIKE PARTS OF the same organism that have to be anatomized together. In both, as with all aspects of life, we must acknowledge the extent to which expediency ultimately accounts for what we do. We are not, however, concerned with short-term, or crass, expediency. Rather, as the products of evolution, our behavior tends to approximate what has been serviceable, in the long run and for the most part, to our ancestors in achieving reproductive success. All this must be hedged and qualified, in ways that all too often such things are not, if we are to avoid serious misconceptions.

When we say that we are the product of some competitive process, we must not conceive of this process in terms of some travesty, especially in terms of mortal combat as suggested by Herbert Spencer's expression "the survival of the fittest." Natural selection would function quite effectively if the only cause of mortality were the infirmities of old age. The fitness of an organism can derive just as well from being a loving parent, a generous friend, and a responsible citizen, as from anything else. We have a vested interest in the welfare of those around us. And so do they in ours. This makes virtue expedient, but not crassly so.

Acting in one's own interest does not necessarily mean acting against the interests of others. We are better off if our neighbors provide for their own needs. In feeding and clothing themselves and caring for their children, they incidentally contribute to our own prosperity. If giving charity be an act of virtue, life is better when there is no need for it. The prosperity of our neighbors creates a market for whatever goods and services our labor may provide. Accordingly it is worthwhile for us—viewed as purely self-interested organisms—to invest some of our resources in the welfare of our neighbors. This is in addition to whatever we might receive in return out of gratitude or through reciprocity.

We are better off if we have healthy neighbors, and it would be utter folly to monopolize the supply of medicine in order to be more healthy than they are. So too with knowledge. Our neighbor's ignorance is as bad for us as his ill health, and may indeed be the cause of it. Industry and all the rest of us benefit from a supply of skilled labor. We rely upon others for their skill and expertise, and are better off if we can hire a plumber or a psychiatrist should we need one. The division of labor relieves us of having to learn more skills than time or inclination, much less talent, permit. So any enlightened and reasonable person acting in his own self-interest ought to act so as to make knowledge and skills generally available.

Knowledge, however, has somewhat the character of a public good. That is to say, we are better off if somebody else foots the bill for putting it into the hands of others. It is also a part of the infrastructure of an economy, like roads and harbors, and is often neglected because its function is not understood. In developing countries factories are often built with inadequate consideration for how the raw materials and the product will be transported, and who will provide the technical expertise. This is true of capitalist and socialist economies alike.

Knowledge is misunderstood partly because it is a peculiar kind of commodity. For one thing, it can be multiplied without the sort of limitation that affects loaves and fishes. If I share a loaf of bread with you, there will be less of it for me to eat. But if I tell you something about fish biology, my store of knowledge is in no way reduced. In this respect knowledge differs profoundly from the ordinary run of material possessions. We can give it away, trade it, or sell it, without depriving ourselves—except insofar as it costs us time and effort to communicate. We must, of course, exempt from this consideration such things as trade secrets, which confer a monopoly upon their possessor.

If we view knowledge from no other point of view than the crassest sort of self-interest, especially short-term pecuniary motives, then we get Philistinism with respect to the arts and the sciences alike. According to the Philistine, resources devoted to culture in the broad sense are justifiable only insofar as they subserve materialistic ends, or at least do not detract from them. Against the Philistines we should argue that since knowledge and beauty are not in short supply, it is an act of virtue to enjoy these rather than their material alternatives. Life in society is better when we are enjoying the innocent pleasures of life, rather than fighting or otherwise competing for sex, money, and similar commodities and tokens thereof. People who enjoy music or a good conversation are much easier to get along with than those whose lives are devoted merely to gain.[98]

The principles here are not without significance for international relations and the search for peace. Science, like art and religion, transcends national boundaries and creates a truly cosmopolitan community. It provides a basis for goodwill and friendship among people by virtue of the fact that they work together for common ends. A scholar visiting abroad receives the sort of warm welcome and intimacy with the local populace that an ordinary tourist, merchant, or governmental emissary rarely experiences. I was first struck with this when I visited Japan while still a graduate student and spent a few weeks doing research at the Seto Marine Biological Laboratory of Kyoto University. Science is held in very high esteem among the Japanese. But Japanese biologists tend to derive a somewhat different kind of satisfaction from their research than we do. I was fascinated by theory, and tried to explain every feature I could observe in the tiny opisthobranch gastropods that I was dissecting. Professor Kikutarô Baba, author of *Opisthobranchia of Sagami Bay, Collected by His Majesty the Emperor of Japan*, was kind enough to read my manuscript. He respected the theoretical aspect of my work, and discussed it with me, but like many Japanese biologists took little interest in theoretical matters himself. What really interested him was my unexpected observations on diet and reproduction. In Japan, the contemplation of nature is esteemed as one of the most worthy of cultural activities. One doesn't have to be Japanese to enjoy that.

It is often asserted that science and art are pursued "for their own sake." What on earth is this supposed to mean? If it is meant that the pleasure we derive is all the justification we need, all well and good. We don't care why we do those things. This does not mean, however, that there are no sound biological or other reasons for such activities. And to pretend that no such reasons exist can serve as a basis for an unrealistic attitude. We derive pleasure from understanding the world around us. Why should this pleasure be any different from that which we derive from eating? It is conceivable that we deal here with a maladaptive or adaptively neutral aspect of our biology. But all too often adaptively neutral features turn out to be failures of the imagination.

If the pursuit of truth and beauty do have advantages to a social organism like ourselves, then various aspects of our lives become more readily intelligible. The trouble is that Philistines take a narrow view of utility. The usefulness of knowledge means more than what is good for General Motors. That scientific knowledge is useful in providing material benefits is not an issue. The question is whether so narrow a conception of utility ought to be our sole criterion for determining how we deal with it. Crass materialism is, indeed, the basic premise in virtually every argument used to justify the existence of science.[99] Science saves lives and earns money, if not directly, at least indirectly.

The purely cognitive aspect of science—understanding what is going on around us—has benefits apart from enabling us to manipulate the world. An enlightened person, or an enlightened society, is better off by virtue of having a realistic view of things. We pity savages for their unfortunate superstitions, but we tend to forget how recently and to what a limited extent the general run of humanity has been relieved of such burdens.

The point may be illustrated by an obscure but venerable science called "teratology"—etymologically the study of monsters, but more appropriately the study of what are generally called "birth defects." This science hardly existed before the nineteenth century, and credit mostly goes to the French zoologist Étienne Geoffroy Saint Hillaire (1772–1844).[100] Prior to his contribution there was no rational explanation for an infant being born with no head, or with two of them, or otherwise defective, and sometimes hideously so. Such happenings were often attributed to supernatural influences, and to prenatal impressions on the part of the mother. Geoffroy's work showed that such monstrosities followed definite rules or laws, and furthermore that

194

abnormal development was a variation upon normal development. Birth defects now can be mitigated by surgery, and in part prevented through prenatal hygiene, with mothers avoiding drugs rather than supernatural influences. Even so, a certain number of birth defects are as unavoidable as an occasional traffic accident. In the old days the birth of a deformed infant was interpreted as a punishment for some kind of sin on the part of the mother. Today there are still vestiges of such attitudes, as in the prejudices against left-handed people. If such truths of biology were more widely known, there would be less misery in the world.

This cognitive value to scientific knowledge is not, strictly speaking, materialistic, but it is nonetheless supremely practical. The world is better off when we need not blame ourselves or others when accidents are misinterpreted as the consequence of sin. And understanding what goes on in the world around us provides a wholesome sense of confidence if it allows us to tell a legitimate fear from one grounded in ignorance. One advantage to being a zoologist is that one can keep the animals that are really dangerous at a distance, and not be frightened by harmless snakes and spiders. Such creatures become innocuous neighbors, and objects of interest, or a mere nuisance to be taken out of the house and dumped in the garden where they belong.

A sense of curiosity would seem to be a normal part of our adaptability as organisms. We are not the only animal species that explores its environment and evidently derives some sort of satisfaction from doing so. An animal is better off when it surveys the habitat for predators, a place to live, and a supply of food. Curiosity seems to be linked to life in environments that are diverse and apt to change. Social creatures like ourselves might well be expected to derive benefits from knowing what the neighbors are up to. It is easy to see how such intelligence might be more readily obtained once language had arisen, giving rise in turn to such abuses as malicious gossip and outright slander. That human curiosity has advantages is all too obvious. Of greater interest perhaps is why so much is done to stifle it. We all know how much pleasure children derive from acquiring knowledge, in spite of educational practices. The desire to know gets suppressed, and one wonders if those who control the behavior of the young find it not entirely to their interest. If so we should expect the suppression of academic freedom to begin, not in the kindergarten, but in the cradle.

Granted that we have at least three kinds of utility derived from scientific knowledge—material, cognitive, and cultural—the question arises of how we ought to invest our resources so as to obtain the optimal return with respect to all three of them. Does maximizing one detract from the others? We need not assume that a conflict exists here, or that one must exist. But discussions about the relative merits of pure versus applied research certainly imply that there is one. The topic deserves to be reconsidered from a different point of view.

It is one thing to regard knowledge from the point of view of demand for goods of a certain kind, another to regard it from the point of view of a resource—as a consumer good or a capital good, if you prefer. In the sense that a theory gets replaced by a better one, knowledge does become obsolete. But in another sense it does not. The earlier stages lead to improvements, so that the return on earlier investments is perpetual. In the long run, what we are trying to optimize is the rate of discovery. That should maximize the total benefits, be these material or not. From the point of cultural utility at least, the best way to maximize productivity in the intellectual sector of the economy is to devote the greatest amount of effort to solving soluble problems. This may seem like a truism, but it is overlooked so routinely that we had better consider it a profound truth. The plain fact of the matter is that scientists as scientists get credit for solving problems, and for nothing else. To work on problems that simply cannot be solved is intellectual suicide. It is true that some problems are soluble but not significant. Maybe it is better not to work on exobiology, when we know so little about life here on earth. But then again, we have to be careful. Knowledge is a system of interrelated parts that evolves as a whole, not a dunghill of fact and theory. The solution to a problem may come from quite unexpected quarters, and, much as in war, it may be better to approach one's objective indirectly.

My own experience is of some relevance here. I wrote my doctoral dissertation on a group of organisms misleadingly called "sea slugs," which, unlike the garden variety, are often spectacularly beautiful and have virtually no economic significance. The choice of a research problem was dictated by purely intellectual considerations. There was an opportunity to find out how the group had evolved by studying the anatomy of their reproductive system. My research was supported by a training grant from the National Institutes of Health, back in the days when Congress was being very generous. One might ask what on earth this had to do with medicine. Perhaps if Senator Proxmire had heard, he might have awarded me one of his "Golden Fleece" awards. However, Eric Kandel, an eminent neurophysiologist, read my paper and sent me the manuscript of a book he was writing on a sea slug called *Aplysia*.[101] It turns out that sea slugs have peculiar nervous systems, with large, readily identifiable cells, making them ideal materials for experimental research aimed at finding out how nervous systems work. If, as seems very likely, the principles that apply to very simple systems apply to all of them, then obviously they apply to our own. I was able to provide Kandel with some useful advice that helped make these organisms easier for neurophysiologists to work with. Among other things, they need a good classification, so that they can compare one kind of sea slug with another on the basis of their real genealogical relationships, and not on the basis of superficial appearances. Hence there is a direct link between my pure research, and something of far more obvious applicability to practical matters. There is no way that either I or the National Institutes of Health could have planned it that way. Things like that just happen.

A more impressive example of how pure science just happens to have unexpected applications comes from the career of Elie Metchnikoff (1845–1916), the Russian embryologist mentioned in an earlier chapter. Metchnikoff was interested in the very earliest stages in the evolution of animals. One possibility suggested by Haeckel was a stage in which the animal was little more than a ball of cells with a simple gut in which food was digested. Metchnikoff proposed as an alternative that the ancestral creature had no gut, but rather had a solid body. Food would be taken up and digested inside amoeba-like cells called "phagocytes." Later Metchnikoff proposed that such phagocytes also play an important role in defending the body from disease, by ingesting harmful bacteria. This notion evolved into a major portion of the modern science of immunology, and earned Metchnikoff a Nobel Prize for medicine and physiology in 1908.

Yet having said this we must avoid falling back into the same old arguments habitually used to justify the existence of pure science. The point is not that pure science can be justified by its benefits for applied science, though of course it can be so justified. Rather the point is that pure science plays a central role in all aspects of intellectual culture. If

197

we are to enjoy the benefits of modern civilized life, we need scientific knowledge about all aspects of the natural world. To this end there can be no substitute for research. Without the constant production of new knowledge, science not only loses its proper character, but altogether ceases to exist. Our educational establishments in particular should not have to justify research on any other basis.

Increasing the supply of knowledge is one thing; responding to a demand for it is another. Considerations on the demand side are notoriously apt to be unrealistic. A few years ago the United States government slopped the trough with funds for research on matters supposedly in the public interest—heart disease, cancer, and stroke, for example. More recently, a lot of money has been made available for research on aging, and reviewers tell me that the applications are of generally low quality. By diverting resources from problems that are soluble now, to ones that are not, we deprive ourselves of the where-withal to solve them in the future. The general public and its representatives are behaving, not like wise philanthropists or sober and responsible investors, but like children. They want immediate results, and cannot work toward long-term goals. To be sure, if one is not apt to live very long, one wants results sooner than if one anticipates many years of life, but this only shows how the decision-making process gets distorted.

A citizen's decision as to how resources used in research should be allocated is of course fired by self-interest, and his interests will tend to conflict to some degree with those of science and the rest of humanity, including those of future generations. Obviously a voter will want what is good for him. If he is afraid of cancer, he will want something done about it. If he is young he will be more amenable to funding certain kinds of long-term projects than older persons who will not personally benefit from them. Since the art of solving problems is poorly understood and very much a chancy affair, the economic decision making is apt to be very inefficient. It seems to be a common human failing that when we are faced with a problem we try not to solve it, but rather to do something that makes us feel better. We are unhappy when a relative dies of some disease, and we contribute to research aimed at providing a cure for that particular disease. So we fail to put the money where it does the most good.

One might hope that a wise and benevolent government, and an

198

equally wise and benevolent private sector, would attempt to produce a maximum return in terms of cultural, cognitive, and material benefits alike, at the least cost in time, suffering, and treasure. Perhaps these interests are not so much in conflict as one might think. In a large measure the conflicts exist as a result of misunderstandings, and from lack of imagination and enterprise. A scientist does his work best by maximizing discoveries here and now, and humanity benefits because that gives us the best results, overall and in the long run. Industry has to fund research in a way that gives it a reasonable return upon investment, and that means investing in only a limited portion of the possible opportunities for the kind of research that needs to be done for the general welfare. But at least there is a disincentive for working on insoluble problems. Again, however, solutions to many of the soluble problems are public goods, and nobody wants to pay the bill for them. The great foundations are in a position to fill this sort of need much better than government, because they are somewhat relieved of the need for immediate and short-term benefits and of the distortions created on the demand side. But they can only act in accordance with this circumstance if those who run them understand the problem. From what I have seen, they could use some help.

It is not simply a matter of the wrong projects getting funded, or of prestige being allocated to the wrong people and thereby resources not being most efficiently utilized. A shift from the more soluble to the less soluble problems means a shift of human resources—that is to say, talent—from the more appropriate to the less appropriate work. Those who work on projects that are attractive simply because there is a demand for their solution are surely going to be the least competent, and the least responsible, members of the scholarly community. The best scientists will surely be attracted to the most soluble problems, irrespective of demand. Only when the two coincide, and that is not unheard of in the least, do we get an appropriate mix of both talent and its support.

A purely demand-side economy of the intellect will be given over to purely academic considerations—to giving the appearance of scholarship, not the reality. The people who meet the demands will be rascals and fools. Among fools I would number fuzzy-minded, often juvenile, persons who misconstrue the role of humanitarian ideals in science. We can indeed justify science in terms of the good it does. That, however, is because knowing the truth is a good thing, not because we should run our lives on the basis of sentimentality. At one time it was esteemed an act of piety to cleanse the sores of lepers with one's tongue, but that never provided a cure.

In science the relationship between supply and demand is not always straightforward. A higher rate of investment on a given problem will not necessarily result in a proportionate increase in the rate of its solution. One doesn't have to be an astute businessman or a professional economist to appreciate this point. The supply of many commodities is notoriously "inelastic"—not much can be done, if anything, to increase it. If we want more wheat, we can plant more acres in wheat, very rapidly, but try increasing the number of whales that fast. Opportunities for research are not something we can produce simply at will.

Furthermore, scientists who have to choose between the desire for knowledge and the desire for money, are not choosing between a pair of readily substitutable commodities. It is not like corn oil and peanut oil to be used in cooking. It is far more like marrying on the basis of love or money. In an ideal situation, of course, one gets both, and the economic aspects of choosing a mate are important considerations. However, a reasonable person does not subordinate everything to pecuniary interests. Now, there is nothing wrong with doing applied research, or working on problems that society wants solved, so long as one really wants to solve those problems and those problems really are soluble. But a scientist who works on problems he knows cannot be solved, simply because money is available for working on them, may reasonably be compared to a prostitute. The problem is not simply that certain people opt for that way of earning a living in a free-enterprise economy out of mere cupidity. Rather, the state of the economy is such that many have no realistic alternative.

An enterprising and generally competent scientist ought to be able to beat the system, particularly if he has no scruples about doing so. The trick is to get money ostensibly to do bad science, and use it to do good science instead. Much "mission-related" research has been justified on this basis. Here is the formula: Decide what you want to do, and what equipment and other resources you will need to do it. Find something that at least remotely resembles what you want to do, and for which support is available. Write an application for a grant, perhaps mentioning what really interests you as a minor part of the project. Have graduate students, postdoctoral fellows, and technicians get the drudgery out of the way, and spend most of the time doing what really interests you. One need not do exactly what the grant was awarded for. Indeed, the really important consideration is to appear productive at one thing or another.

There are infinite variations on this theme, but they all boil down to the misappropriation of funds. Of course funds are misappropriated from a bad cause to a good one, and it is very hard to condemn such an act because of its immediate consequences. One can always say that a certain amount of flexibility gets built into budgets and programs in general. Money intended for teaching has often been used for both research and teaching. And conversely, money intended for research has often been used for both teaching and research. After all, both students and professors are supposed to read the same books. And since at a graduate or even advanced undergraduate level there is little distinction between the two, there need be no contradiction.

While we must recognize some advantages to this arrangement, it has at least two obvious disadvantages. In the first place it is inefficient. In the second place it leads to abuses and to corruption.

When I was at Berkeley there was a little fund for research, in addition to what was available within the department. Every year I was asked to apply for it, and the funds were indeed useful. If I knew what I was going to do the next year, I wrote down what I anticipated spending the money for. If not, I had no choice but to write up some fundamentally bogus proposal. In either case I had plenty of discretion as to how the funds were spent. This was perfectly reasonable. A scientist ought to be able to shift from one activity to another as opportunities permit. But the arrangement was preposterous. Why didn't they just give me a few dollars to be spent as petty cash? Why waste several hours of one's valuable time writing a phony proposal? As a junior member of the faculty I had every reason to allocate the funds efficiently. I had to do research in order to get tenure, and it really made a difference how the money got spent. Things did not change in any fundamental way after tenure was awarded. This example is, of course, trivial. But suppose that about 10 percent of good science is smuggled into a project in which 90 percent is a waste of time. These figures are purely conjectural, but they suggest the level of inefficiency that could result. However, it is not a bad thing at all, if what one wants is to keep a lot of administrators and marginal scientists and technicians on the dole.

Obtaining funds for research has become a major determinant of academic prosperity, not only for institutions but for individuals as well. A scientist is expected to spend a large amount of time writing grant proposals. Whatever may be the merits of the proposals from a scholarly point of view, applying for grants reduces the amount of time available for work in the laboratory. The pecuniary rewards will inevitably result in a conflict of interest with every other utility. For one thing there will be an effort to produce the maximum return in money per unit of effort devoted to grant applications. For another fundable projects will be preferred.

A more insidious problem is that scholars will be judged as fundraisers. To meet this demand, they will need to devote much time and effort to developing the skills needed for such activity. This means not doing something else. If a graduate student has to choose between taking a course that will enable him to read German and taking one on how to write a grant proposal, there is a serious problem here. Potential employees are evaluated on the basis of their fundraising abilities, and this is stated explicitly in advertisements for academic positions. Of late there has developed a practice of asking job applicants to submit grant proposals along with *curricula vitarum*. Just as with scholarship and pedagogy, there is some correlation between an ability to do good research and an ability to write grant proposals. However, it does not seem inevitable that the two skills will coincide, much less all three. The more emphasis is placed upon fundraising ability, the less can be placed upon scholarship and pedagogy.

Shady practices with respect to grantsmanship can lead to a general distortion of values. From selling one's body, one proceeds to sell one's soul. If we allow a little money to be siphoned off from bad research to good research, who is to say that we shall not divert it from research to carpeting the office of the dean? If someone is forced to pad the budget in his grant proposal, can he be blamed for padding his expense account? Addressing a yet more general problem, it is very hard to keep dishonesty from becoming habitual when it is routine in large areas of one's daily life. If it is all right to lie to the public, and to the administration, why not lie to one's colleagues, to one's students, and to one's self? Bad company corrupts good morals. A child who grows up in a neighborhood in which pimps and dope dealers flourish, and in which nobody rises to prosperity through honorable labor, is not apt to fulfill his potential as a responsible citizen. It is the same with the students at our great universities when they are exposed to corrupt role models. And with the entire society in which they live.

How the universities become corrupt is not very evident on the surface. Semieducated people are very good at maintaining appearances. And it takes a lot of effort to figure out how the system works. At Berkeley I twice applied for funds from the administration for what was called "innovative teaching." When some of us tried to get a new course in marine biology going, our request for support from this fund was turned down, but we managed to teach the course thanks to the enthusiasm of the faculty and a little creative financing. The students were delighted, and performed very well indeed, so that the experiment was by any reasonable criterion a great success. It was in fact innovative, because the students were provided with an opportunity to do original research. Later it was easy to get a few dollars from the same source for modifying my course on invertebrate zoology. Yes, there was a little bit of innovation involved, but what was really going on was that the money earmarked for better teaching was actually used for routine maintenance. Innovation was mere pretext, a hypocritical response to the demands of a student body that was rightly indignant at the shoddy education it was receiving.

In another case, money was provided for improving undergraduate education. Professors from various campuses of the University of California were given reduced teaching loads, and got together in pleasant places to talk about teaching instead of doing it. I am too cynical to regard this as a real effort on the part of the members of the faculty to do their job better. Professors spend plenty of time discussing teaching on an informal basis as it is.

I was once turned down for an in-house fellowship that was supposed to provide time off to do research. That obviously was the intent of the person who endowed it. Had I known the real criterion for awarding such fellowships, I would never have wasted my own time or anybody else's by applying. The real function of the fellowship is as a reward for doing certain administrative chores. One works in a dean's office or something for a couple of years, and the fellowship is bestowed as indirect compensation. In other words, funds earmarked for research are used to fund administration. I am not questioning the wisdom of this arrangement. At least money gets used to support the faculty, whatever they may be asked to do. Nonetheless there are serious problems for anyone who tries to bestow philanthropy upon a public institution. One may wind up donating to taxpayers and politicians instead of students and faculty. At a faculty meeting my colleague Max Alfert once pointed out that if we used our grant money to purchase a book for the library, the administration would deduct the value of the book from the library's budget.

So it is that external considerations of economic utility create internal diseconomies with respect to the acquisition of knowledge. We must emphasize, however, that not all such external considerations are materialistic. Indeed, they can be spiritual. It is all too notorious that much resistance to science has arisen because its findings have seemed to undermine religion. One doesn't have to know much history to realize that religion has accommodated itself to such heresies as the heliocentric theory of the solar system. Often people feel disoriented when it may be necessary to revise their beliefs—even learning the truth about Santa Claus can be upsetting. Much of the resistance to intellectual change has been based upon the assumption that traditional beliefs are the expedient way to control those whom we treat as our inferiors, be they children, women, or the poor. The trouble here is that children mature, and to control their behavior by lying ill prepares them for dealing with truth as adults. As to women and the poor, one might question the propriety of disadvantaging such persons by denying them knowledge of the truth.

The same problems arise with respect to scientific issues that relate to matters of political and economic policy. I freely admit, for example, that scientific and pseudoscientific discussions about such matters as race have done a lot of harm. But that does not mean that the end of protecting democratic values and institutions justifies the means of thought control. If academic freedom is to exist, it has to be more than just academic. It has to be freedom.

Maturity can almost be defined as the ability to work toward long-term goals. It indicates strength of character, and is a key constituent of scholarly discipline. Young people have to gain such qualities through experience, precept, and example. When academia knuckles under to pressures that would have it reject scholarly values, it abandons responsibility for leadership. The same mentality that leads to doing trendy research leads to teaching trendy courses. And to mixing trendy politics with trendy science. At Berkeley, after all, that was precisely what the kiddies wanted.

Chapter 13

ON KEEPING
SCIENCE PURE

THE ABUSES ENUMERATED IN PREVIOUS CHAPTERS MIGHT BE LESS pervasive were their causes generally understood. If everybody knew how science really works, the subterfuge and lying would lose much of their effectiveness. If everybody knows how a confidence game is perpetrated, people cease to be taken in, and only because new suckers keep getting born do the old tricks continue to work. If customers purchase only superior goods, shoddy ones will be driven off the market; but then again, this depends upon their knowing the one from the other.

Perhaps we should excuse society as a whole from any responsibility for a base coin getting passed in the intellectual marketplace. One might argue that such is the inevitable result of the complexity of modern life, and that only an expert can participate in scientific quality control. However much truth there may be to this argument, let us not forget how convenient an expert finds it when others have no choice but to take his word for it that he has done his job properly. Again, I am not myself a medical doctor, but I know enough biology that a physician had better not try to fake it when I ask him a question, and if I doubt his competence, I can ask a few questions to which I already know the answer. Goods and services are not evaluated properly if it is expensive to evaluate them, or to acquire the capacity to do so, or if we are unaware of the advantages.

So far as the problems of academia go, one solution might be to adopt a more favorable attitude toward honesty in all of our conduct, and not just in the scholarly life. This may not be feasible in a society that trades so heavily in lies. To market an honest intellectual product may take a considerable amount of courage, not just hard work. To admit that one does not know all the answers may be painful. Furthermore it is difficult to be candid and open about just one aspect of life. If the general public becomes adept at critically evaluating science, what about politics, religion, morals, and everything else? One reason why some people think that science is a bad thing is that it tends to undermine authority.

Let us face it. Lies are cheap, and they all too often substitute for the truth in our daily lives. They are one of the easiest ways of getting our neighbors to act in our interests. Lies are especially popular in dealing with the young, and such lies are excused on the grounds that parents and teachers always act in the interests of their charges. Would that this were so! When there are good biological and economic reasons for an identity of interest between parent and child or teacher and pupil we can be confident that the older generation will act in the interests of the younger. Often such an identity of interest does exist, but everybody knows that conflicts are a part of daily life. (The gentle reader of course is an exception, and always acts with perfect benevolence toward his ungrateful offspring!)

Therefore it becomes suspect when lies are told in the purported interest of the young. This does not imply that parents ought never to lie to their children, but only that there should be no question in whose interest the lies get told. There are white lies and black lies, and gray ones, and the distinction has to do with just that point. We don't tell the truth in a way that hurts people's feelings or invades their privacy. That is bad manners if nothing else. Nonetheless, one cannot make a general practice of lying to the young without holding oneself up as an example of a liar. If one tells a child that honesty is the best policy, but does not practice honesty oneself, one teaches hypocrisy. If the child decides that it is good to lie, the next generation will be all the more populous in liars. If, on the other hand, the child decides that it is bad to lie, but sees his elders lying anyway, he will lose respect for them, and will not believe them even when they tell the truth. One cannot have it both ways. The depth of cynicism would be to suppose that a parent wants his child to be the only liar in a society of honest citizens, but one who doesn't get caught, and who always tells the truth to that one of his two parents. Thus conditions arise that produce a community of skillful liars. But the cost of lying may outweigh the benefits. The more one benefits from lies, the less one benefits from truth.

A good scientist has to be truthful. That does not mean that he cannot be tactful and diplomatic. It does mean that dishonesty as a general practice and as a trait of character will cause his work to suffer. Honesty is particularly valuable among scholars because of the kind of job they are supposed to do, but it benefits others as well. We all suffer once in a while from the results of our own wishful thinking—as we sometimes realize a few months after an election. The best way to avoid being disillusioned is to not have all those illusions in the first place. It takes a great deal of time and effort to decide when it is appropriate to lie and when it is appropriate to tell the truth. And if, in order to lie successfully, one has to believe one's own lies, it may diminish one's capacity to distinguish truth from error.

Therefore, if one wants to be a good scientist, one ought to cultivate honesty in everything that one does, not excepting the non-scientific aspects of one's life. It helps to avoid any entanglement with endeavors that might compromise one's purity as a scholar. This means avoiding fanaticism and intolerance in politics and religion. It does not mean that a scholar should withdraw entirely from the world of practical affairs like a monk to his cell. He ought to be active in society to the extent that his values contribute to the welfare of society, but not in a way that they are corrupted by it.

Scientists ought to be recruited from the ranks of the honest. Someone whose values and attitudes are not conducive to the pursuit of truth has no real vocation as a scholar, and ought to find a more appropriate way of earning a living, and indeed he should do so for his own benefit, not just that of the rest of us. A more widespread understanding of how science really works should make it easier to recruit the appropriate sort of person into the scientific community. This suggests that we should tell the truth about science when we present it to the young. But there is some question as to how eager we will be to pay the price.

As was already suggested, a scientific education tends to erode the power of authority. If teachers do not know all the answers, what about parents? The answer is that the young find out what is going on in due course, and are ill counseled as to what they should do when that happens. Having discovered that parents and teachers have lied to them, they are left with nothing but the example of lying itself. They come to disrespect even the most legitimate kinds of authority—the authority of duly constituted leaders, the authority of mature judgment based upon broad experience and much reflection, and even the authority of reason and common sense. If they turn to drugs, cults, and pseudoscience, it may have something to do with poor leadership.

Academia, in all its ramifications, has become one vast buck-passing mechanism. We all want somebody else to take responsibility. So pervasive is the practice of getting others to shoulder our burdens that the very notion of responsibility has been perverted. In scholarship, taking responsibility means seeing to it that one's research is done, and done well, and made available to others. In academia, taking responsibility means being he to whom the buck gets passed. A parent who never reads a book curses the schools for his child's illiteracy. A politician votes himself a raise, and denounces waste in the university. A professor spends his time consulting instead of preparing his lectures, and expects his students not to cheat on their examinations. Everything is structured so that somebody is blamed for what goes wrong, but is not given the authority to do anything about it. Finding fault, in and of itself, will never solve the problems, especially if finding fault is a means of evading one's own responsibilities.

In the dark years at Berkeley, we were told by the media and by politicians that the faculty ought to "take responsibility" for the students' misbehavior. Nobody ever discussed what this was supposed to mean. Did they want me to lead a regimental combat team onto the campus, and clean the place out with tanks and flamethrowers? Another time we received a pronouncement from on high that there were not enough blacks on the faculty, and devoted several hours in a faculty meeting to talking about the problem. I made the mistake of nominating one, a friend of mine from Jamaica, but of course it never got past the department chairman. The reason was that the administration did not want to have us solve the problem. Rather it wanted an excuse for saying that we had given the matter a great deal of thought but, try as we did, we had failed to come up with a solution. If a solution was found, they would get credit; if not, we would share the blame.

From time to time it is said that scientists have a "responsibility" to do something about the problems that science and technology are supposed to have created for us. Somehow we are responsible for the effects of what we do. In some cases this makes a certain amount of sense. If one spills something, it is one's responsibility to clean up the mess. A parent has a responsibility in seeing to it that a child is properly cared for. But if one receives a letter containing bad news, the person who delivers the mail is in no way responsible for any suffering or for what causes it. Blaming the messenger, however, is very common behavior, like kicking a chair that assaults us in the dark. The question is, therefore, whether scientists who tell us truths we find hard to cope with are any more responsible than anybody else. The answer is that, at the very least, there is no excuse for passing the buck to them.

Scientists are not politicians. They are not in a particularly good position to exercise leadership outside of their profession. And if they spend their time doing politics instead of scholarship and pedagogy, their talents are not being effectively utilized. But scholars are citizens, and as citizens they have the same duties as everybody else. Some people, including some scientists, have more leadership ability than others, and this affects how they might reasonably allocate their time, but the same may be said of every vocation. So too a scientist perhaps has special knowledge that ought to be made available in deciding what is good for society. But this is also true of farmers. Therefore a scientist's place is in the laboratory, just as a farmer's place is at the plow. Just as the farmer helps to put bread on the table and milk in children's mouths, seeing to it that knowledge gets produced and used properly is everybody's responsibility.

Science is by no means the only important activity in which our civilization is engaged. The effective division of labor depends upon people engaging in a variety of different activities. As a part of culture, however, science does not exist in a little world all by itself. It influences, and is influenced by, the rest of what we do. Its values are an integral part of our lives. When someone who wants to do good work can only get the support of his neighbors by lying to them, we create a circumstance that corrupts good morals. On the one hand, the telling of lies becomes a general practice. On the other hand, it encourages the habit of expecting to be told the kind of lies we want to hear. The one is especially pernicious for the practitioner of science, the other for its beneficiaries, but both are affected.

Good scientists do not lie, and a flourishing scientific enterprise cannot exist in a community of liars. If civilization is to prosper, not everybody need become a scientist, any more than we need all become artists, statesmen, or captains of industry. It is necessary that honesty be esteemed and cultivated, and that reason be treated with due respect. And if science is not just allowed, but encouraged, to set a good example, the effects might spread to other aspects of our lives. For the same basic reason that the enemies of civilization are the first to attack science, the friends of civilization should be the first to defend it.

Notes

1. Thomas S. Kuhn, *The Structure of Scientific Revolutions* (Chicago: University Press, 1962; 2nd ed., 1970). Paul Feyerabend, *Against Method* (London: New Left Books, 1975).
2. Imre Lakatos, *The Methodology of Scientific Research Programmes* (Cambridge: University Press, 1978). Larry Laudan, *Progress and Its Problems: Toward a Theory of Scientific Growth* (Berkeley: University of California Press, 1977).
3. K. R. Popper, *The Logic of Scientific Discovery*, 3rd English ed. (New York: Harper Torchbooks, 1965; 1st German ed., 1934; 1st English ed., 1965; 2nd English ed., 1960). For critique of Kuhn, Feyerabend, Lakatos, and Popper, see H. Newton-Smith, *The Rationality of Science* (Boston: Routledge & Kegan Paul, 1981).
4. Thorsten Veblen, *The Higher Learning in America: A Memorandum on the Conduct of Universities by Business Men* (New York: Viking Press, 1918). Burton J. Bledstein, *The Culture of Professionalism: The Middle Class and the Development of Higher Education in America* (New York: W.W. Norton & Co., 1978) is a worthy successor.
5. Michael T. Ghiselin, *The Economy of Nature and the Evolution of Sex* (Berkeley: University of California Press, 1974).
6. Michael T. Ghiselin, "The Economy of the Body," *American Economic Review* 68:233–237 (1978).

211

7. Michael T. Ghiselin, "Principles and Prospects for General Economy," in G. Radnitzky and P. Bernholz, eds., *Economic Imperialism: The Economic Approach Applied Outside the Field of Economics* (New York: Paragon House, 1987).
8. Alfred Marshall, *Principles of Economics*, 9th (Variorum) ed. (New York: Macmillan, 1961; 1st ed., 1890; 7th ed., 1916). Two volumes.
9. Michael T. Ghiselin, *The Triumph of the Darwinian Method* (Berkeley: University of California Press, 1969). Other references below in Chapter 2.
10. J. E. R. Staddon, ed., *Limits to Action: The Allocation of Individual Behavior* (New York: Academic Press, 1980).
11. Proceedings in *Research in Law and Economics*, vol. 4 (1982).
12. Richard R. Nelson and Sidney G. Winter, *An Evolutionary Theory of Economic Change* (Cambridge: Harvard University Press, 1982).
13. Armen A. Alchian, "Uncertainty, Evolution, and Economic Theory," *The Journal of Political Economy* 58:211–221 (1950).
14. Robert Boyd and Peter J. Richerson, "Sociobiology, Culture and Economic Theory," *Journal of Economic Behavior and Organization* 1:97 121 (1980).
15. A good anthology on applied research is Christopher Freeman's, *The Economics of Industrial Innovation* (Harmondsworth: Penguin Books, 1974). Also of interest are works that might be characterized as dealing with political, bureaucratic, and organizational matters. Henry W. Menard, *Science: Growth and Change* (Cambridge: Harvard University Press, 1971). D.S.L. Cardwell, *The Organisation of Science in England*, 2nd ed. (London: Heinemann, 1972). A. Hunter Dupree, *Science in the Federal Government: A History of Policies and Activities to 1940* (Cambridge: Harvard University Press, 1957).
16. Gordon Tullock, *The Organization of Inquiry* (Durham: Duke University Press, 1966). Significant, but quite different, is Nicholas Rescher, *Scientific Progress: A Philosophical Essay on the Economics of Research in Natural Science* (Pittsburgh: University of Pittsburgh Press, 1978). Also, Michael Gibbons and Björn Wittrock, eds., *Science as a Commodity: Threats to the Open Community of Scholars* (Harlow: Longman, 1985). I should also mention preliminary statements by Gerard Radnitzky and myself. Gerard Radnitzky, "Cost-Benefit Thinking in the Methodology of Research: The 'Economic Approach' Applied to Key Problems of the Philosophy of Science," Radnitzky and Bernholz, cited in note 7, above. Michael T. Ghiselin, "The Economics of Scientific Discovery," Radnitzky and Bernholtz, cited in note 7, above.
17. Alvin Weinberg, *Reflections on Big Science* (Cambridge: M.I.T. Press,

1967). W. Henry Lambright, *Governing Science and Technology* (London: Oxford University Press, 1976). Many articles on science policy have been published in the scholarly journal *Minerva*.

18. Michael T. Ghiselin, "A Radical Solution to the Species Problem," *Systematic Zoology* 23:554–556 (1974).

19. David L. Hull, "Are Species Really Individuals?" *Systematic Zoology* 25:174–191 (1976).

20. David L. Hull, "Central Subjects and Historical Narratives," *History and Theory* 14:253–274 (1975).

21. Niles Eldredge, *Unfinished Synthesis* (New York: Oxford University Press, 1985).

22. Michael T. Ghiselin, "Categories, Life, and Thinking," *The Behavioral and Brain Sciences* 4:269–313 (1981). Includes commentaries.

23. John Dewey, *The Quest for Certainty: A Study of the Relation of Knowledge and Action* (New York: G.P. Putnam's Sons, 1929).

24. Karl R. Popper, reference cited above, note 3, and consistently throughout his other works. In spite of some reservations, for many years I have endorsed Popper's enthusiasm for the H–D model, and continue to do so.

25. Michael T. Ghiselin, note 9, above.

26. Karl R. Popper, "Natural Selection and the Emergence of Mind," *Dialectica* 22:339–355. See also Edward S. Reed, "The Lawfulness of Natural Selection," *The American Naturalist* 118:61–71 (1981).

27. For social aspects of science, I particularly recommend Jerome K. Ravetz, *Scientific Knowledge and its Social Problems* (Oxford: Clarendon Press, 1971), and Joseph Ben-David, *The Scientist's Role in Society: A Comparative Study*, 2nd ed. (Chicago: University of Chicago Press, 1984). I have also made good use of the following: Warren O. Hagstrom, *The Scientific Community* (New York: Basic Books, 1965). Augustine Brannigan, *The Social Basis of Scientific Discoveries* (Cambridge: Cambridge University Press, 1981). Diana Crane, *Invisible Colleges: Diffusion of Knowledge in Scientific Communities* (Chicago, University of Chicago Press, 1972).

28. Reference cited in note 22, above. Kuhn evidently makes this mistake in works criticized here.

29. Kuhn, reference cited in note 1, above.

30. Michael T. Ghiselin, "The Individual in the Darwinian Revolution," *New Literary History* 3:113–134 (1971).

31. I. Bernard Cohen, *The Newtonian Revolution: With Illustrations of the Transformation of Scientific Ideas* (Cambridge: Cambridge University Press, 1980).

32. Peter Munz, *Our Knowledge of the Growth of Knowledge: Popper or Wittgenstein?* (London: Routledge and Kegan Paul, 1985).

33. S. Toulmin, *Human Understanding* (Princeton: Princeton University Press, 1972).
34. David L. Hull, "Darwinism as a Historical Entity: A Historiographic Proposal," pp. 773–812 in David Kohn, ed., *The Darwinian Heritage* (Princeton: Princeton University Press, 1985).
35. Thomas S. Kuhn, "Reflections on My Critics," in Imre Lakatos and Alan Musgrave, eds., *Criticism and the Growth of Knowledge* (Cambridge: Cambridge University Press, 1970).
36. See especially John Dewey, *Reconstruction in Philosophy* (New York: Henry Holt, 1920). The views of Laudan (note 2 above) are also pragmatist in spirit.
37. David L. Hull, Peter D. Tessner, and Arthur M. Diamond, "Planck's Principle: Do Younger Scientists Accept New Scientific Ideas with Greater Alacrity Than Older Scientists?" *Science* 202:717–723 (1978).
38. Edward Bailey, *Charles Lyell* (London: Thomas Nelson and Sons, 1962).
39. Howard P. Tuckman and Jack Leahy. "What Is an Article Worth?" *Journal of Political Economy* 83:951–967 (1975).
40. W.W. Rostow, *The Stages of Economic Growth: A Non-Communist Manifesto* (Cambridge: Cambridge University Press, 1960).
41. Ernst Mayr and William B. Provine, eds., *The Evolutionary Synthesis: Perspectives on the Unification of Biology* (Cambridge: Harvard University Press, 1980).
42. Ernst Mayr, *The Growth of Biological Thought: Diversity, Evolution, and Inheritance* (Cambridge: Harvard University Press, 1982) provides an outstanding discussion, in spite of its autobiographical character, and in some ways because of it.
43. Mae-Wan Ho and Peter T. Saunders, eds., *Beyond Neo-Darwinism: An Introduction to the New Evolutionary Paradigm* (London: Academic Press, 1984).
44. Frank J. Sulloway, *Freud, Biologist of the Mind: Beyond the Psychoanalytic Legend* (New York: Basic Books, 1979).
45. Sidney G. Winter, "Satisficing, Selection and the Innovating Rudiment," *Quarterly Journal of Economics* 85:237–261 (1971).
46. A. Hallam, *A Revolution in the Earth Sciences: From Continental Drift to Plate Tectonics* (Oxford: Clarendon Press, 1973) provides a good brief history.
47. P. C. Wason, "On the Failure to Eliminate Hypotheses in a Conceptual Task," *Quarterly Journal of Experimental Psychology* 12:129–140 (1960).
48. Fred Helsebeck, Jr., "Syllogistic Reasoning: Generation of Counterexamples," *Journal of Educational Psychology* 67:102–108 (1975).
49. Cameron R. Peterson and Lee Roy Beach, "Man as an Intuitive Statistician," *Psychological Bulletin* 68:29–46 (1967).

NOTES

50. R.E. Johannes, *Words of the Lagoon: Fishing and Marine Lore in the Palau District of Micronesia* (Berkeley: University of California Press, 1981).
51. Hillel J. Einhorn and Robin M. Hogarth, "Behavioral Decision Theory: Processes of Judgment and Choice," *Annual Review of Psychology* 32:53–88 (1981).
52. Norwood Russell Hanson, *Patterns of Discovery: An Inquiry into the Conceptual Foundations of Science* (Cambridge: Cambridge University Press, 1965).
53. George Kingsley Zipf, *The Psychobiology of Language: An Introduction to Dynamic Philology* (Cambridge: M.I.T. Press, 1965; 1st ed., 1935).
54. Michael T. Ghiselin, Elaine de Man, and John P. Wourms, "An Anomalous Style in the Gut of *Megatebennus bimaculatus*, a Carnivorous Prosobranch Gastropod," *Veliger* 18:40–43 (1975).
55. Philip Steadman, *The Evolution of Designs: Biological Analogy in Architecture and the Applied Arts* (Cambridge: Cambridge University Press, 1979).
56. Michael T. Ghiselin, "Reproductive Function and the Phylogeny of Opisthobranch Gastropods," *Malacologia* 3:327–378 (1966).
57. E.H. Gombrich, *Art and Illusion: A Study in the Psychology of Pictorial Representation* (London: Phaidon Press, 1960), 78.
58. Karl R. Popper, *The Poverty of Historicism*, 3rd ed. (New York: Harper Torchbooks, 1964), 155–156.
59. William B. Provine, *The Origins of Theoretical Population Genetics* (Chicago, University of Chicago Press, 1971), 73–80.
60. William Harvey, *De Motu Cordis et Sanguinis in Animalibus*, translated in Robert Willis, *The Works of William Harvey, M.D.* (London: The Sydenham Society, 1847).
61. Robert K. Merton, *The Sociology of Science: Theoretical and Empirical Investigations* (Chicago: University of Chicago Press, 1973).
62. Douglas P. Peters and Stephen J. Cecci, "Peer-Review Practices of Psychological Journals: The Fate of Published Articles, Submitted Again," *The Behavioral and Brain Sciences* 5:187–258 (1982).
63. David N. Laband, "The Review Process in Economics: Empirical Findings." [In press.]
64. See discussions in references in notes 5 and 6, above.
65. Emile Durkheim, *The Division of Labor in Society*, translated by George Simpson (New York: Macmillan, 1933). Based on several editions, the first of which appeared in 1893.
66. Burton R. Clark, *Academic Power in Italy: Bureaucracy and Oligarchy in a National University System* (Chicago: University of Chicago Press, 1977).

67. Silvan S. Schweber, "Darwin and the Political Economists: Divergence of Character," *Journal of the History of Biology* 13:195–289 (1980).
68. Jack Hirshleifer, "Economics from a Biological Viewpoint," *Journal of Law and Economics* 20:1–52 (1977).
69. Henri Milne-Edwards, *Introduction a la zoologie générale, ou considérations sur les tendances de la nature* (Paris: Victor Masson, 1851). (Earlier publications not seen.)
70. Ernst Haeckel, *Ueber Arbeitstheilung in Natur- und Menschenleben* (Berlin: Luederitz, 1869).
71. Michael T. Ghiselin, "The Evolution of Hermaphroditism Among Animals," *The Quarterly Review of Biology* 44:189–208 (1969).
72. Eric L. Charnov, *The Theory of Sex Allocation* (Princeton: Princeton University Press, 1962).
73. Robert Olby, "Mendel No Mendelian?" *History of Science* 17:53–72 (1979).
74. William Broad and Nicholas Wade, *Betrayers of the Truth* (New York: Simon and Schuster, 1982) deserves to be singled out for negative commendation.
75. See references cited in notes 27 and 61, above.
76. Bertrand Russell, *Authority and the Individual, With a Terminal Essay Philosophy and Politics* (Boston: Beacon Press, 1960), 93.
77. J.S. Weiner, *The Piltdown Forgery* (Oxford: Oxford University Press, 1955).
78. Stephen Jay Gould, *The Mismeasure of Man* (New York: Norton, 1981).
79. Ernst Mayr, "Speciation and Natural Selection," *Evolution* 36:1119–1132 (1982).
80. Charles Darwin, *The Variation of Animals and Plants under Domestication* (London: John Murray, 1868). Two volumes.
81. Stephen Jay Gould, *Ontogeny and Phylogeny* (Cambridge: Harvard University Press, 1977). See my review in *Isis* 69:263–264 (1978).
82. Richard Goldschmidt, *The Material Basis of Evolution* [with an introduction by Stephen Jay Gould] (New Haven: Yale University Press, 1982; originally published in 1940).
83. Richard Dawkins, *The Blind Watchmaker* (Oxford: Clarendon Press, 1986).
84. Olga Metchnikoff, *The Life of Elie Metchnikoff* (London: Constable and Company, 1921).
85. Charles Darwin, "Geology," in John F. W. Herschel, ed., *A Manual of Scientific Enquiry; Prepared for the Use of Her Majesty's Navy: And Adapted for Travellers in General* (London: John Murray, 1849). The passage quoted differs in some other editions.

NOTES

86. Merton, reference cited above in note 61.
87. Richard Levins and Richard Lewontin, *The Dialectical Biologist* (Cambridge: Harvard University Press, 1985).
88. Reference cited above in note 41.
89. R.C. Lewontin, *The Genetic Basis of Evolutionary Change* (New York: Columbia University Press, 1974), and reference cited above in note 5.
90. Frank J. Sulloway, "Darwin and the Galapagos," *Biological Journal of the Linnean Society* 21:29–59 (1984).
91. Reference cited above in note 44.
92. Michael T. Ghiselin, "William Harvey's Methodology in *De Motu Cordis*, from the Standpoint of Comparative Anatomy," *Bulletin of the History of Medicine* 40:314–327 (1966).
93. Sir Gavin De Beer, *Embryos and Ancestors*, 3rd ed. (London: Oxford University Press, 1958); Jane M. Oppenheimer, "Problems, Concepts and their History," in Benjamin H. Willier, Paul A. Weiss, and Viktor Hamburger, eds., *Analysis of Development* (Philadelphia: Saunders, 1955).
94. William Coleman, *Biology in the Nineteenth Century: Problems of Form, Function, and Transformation* (New York: Wiley, 1971). Garland E. Allen, *Life Science in the Twentieth Century* (Wiley, 1978).
95. Ernst Haeckel, *Zur Entwickelungsgeschichte der Siphonophoren* (Utrecht: C. Van Der Post, 1869).
96. Theodosius Dobzhansky, "On Some Fundamental Concepts of Darwinian Biology," *Evolutionary Biology* 2:1–34 (1968).
97. Bruce Kuklick, *The Rise of American Philosophy: Cambridge, Massachusetts 1860–1930* (New Haven: Yale University Press, 1977).
98. I have speculated on such matters in chapter 9 of the reference cited above in note 5.
99. See above, note 17.
100. Théophile Cahn, *La Vie et L'Oeuvre d'Étienne Geoffroy Saint Hillaire* (Paris: Presses Universitaires de France, 1962).
101. Eric R. Kandel, *Behavioral Biology of Aplysia: A Contribution to the Comparative Study of Opisthobranch Molluscs* (San Francisco: W. H. Freeman and Company, 1979).

Index

INDEX

"Demand-side economics," 27
De Motu Cordis et Sanguinis in Animalibus (Harvey), 51
Deseret News, The, 89
"developmental mechanics," 179
Dewey, John, 11, 18–19
dexterity, practice and, 91, 92, 108
Die Coelomtheorie (Zimmerman), 159
Die Telomtheorie (Zimmerman), 159
"divergence of character," 98, 185
diversity: in books, 80; among courses, division of labor and, 93; in graduate school, 85
division of labor: academic, 91–114; competitive, 98, 117–118; cooperative, 98, 117; designing optimal policy for, 118–120; extent of market and, 95–96, 116–117; history of, 91, 95–98; improvement and, 93; as limited, 115–131; Marxist view of, 94; principle of, 2; Smith on, 79; social cohesion and, 94
Dobzhansky, Theodosius, 24, 182
downtime, 92
Driesch, Hans, 174–175
"duck-rabbit," 38
Dürer, Albrecht, 41
Durkheim, Emile, 94

economic thought, extensions of, 4–5
Economy of Nature and the Evolution of Sex, The (Ghiselin), 2
Economy of the Body, The (Ghiselin), 2
economy of the intellect, demand-side, 199
editor, responsibility of, 61–62
Ehrlich, Prof., 25

embryology, comparative/experimental, 179, 180
empirical sciences, complementarity in, 120
empiricism, 172
epistemological nihilism, 15
error, in science, 19
espionage, in reviewing process, 145
Essay on the Principle of Population (Malthus), 97
essentialism, 37
evaluation: cutting corners in, 71–72; incentives and, 61–76
evolution, 24–26, 177; cultural, 3; embryology and, 139; first presented, 52, 53. *See also* Darwin, Charles; natural selection
evolutionary biology: exploratory stage of, 25–26; future of, 169; history of, 23–25
experimentalism, 170–171
Expression of the Emotions (Darwin), 111
externalist historians, 14

fads, 157
Feyerabend, Paul, 2, 15, 72, 176
Fisher, R. A., 23–24
fixed costs, 102–103
Forbes, Edward, 33
foreign language, diminishing returns and, 108–109
fraud, 133; in medical research, 134; in science, 138; in scientific literature, 138; in scientific publications, 135–137
"free ride" principle, 103
Freud, Sigmund, 177, 178
funds, misappropriation of, 201
futurology, 169

INDEX

INDEX

natural selection, 178, 191; evolution by, 52; as inductive process, 34–35
naturalism, 171
Nautilus, 16
Nelson, Richard R., 3
nidamental glands, 43
nominalism, 6
noninterference, principle of, 101
novelists, integration among, 124–126
novelty: as inducement to change, 26; as product, 112

occupations, as hereditary, 95
"ocular demonstrations," 51
On Growth and Form (Thompson), 116
On the Origin of Species (Darwin), 111. *See also Origin of Species, The*
Ontogeny and Phylogeny (Gould), 139
Opisthobranchia of Sagami Bay, Collected by His Majesty the Emperor of Japan (Baba), 193
Oppenheimer, Jane, 180
"optimal foraging strategy," 113
Origin of Species, The (Darwin), 24, 52, 53
orthogenesis, 26

paradigm theory, 16–17; stages in economic history of, 22–23; versions of, 18
Pasteur, L., 112
pedagogy, novelist and, 125–126
Peters, Douglas P., 65–67
Philistinism, 193, 194
philosophy: contemporary, 188–189; as weapon, 175

Piltdown hoax, 138
piracy, intellectual, 142–143
plagiarism, 133, 141–142; borderline, 145–147; scholarship and, 142–143
Playfair, John, 154
Popper, K. R., 2, 175; on objectivity of science, 47; on refuting hypotheses, 12, 13; on theories as scientific, 172
principles, mastery of, 173
Principles of Animal Taxonomy (Simpson), 137
Principles of Biology (Spencer), 98
Principles of Geology (Lyell), 97, 154
Principles of Political Economy (Mills), 97
priority, scientists' concern for, 55–56
prizes, as reward, 164
"product diversification," 185
progress: erroneous conception of, 16; innovation and, 91–92, 93, 112; specialization and, 96; technological change and, 93
Provine, William B., 48
Proxmire, Sen. William, 197
Pruvot-Fol, Alice, 160
psychic income, 152
punctuated equilibria, 139
pycnogonids, 103
pyrrhonism, 15

quantification, 170
quantity of publication, 81–82

rationalism, 172
reductionism, 122, 181–182
redundancy, 82–83
"refutationalsim," 12–13

INDEX

Rensch, 24

requirements, academic, 185

research: changing fashions in, 156; justification for, 198; mission-related, 200–201; obtaining funds for, 201–204; resources used in, 198; teaching and, 105–107, 187–188; U.S. government and, 57–58

resources, as subject matter of economics, 3–4

retooling, cost of, 20, 101, 110

reviewer, disincentives/incentives of, 62–64

reviewing process: anonymity and, 63–64; "blind," 64; opportunities for sabotage in, 144–145; problems in, 59

reviews: experimental study of, 65–67; incentives for good, 67; kinds of "helpful," 65

revenge, 147

Richerson, Peter J., 3

"right," authority and, 56–57

Rostow, W. W., 22

Russell, Bertrand, 137

sabotage, 133, 145

saltations, 139

"satisficing," 32–33

scandal-management, 147, 148

scholarly world, 5

scholars, as fundraisers, 202

science: approaches to explication of, 11–28; authoritarian image of, 72; authority and, 206, 207–208; cognitive aspects of, 194–195; commoditization of, 169; cosmopolitan community and, 193–194; as free-enterprise economy, 169; history of and ideological controversy, 176–181; intellectual culture and, 197–198; keeping it pure, 205–210; myth and legend in, 177; normal, 16–17; philosophy of and ideological controversy, 174–176; rationality of, 1–2; revolutionary, 16; social constructionist view of, 136; technology and, 74

Scientific Citation Index, 158

scientific method, "common sense" theory of, 36

"scientific paper," 80–83

scientific publications, role of, 52–53

scientists: as explorers, 19–21, 57; politics and, 209; sources of information and, 52–55; specialization of, 153; as users and producers, 55

Scott, John, 178

Sea of Cortez (Steinbeck), 125

sea slugs, 196–197

self-citation, 161

Seto Marine Biological Laboratory, 193

"sex-allocation theory," 100

Simpson, George Gaylord, 24, 137, 182

siphonophores, 180

"size-advantage model," 100

Smart, J. J. C., 8

Smith, Adam, 2; on division of labor, 79; "invisible hand" of, 30, 99; on principles of division of labor, 91–93, 95, 98–99, 101, 108, 110–111, 112; on progress, 16; on research and teaching, 105

Snow, C. P., 125

social cohesion, division of labor and, 94

225

INDEX